EXHUMING LOSS

Publications of the
Institute of Archaeology, University College London

Series Editor: Ruth Whitehouse
Director of the Institute: Stephen Shennan
Founding Series Editor: Peter J. Ucko

The Institute of Archaeology of University College London is one of the oldest, largest, and most prestigious archaeology research facilities in the world. Its extensive publications programme includes the best theory, research, pedagogy, and reference materials in archaeology and cognate disciplines, through publishing exemplary work of scholars worldwide. Through its publications, the Institute brings together key areas of theoretical and substantive knowledge, improves archaeological practice, and brings archaeological findings to the general public, researchers, and practitioners. It also publishes staff research projects, site and survey reports, and conference proceedings. The publications programme, formerly developed in-house or in conjunction with UCL Press, is now produced in partnership with Left Coast Press, Inc. The Institute can be accessed online at http://www.ucl.ac.uk/archaeology.

Critical Cultural Heritage Series, Beverley Butler, Series Editor

Other Recent Titles

EXHUMING LOSS

Memory, Materiality, and Mass Graves of the Spanish Civil War

Layla Renshaw

Routledge
Taylor & Francis Group

LONDON AND NEW YORK

First published 2011 by Left Coast Press, Inc.

Published 2016 by Routledge
2 Park Square, Milton Park, Abingdon, Oxon OX14 4RN
711 Third Avenue, New York, NY 10017, USA

Routledge is an imprint of the Taylor & Francis Group, an informa business

Library of Congress Cataloging-in-Publication Data:

Renshaw, Layla.
  Exhuming loss : memory, materiality, and mass graves of the Spanish Civil War / Layla Renshaw.
    p. cm.—(Critical cultural heritage series)
  Includes bibliographical references and index.
  ISBN 978-1-61132-041-1 (hardback) — ISBN 978-1-61132-042-8 (paperback)
  1. Spain—History—Civil War, 1936–1939—Atrocities. 2. War victims—Spain—History—20th century. 3. Mass burials—Spain—History—20th century. 4. Human remains (Archaeology)—Spain. 5. Forensic archaeology—Spain. 6. Exhumation—Social aspects—Spain. 7. Collective memory—Spain. I. Title.
  DP269.5.R46 2011
  946.081'1—dc22
                    2011006965

ISBN 978-1-61132-042-8 paperback
ISBN 978-1-61132-041-1 hardback

Contents

List of Illustrations

Acknowledgements

I wish to thank my informants in all of the exhumation sites that I visited and worked on in Spain. I would like to thank my friends and informants in the two communities in which I conducted the ethnographies upon which this book is based. Many individuals showed me remarkable kindness, patience, and openness, as well as unstintingly generous hospitality and practical help, particularly those of the Peña Las Cebollas, as well as Jose Ignacio, his family, and his friends in "Villavieja." It was a privilege to listen to the accounts of the older generation of residents in my field sites. I also wish to thank the coordinators of ARMH for granting me remarkable access to the operation of their campaign and their exhumations. I would like to thank both Emilio Silva and Jose Maria Pedreño for sharing their perspectives on the Republican memory campaign. Numerous individuals participated as expert practitioners in this campaign and I would like to acknowledge the invaluable help of Francisco Etxeberria Gabilondo, Jimi Jiménez, Luis Ríos, Francisco Ferrándiz, Andrea Alonso, Andrés Devesa, Derek Congram, and Inma López Flores among many. Many excavation volunteers were patient with my participant observation while we undertook demanding work. I am forever indebted to Javier Mije for enabling me to overcome problems with translation and transcription of interview material, for his support in undertaking this work, and for the many cultural and political insights he furnished.

I acknowledge the support of a doctoral award from the Arts and Humanities Research Council in undertaking this research.

I wish to thank the supervisors of my doctoral thesis, Professor Chris Tilley and Dr. Victor Buchli, for their consistent help and encouragement. I would also like to thank the anonymous reviewers who read an earlier version of this book and gave immensely constructive and detailed feedback.

Finally, I am grateful every day to Patrick and my family for their love, support, and patience.

EXHUMATION AND THE TRAUMATIC PAST

It is difficult to verify the competing truth claims of antagonists in social conflicts, particularly in a moment of intellectual history when political leaders are as likely as postmodern professors to claim that truths are multiple, perspectival and partial, and when public relations and information management teams are standard features of every political organization. But there is one way... familiar to anyone who follows cases of political violence, in which adjudicators can establish definitive and reliable evidence: get to the dead bodies, the corpses whose materiality cannot be denied.
—Eric Klinenberg, *Bodies that Don't Matter*

The systematic use of forensic exhumation to investigate deaths that occurred during periods of war or mass human rights violations came to the fore in South and Central America in the late 1980s and 1990s in conjunction with the various truth and reconciliation hearings that investigated the periods of state terror in countries including Guatemala (Sieder 2001) and Argentina (Brysk 1994). Prior to the 1980s, with the exception of cases such as the Katyń Forest Massacre (Raszeja and Chroscielewski 1994) and the repatriation of American casualties from Southeast Asia (Hoshower-Leppo 2002), exhumation, and particularly human identification, did not have a primary role in processes of postconflict mourning, reconciliation, and reconstruction. This was due, in part, to the scale of fatalities in the two world wars and to limitations in the available investigative techniques, but also to changing attitudes toward individual identity, death, and memorialisation (Laqueur 1994, 1996), as I will discuss at greater length.

The Nuremberg trials following World War II used primarily textual, verbal, and photographic evidence, rather than forensic recovery and analysis of human remains (Douglas 1998). However, these trials represent a pivotal point in both the development of international law and the public understanding of the concepts of human rights and war crimes, particularly crimes against civilian populations. Another legacy of Nuremberg was the creation of a key precedent, namely the notion that a legalistic investigative framework could be applied to the traumatic past. While this legacy has been problematised (Arendt 1994; Felman 2001), in the decades since Nuremberg the framework in which issues of justice are addressed between nation states has broadened to include collectives within the nation among the subjects entitled to pursue investigations into atrocities. A key departure from the world wars has been the differing response demanded by clandestine killings perpetrated by the states against their own citizenry or between opposing sides in a civil war, as these required not just a simple account of the dead and missing, but also a more detailed investigation to counter revisionism and denial and to lay the foundation for a new social order with the potential for reconciliation (Saunders 2002). To this end, these investigations have placed a much greater emphasis on locating and exhuming human remains and subjecting them to detailed forensic analysis. Physical evidence and scientific analysis have assumed an ever-greater role in the investigation of the traumatic past (Corillon 1989). The body-as-witness has become a trope of the reckonings that follow acts of violence. Representations of amassed and comingled human remains have become icons of the twentieth-century mechanised violence, particularly against civilian populations, and specific images of human remains have become shorthands for particular historical events (Laqueur 2002; Sontag 2004)—such as Lee Miller's photographs of Buchenwald and Dachau, the skeletons of the victims of Pol Pot's regime in Cambodia, or the Kibuye Church Memorial in Rwanda where some of the victims' bones remain displayed under a crucifix.

Since the late 1980s, the practice of exhumation and scientific analysis of human remains has become the dominant paradigm for the investigation of atrocities. Since its foundation in 1984 (Doretti and Fondebrider 2001), the Equipo Argentino de Antropología Forense (EAAF), composed of leading practitioners of forensic archaeology and anthropology, has investigated abuses in more than thirty countries around the world. The atrocities against civilians committed during the breakdown of the former Yugoslavia between 1991 and 2001 prompted the systematic and most sustained use of forensic exhumation to date. The extensive media coverage of these investigations has been instrumental in raising a popular awareness of the investigative process and in shaping the public perception and knowledge of the conflict. The speed of implementation of forensic exhumation in Iraq in 2003, ahead of the reconstruction of war-damaged infrastructure, indicates the primacy that forensic investigation has assumed in structuring representations of the recent past and the potential political and symbolic power of those representations.

The political and symbolic power of exhumation, and the many factors that contribute to it are themes explored throughout this book. I contend that acts of exhumation and human identification lie at the intersection of different moral, metaphysical, and psychological preoccupations and anxieties concerning mortality, individuality, the fallibility of memory and historical narrative, the infallibility of physical proof, and the possibility of redemption and closure in the wake of trauma. Exhumation and human identification have accrued a set of largely positive associations in public perception, and above all in media representations. Investigations into mass deaths are understood as an assertion of the sanctity or worth of an individual life and the victory of individual identity over anonymity. The systematic investigation of the traumatic past can serve to allay anxieties around memory and forgetting. It reflects the modern impulse to capture and contain the past, as well as an empiricist association between physical evidence and objectivity. It satisfies the widely held belief that the recovery of human remains is indispensable in order to enact death rituals, enable healthy mourning, and achieve psychological closure. Positive evaluations of exhumation are also fed by a narrative of technical and scientific progress with respect to the methodologies employed to find bodies and reassign their identities (along with a fascination within crime fiction or drama that detail these cutting-edge technical capabilities), offering the possibility of technical mastery over death and decay. Advances in investigative techniques are perhaps a necessary correlate to the development of destructive technologies that obliterate bodies, one that now finds particular resonance amongst broader fears of falling victim to crime and terror. Investigations also signify the end of impunity for those wielding repressive power, and reflect the redemptive ideal that the rematerialisation of missing people can achieve some kind of posthumous reversal of the wrongs perpetrated against them.

Since the inception of exhumation and human identification, practitioners of forensic archaeology and anthropology have reflected on their multiple meanings, their transformative nature, and the clear fascination they exert on the wider public (Cox 2001; Hanson 2007). Exhumation appears to serve as a magnet for media coverage, above all photographic depictions, generating a supply of disturbing and thought-provoking visual images in which the viewer may readily decode metaphors for the exposure of concealed crimes (Congram and Bruno 2007; Hunter 1999; Renshaw 2007). Public fascination is discernable in an appetite for accessible, first-person accounts of forensic exhumations (Koff 1994) and works of photojournalism and reportage (Stover and Peress 1998). The practice of forensic archaeology and anthropology has provided a rich seam, both dramatically and figuratively, for novelists such as

Kadare (2000) and Ondaatje (2001), who use exhumation and human identification as tropes through which to examine memory, identity, and the traumatic past.

There are a growing number of more sustained scholarly engagements with the symbolic and political potency of exhumation and with the experiences of those who participate in these investigations, including relatives, community members, witnesses, and expert practitioners (see Crossland 2000; Sanford 2003; Sant Cassia 2007; Verdery 1999; Wagner 2008). With this growing attention come increasingly interrogative and critical evaluations of exhumation. Sanford (2003) conducted an ethnographic study of a remote Mayan community as it was undergoing an investigation into gross human rights abuses perpetrated by the Guatemalan government in the 1980s. For Sanford's informants, the investigation of these atrocities was explicitly linked to the status of indigenous communities within Guatemala and was challenging a culture of official denial, revisionism, and impunity. The author illustrates the power of physical evidence to support the claims of those who have been marginalised and silenced. Sant Cassia's ethnographic work among Greek Cypriot survivors of Turkish military action (2007) shows how an unauthorised act of exhumation that disturbs bodies and soil can function as a highly visible form of protest or direct action, forcing the authorities to formulate an official response to constituencies they had hitherto ignored. A demand to accord due process to the dead can also function as a demand to accord due care and attention to the survivors or mourners. The rights and status of the living and their dead are inextricably linked.

Sant Cassia identifies the dissonance experienced by some Cypriot families between the material reality of the skeletal remains and the representations of the dead they had carefully constructed. Crossland's analysis of the human rights investigations in Argentina (2000, 2002) exposes the potential existence of divergent goals and understandings of the exhumation amongst the relatives of the dead, expert practitioners, and state authorities. Crossland's work (2002) highlights the prevailing orthodoxies of forensic discourse that present the return of human remains as a redemptive narrative of psychological closure, and explores the degree to which this orthodoxy is imposed on the relatives of the dead. Both Crossland and Sant Cassia identify the potential tension between the promise of closure and the reality of exhumation and reburial. The Argentinean case, in particular, exposes how ideology-laden the notion of closure may be, and shows that unclosed or unhealed wounds may remain as a site of active political tension and contestation, fuelling a broader critique of authority. Steele (2008) warns against the potential for even the most objective forensic practitioners to become implicated in postconflict judicial structures that pursue a victor's justice.

Kwon's ethnography of mourning, memorialisation, and notions of haunting in contemporary Vietnam (2008) implicitly draws comparisons between the Vietnamese and American responses to losses during the period his informants refer to as "the American War," exposing how culturally specific the role of the body in mourning may be and revealing the different value placed on "closure" as opposed to a sustained relationship with the dead through ghosts and haunting. The American pursuit of closure in Vietnam is achieved through the rigorous scientific investigation of death as conducted by the US military's forensic personnel. The Vietnamese investigative idiom may take the form of an ongoing conversation and reconciliation with the dead via spirit mediums.

The South African Truth and Reconciliation Commission (TRC) has provided a fascinating example of how the traumatic past can be confronted using an investigative paradigm that simultaneously structures a process of profound societal and political change (LaCapra 1999; Wilson 2001), but it is also open to criticism. Wilson (2001) identifies the way an investigative paradigm may constrain or overrule subjective experiences of the traumatic past. Wilson shows how the forensic paradigm, which depends on the meticulous gathering of detailed evidence on a case-by-case basis, may demonstrate the reality of an individual crime, but masks the conditions of "structural violence" (2001, 59) or the "logics of violence" underpinning the crime (Fernández de Mata 2004). Wilson's critique of the forensic paradigm in the South African TRC is of clear relevance to the scientific practices of exhumation and human identification: "Meaningful knowledge about the past is only possible when scientific positivism assumes its proper, subordinate place within the more profound application of historical analysis" (Wilson 2001, 58). The attempt to bring objectivity to such complex subjective experiences as violence and loss exposes the limitations of a forensic investigative paradigm that cannot encompass the totality of these experiences.

Wagner's work in Srebrenica (2008) is an excellent illustration of a sensitive negotiation of power relations between expert practitioners and relatives of the dead. Investigators working in Srebrenica strive to find a form of practice and communication that may bridge the gaps in scientific understanding between them and the community, in order to produce an outcome of the exhumation that is scientifically and legally rigorous, yet fully engaged with the relatives of the dead. Wagner also problematises the apparent neutrality of key concepts in the forensic investigative paradigm such as "identity" and "proof," showing that an investigation's findings must be made not only comprehensible to the layperson but also culturally meaningful, in order to satisfy the relatives of the dead.

Current anxieties around memory, truth, and the traumatic past can be traced, in part, to debates within the historiography of the Holocaust and the claims and counterclaims that followed World War II (Braun 1994; Friedlander 1992). White's notion of "emplotment" (1992) demonstrates how scholarly history and personal memory are subject to literary tropes or devices, particularly to the selection or framing of events to produce a narrative arc that will alter the significance of an account even if the individual events related are objectively "true." The privileging of physical evidence, including human remains, in investigations into the traumatic past is thought to counteract some of the anxieties around the fallibility of human memory, the act of witnessing, and the construction of narratives about the past in testimony. This is arguably naive, since representations of the past based on physical evidence can still exhibit authorship and mediation through acts of selection and framing.

Douglas's work on the "Buchenwald head" (1998) is an example of the emplotment of physical evidence in the Nuremberg trials, a seminal moment for the application of the forensic gaze to atrocities. This example shows how, despite the mass of material evidence of the Holocaust, the Nuremberg exhibits were selected to support a particular representation of Nazism as an evolutionary step backwards to a perceived primitive and barbaric past redolent of cannibalism or headhunting. A shrunken head from Buchenwald was shown to the court, rather than material evidence of the utilitarian or capitalist "logic" that underpinned the use of victim's hair or dental fillings in manufacturing processes. The naivety of a simple correlation between material evidence and objectivity is convincingly illustrated by Paperno's analysis of the exhumation of mass graves in the former Soviet Union (2001), in which the same documents—photographs, excavation records, and pathologists' reports—resurface in three accounts of the massacre: a Soviet report on the crimes of Nazism; a report on the crimes of Stalin authored by local investigators; and an American report of the McCarthy era on the crimes of Bolshevism. This is a salutary reminder that bodies and objects from mass graves are not simply "revealed" during exhumation, but are continuously represented and framed to support particular historical narratives.

Part of the reason for the growing dominance of a forensic investigative paradigm is the broader "turn toward the body" identified within the academic, including archaeological, discourse by Sofaer (2006). A growing number of works have addressed fragmentary and damaged bodies and our comprehension of the body as a site of pain and suffering (Canter 2002; Das 1997; Scarry 1985a, 1985b). These works move away from a primarily psychological perspective on memory and the traumatic past, and consider our shared physicality as a basis for the study of human empathy and its limits. Crossland (2009a, 2009b) situates the contemporary forensic investigative paradigm within the longer evolutionary trajectory of the biological and human sciences—particularly anthropology, criminology, early psychiatry, and more recently neuroscience. These disciplines all share a preoccupation with the exposure of concealed human characteristics and explore the knowability of all aspects of human identity through the physiognomy and anatomy of the living or the mortal remains of the dead, echoing the enjoinder to "open up a few corpses" (Foucault 2003, 180).

Taking a historical overview of changing attitudes to death, and its investigation and commemoration, Laqueur (2002) identifies the notion of the corpus delicti, the tangible facts of a crime, as crucial to understand the role of the body in contemporary postconflict and human rights investigations. Human remains appear more enduring than witness testimonies, which can be contested, and memories, which may be altered by both their retelling and their suppression. The human body has attained the status of definitive corpus delicti of historical crimes, and as such functions as a "kernel of truth" from which forensic practitioners, lawyers, and the international public, via the news media, can "write a narrative with political, juridical, and more intimate memorial, therapeutic consequences" (ibid., 72).

Mass Graves from the Spanish Civil War and the Republican Memory Campaign

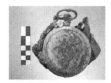

In 2000 Emilio Silva, a Madrid-based journalist, returned to his family's ancestral village of Priaranza del Bierzo in León, ostensibly to investigate details of his family's recent history with the intention of writing a novel about it. Visiting the graves of other deceased family members in the village cemetery caused Silva to reflect on the absence of his paternal grandfather's grave. His grandfather, also called Emilio Silva, was known to have been killed by Francoist forces in one of the thousands of extrajudicial political killings of civilians that characterised the Spanish Civil War. The details surrounding this death were not known to the family, and the grandfather's remains were one of the estimated thirty to forty thousand bodies located in clandestine mass graves throughout Spain (Tremlett 2006). Silva made preliminary investigations amongst the older inhabitants of the village and surrounding area, including his own elderly uncles and an oral historian active in the area, Santiago Macías. They began an informal collaboration and soon encountered informants who told them the circumstances of Silva's grandfather's death and the probable locations of the body (Silva and Macías 2003). Silva's journalistic response was to prove pivotal to the outcome of these initial enquiries, as seen in this extract from an extended interview that I conducted with him:

> In September of 2000, I published an article in the newspaper *León Chronicle* that was entitled: "My Grandfather, too, was a *Desapareci-do*," and in this I complained that Spain has applauded the detention of Pinochet; Garzón has initiated trials in Argentina and Chile; others in Guatemala; and here we have *Desaparecidos* but they don't exist. I wrote this without knowing the dimension of the problem or anything. I wrote this article very angrily and I put my phone number at the bottom. The

article was published on a Sunday, and that afternoon a guy rings me and says, "I'm an archaeologist and my mother is from the village where your grandfather is buried. I read your article and I want to help you. My wife is a physical anthropologist and a few times we thought about opening the grave. Its location is known because there is a spot that the children always go past running, they call it the 'place of the group's *paseo*' and say there are dead people there." With that I felt like I had won the lottery. (Emilio Silva, cofounder of La Asociación para la Recuperación de la Memoria Historica, Madrid)

The exhumation in Priaranza del Bierzo was successfully undertaken in October 2000, resulting in the location and ultimate identification of Silva's grandfather as well as those buried alongside him. In December of that year Emilio Silva and Santiago Macías cofounded the Association for the Recuperation of Historical Memory, registered as a charity with the Ministry of the Interior. In Spanish the organization is called La Asociación para la Recuperación de la Memoria Historica, popularly known by its Spanish acronym ARMH, which is how it shall be referred to throughout this book. Silva and Macías began to receive messages from across Spain, primarily expressions of solidarity, but also requests for advice and support from those seeking to undertake the same process for their own missing relatives.

In September 2001 ARMH opened a second grave containing four bodies in Fresnedo. This time the national and international press was present at the exhumation, [and the] leading Spanish newspaper *El País* published half a page on the exhumation. In early 2002 ARMH set up a website which was to become a decisive communication tool. On March 16, 2002, DNA tests were performed on four of the bodies recovered from Priaranza, again exciting media interest. ARMH later contacted the UN Task Force for Forced Disappearances to inform it of the Spanish Civil War case. Other exhumations followed. By this time ARMH was overwhelmed by communications from relatives of disappeared people asking for help. (Ferrándiz 2006, 8)

Inspired by the press coverage and sustained by a growing internet presence, there was a florescence of regional chapters and affiliated Republican memory organisations, including special interest groups for Republican sailors, miners, and trade unions. The significance of the internet to this campaign lies in part in the way it has facilitated loose affiliations through links and shared participation in online forums. Campaign groups can exist simultaneously as local grassroots initiatives and as participants in a larger nationwide campaign. A number of these groups established relationships of varying degrees of permanence and formality with academics and expert practitioners, including oral historians, archaeologists, anthropologists, and forensic scientists who volunteered on the growing number of exhumations throughout Spain. These expert practitioners also prompted the involvement as volunteers of a growing network of students, primarily of archaeology and physical anthropology, and enabled access to university resources, particularly laboratory space for postexhumation analyses.

> New associations started to spring up in different parts of Spain, some of them as regional or provincial sections of ARMH, or loosely linked to it. Other associations clustered around a second NGO, Foro por la Memoria (Forum for Memory), linked to the Communist party; still others were autonomous. In May 2003 the DNA tests on the exhumed remains of Emilio Silva Faba, Silva's grandfather, were confirmed as positive and he became the first "disappeared person" of the Spanish Civil War to be identified by this means. By the end of 2005 more than five hundred corpses had been recovered in over sixty exhumations. (Ferrándiz 2006, 8)

In addition to conducting mass grave exhumations and reburials, these diverse groups have organised a steadily increasing number of *actos*, a wide range of commemorative acts including vigils, processions, readings, theatrical performances, concerts, and the laying of plaques and monoliths on sites of mass burial and execution across Spain. Collaborations between campaign groups and university departments have developed through conferences, seminars, doctoral projects, and publications (González 2006; Preston 2004a). The number of exhumations conducted each year has risen exponentially, and while the total number of individuals involved is hard to calculate, two hundred graves and close to five thousand bodies have been exhumed and reported on by leading forensic specialist Francisco Etxeberria and his team of expert practitioners from the Aranzadi centre (see Etxeberria et al. n.d. for examples of these reports). Hundreds of graves across Spain have been opened, ranging in size from single burials to sites containing several hundreds. Ferrándiz and Baer (2008) note that the San Rafael cemetery in Malaga may contain the clandestine graves of four thousand people.

In addition to gaining recognition by the United Nations for the status of missing people from the Spanish Civil War, ARMH collaborated with Amnesty International to draw up a series of recommendations to the Spanish government on how to approach to the experience of political repression during the Civil War and subsequent dictatorship.[1] In November 2002 the Spanish parliament passed an unprecedented motion condemning Franco's 1936 military uprising—the act that triggered the Civil War and was to place Franco in power for nearly forty years—as an illegal act of aggression against a democratically elected government

(Ferrándiz 2006). At the same time, an interdepartmental commission was established to hear testimonies from a range of groups in the Republican memory campaign, the most influential of which was ARMH (Espinosa 2006). The culmination of this sustained pressure on the Spanish government to engage with the demands of relatives of the Civil War dead and provide a legal framework for future exhumations was the passage of the so-called Law of Historic Memory, or Ley de Memoria Histórica.[2] This is a complex piece of legislation and has provoked a divided response across Spain's political spectrum (Cue 2007; Moreno 2006).

Overall, the sudden emergence of the Republican memory campaign and the momentum with which it has developed since 2000 can be characterised as an "explosion of interest" (Ferrándiz 2006), constituting the kind of unexpected shift in memory politics that Wilde (1999) has called an "irruption of memory." Fernández de Mata (2004) has characterised the radical rupture in the prevailing Spanish memory politics achieved by these exhumations as the "mass grave phenomena," and González-Ruibal (2007) has noted the high levels of popular awareness and interest in these exhumations. The fieldwork that forms the basis for this book primarily relates to the exhumations organised by ARMH and their wider campaign activities and discourse; however, the alternative model offered by the Communist Republican memory campaign group, Foro por la Memoria, will also be considered in order to highlight points of tension and dispute in their respective approaches to the past. The explicitly ideological rationale for exhumation offered by the Foro will be contrasted to the personal rationale emphasised by ARMH, which focuses on affective familial bonds between the living and the dead and the necessity of mourning and psychological closure. In chapter 1, these differences are highlighted by Foro's sustained critique of ARMH's exhumation practices via the news media and internet.

The starting point for this book is that this momentous rupture in Spanish memory politics and the breaking of the pact of silence have been produced by the opening of the graves, the subsequent encounters and interactions between the living and the dead, and the multiple representations of the human remains and objects that were brought to light. I explore the relationships amongst the materialisation of the traumatic past achieved through the exhumation of bodies and objects from Republican mass graves from the Spanish Civil War, individual and collective memories of Spain's past, and the attribution of individual and collective identities to the Republican dead. I also examine the creation of new individual and collective identities in the present, formed in relation to the dead through the process of their materialisation. This book sets out a detailed material analysis of the exhumation process by considering the opening of graves and subsequent encounters with bodies, objects, and images as a series of transformations that progress through different material indices of the dead and of the traumatic past, or as a series of shifts in the register through which the dead are being materialised. Although acts of extreme violence, on and off the battlefield, were perpetrated by both sides during the Spanish Civil War, this book will discuss solely the exhumation of mass graves containing Republican civilian victims killed by supporters of Franco's coup. The decision to focus on Republican victims is not partisan or politically motivated, but rather is prompted by contemporary events in Spanish society, namely the dramatic resurgence of Republican memory since 2000. The historical background and chronology of events presented in this work should communicate the very different trajectories in burial and memorialisation that befell the casualties from the two sides of the war. The majority of the civilians who died as victims of revolutionary or leftist violence, or at the hands of Republican forces, have been incorporated into the state-orchestrated commemorative practices. As I will discuss, under Franco these commemorative practices included the large-scale exhumation and reburial of those who had died in support of the military uprising (Rodrigo 2008, 200). The dominant memory politics of Franco's regime gave public space and recognition to these losses, while those on the losing side were marginalised and silenced. This disparity in treatment, which endured for over sixty years, was the starting point for the Republican memory campaign analysed here.

SPAIN'S CIVIL WAR, DICTATORSHIP, AND TRANSITION TO DEMOCRACY

An outline of Spain's recent history is indispensable to understand Spain's memory politics and the significance of current exhumations. The Spanish Civil War was triggered by a military coup led by General Francisco Franco in July 1936. This uprising was the culmination of a turbulent five-year period during which Spain had become a Republic and had experienced successive waves of strikes, public protest, and violent civil unrest, which were put down by mass arrests and violently repressive measures such as the massacre at Casas Viejas (Mintz 1982). The three national elections between 1931 and 1936 produced swings in political control between blocs of left- and right-wing parties that resulted in a succession of ineffectual coalition governments, revealing the degree to which Spain was polarised along intersecting lines of socioeconomic class, ideology, and geographical region (Preston 1996). Franco's uprising was against a left-wing government known as the Popular Front, primarily a coalition of the Socialist Party and the Republican Alliance. With the onset of the Civil War, the two sides emerged as the *Nacionales* (a self-definition as Nationals because they considered themselves the true Spaniards and patriots) and *Republicanos*, usually referred to in Anglo-Saxon accounts as the Nationalists and the Republicans. The two sides referred to each other as *Fascistas* and *Rojos* (meaning Reds). In my field sites, the supporters of the military uprising are described as Fascists, Falangists (from the preexisting right-wing movement that merged into Franco's overarching political organisation, the *Movimiento*), or pejorative terms. Due to the complexity of political affiliations amongst both sides during the war, the further blurring of these associations on a local level, and the very long time span encompassed in this book, I refer to those supporting the winning side, and the supporters of Franco's subsequent regime, simply as "Francoists." The war was conducted by opposing armies who fought extended battles for the major cities and strategically significant territories throughout Spain, but a large proportion of the dead were unarmed civilians, killed for a continuum of ideological-religious-class reasons (Fernández de Mata 2004). Many of these killings took the form of extrajudicial abductions and executions, known euphemistically as *paseos* or "taking a stroll." These were perpetrated by militias rather than soldiers, on a highly localised, intimate, and sometimes fratricidal level, as was the case in my field sites.

The scale of the trauma experienced by the country as a whole is indicated by a consideration of the statistics on death, incarceration, and exile:

> It has been calculated that there were some 350,000 deaths during the Civil War period of 1936–1939 in Spain in excess of the number that might have been expected had there been no war. A disturbingly high proportion of these were deaths away from the battlefield. An additional 214,000 excess mortalities have been calculated for the period 1940–1942, as a result of hunger, disease and political repression related to the conflict, though the real effects may have been worse still. Around 500,000 people fled into exile at the end of the war. At the end of 1939, according to government statistics, there were more than 270,000 held in the regime's prisons where political executions took place and where punishment beatings, starvation and lethal epidemics were commonplace. (Richards 2002, 93)

It has been estimated that 200,000 of the 350,000 war deaths were of Republicans. Of 270,000 Republican prisoners, 100,000 died in prisons and concentration camps in the postwar period (Preston 1989).

It is the victims of the *paseos* or extrajudicial killings of Republican civilians, killed during the war period but away from battle lines and buried in unmarked mass graves, that form the primary focus of the ARMH campaign for the exhumation and reburial of human remains.

However, alongside these clandestine executions and disappearances there were also public, highly ritualised manifestations of violence, often drawing on religious motifs of *auto da fé*, and even crucifixions, highly redolent of practices of the Inquisition (Graham 2004). There was a high incidence of exemplary violence and public exposure of human remains. Large numbers of people were internally displaced, and systematic aerial bombardment of civilian settlements was used for the first time on mainland Europe. It has been documented that rape and systematic acts of gendered or sexual violence were perpetrated in communities that fell to Francoist forces. In addition, civilians were subject to psychic violence in the form of print and radio propaganda that consisted of highly elaborated and obscene descriptions of violence, particularly threats of sexual violence (Preston 2004a). The period from 1936 to 1939 can be characterised as a time of extreme violence, trauma, and loss that directly affected a large proportion of Spain's civilian population. Espinosa (2002, 103) has been at the forefront of historians who have characterised this violence as "genocidal." He asserted that the working-class population of some regions of Spain, particularly in the south, was subject to a systematic extermination.

Spain was ruled as a dictatorship between 1939 and the death of General Franco in 1975. During this period there were a severe repression of political dissenters and reprisals against the families and supporters of Republicans who had died in the war and in the wave of postwar political executions. Tens of thousands of Republicans remained in labour camps or prisons until the 1950s, where they received political and religious reeducation. A bureaucratic framework of surveillance, conduct reports, and travel passes evolved in order to control the movements and livelihoods of politically suspect families, often causing them to be divided and subjected to economic hardship. Franco's government instigated a postwar autarky reflecting Spain's isolation from Europe. This triggered intense economic scarcity and rationing, which disproportionately affected the losing Republican side (Richards 1995). Requisitions of assets by the state left Republican families destitute, and a system of crippling fines for "political crimes," levied retrospectively and even posthumously for political activities throughout the 1930s, further exacerbated the material hardship for Republican families (Graham 1995a, 1995b). In line with other totalitarian regimes, there was a highly evolved state propaganda machine demonising the Left, as well as a state censorship of all forms of public expression. A detailed account of the development and functioning of this propaganda machine, both during and after the war, can be found in Sevillano (2007).

Significantly, the areas in which my fieldwork took place returned Popular Front politicians to the Spanish parliament in 1936. Moreover, the mayor and town council in both field sites were of the Popular Front, although local political activity in the area was also strongly informed by anarchist and communist groups, particularly trade unions. This meant that with the onset of war, the working-class populations of my field sites were targeted for severe reprisals. In my first field site of Villavieja, the major episode of political violence occurred in 1936 with the killing of twenty-two men and their burial in two mass graves. The nucleus of the victims were members of the village council and the working men's club, including the mayor, as well as their close male relatives and associates from the surrounding area. In my second field site of Las Campanas, a more extended episode of roundups and incarcerations during the first week of September 1936 culminated in the execution of forty-six men from the site and surrounding villages and hamlets, whose remains were concealed in a single mass grave on the outskirts of Las Campanas. The victims were once again politically active working-class, and liberal middle-class men and their male kin.

The opening up of Spanish society began in the 1960s. This has been linked to the boom in mass tourism and the associated increase in contact with northern Europeans who introduced progressive social trends, particularly around popular culture, fashion, and sexual behaviour (Tremlett 2006). Admittance to the United Nations in 1955 ended the initial phase of postwar isolation. A greater level of international engagement was attained via admittance to NATO in 1982. Some liberalisation in Spanish politics occurred in the 1960s, although political incarcerations and executions continued into the 1970s (Preston 1989). Some commentators argue that the regime actually hardened during the 1970s, and that the ultimate transition to democracy was certainly not a progressive or linear evolution from the dictatorship (Ferrán Galleg 2008). Economic development fuelled a growing political confidence amongst the Spanish population, spearheaded by the new trade unions that formed around the rapidly expanding construction and service industries (Tremlett 2006). The death of Franco in November 1975, preceded in 1973 by the assassination in an ETA bombing of his appointed successor, the right-wing hard-liner Carrero Blanco, precipitated the transition to a parliamentary democracy in 1977 with the monarch, Juan Carlos, as the new head of state.

The form of this democratic transition, a so-called "pacted" transition, was hailed by international commentators as a model of compromise and cooperation between formerly implacable enemies (Aguilar 2001; Desfor Edles 1995, 1998). It is now increasingly seen by critics on the Left as the old guard's grudgingly relinquishing power, primarily as an act of self-preservation to avoid the kind of mass uprisings witnessed in Portugal and Greece (Díaz 1995; Rey 2001). The rhetoric of this transition is highly indicative. A political amnesty was granted, indicating the desire for a clean break from the past. The period of consensus that emerged is popularly characterised within Spain as "the pact of silence" or, most tellingly, "the pact of amnesia" (Aguilar 2002). Contemporary critics argue that the compromises and concessions made by the Left in order to be granted the legal status of a recognised political faction and the right to participate in the transition has in fact rendered these political parties paralysed, impotent, and even morally bankrupt. Critics argue that their complicity in the amnesia regarding the killing and repression of civilians during the Civil War and the dictatorship has undermined their symbolic capital and political raison d'être as parties of popular resistance; or, worse, that their "pacting" constitutes a betrayal of the victims of Francoism (Díaz 1995; Rey 2001). The examples of recent, more open transition processes, such as the South African model of truth and reconciliation, provide an unfavourable comparison (González-Ruibal 2007). The investigations into the "Dirty War" in Latin America, particularly the exhumations in Argentina (Robben 2005) and the legal pursuit of General Pinochet, also stand in stark comparison to the timidity of the Spanish transition, as highlighted by Emilio Silva's reference to Latin America in his first newspaper article and explored in some detail by Davis (2005) and Golob (2008).

The fragility of the emergent consensus of the late 1970s and 1980s was underlined by the failed military coup of 1981, when a small core of Francoist army officers staged an armed occupation of the parliament and declared the return of military rule. This armed occupation occurred during a televised debate, and the country was transfixed by the images broadcast from within their new parliament. The abortive coup was defused within twenty-four hours, in large part thanks to the decisive action taken by King Juan Carlos, who cemented his new role as the figurehead of democratic Spain. Although in popular mythologising this event has come to be seen as a rite of passage or "baptism of fire" that ultimately strengthened the new regime, it was a highly traumatic and destabilising experience for many of my informants, as right-wing vigilantes in communities throughout Spain drew up blacklists targeting renowned left-wingers, and for twenty-four hours the country appeared on the verge of stepping back to the *paseos* of 1936.

The formation of ARMH created a rupture in Spanish memory politics and marked a clear departure from earlier and comparatively muted attempts to open a debate on Francoist repression or even simply generate a climate in which the topic could be publicly addressed by the government, the media, or the academia. Prior to 2000, the Republican experience of Francoist repression was documented mainly in memoirs and scholarly historical work based on textual or archival sources, but this had little impact on mainstream opinion within Spanish society as it was mainly produced by the vast diaspora of Spanish intellectual and political exiles (Fidalgo 1939; García 1972), or written by Anglophone historians and primarily circulated within Europe and North America (Fraser 1979; Preston 1996; Thomas 1990). (However, Juliá [2010] makes a reappraisal of Spanish historiography and suggests that substantial critical scholarly work was undertaken, even under dictatorship.) Outside of Spain, popular understandings of the Civil War were shaped by the prolific output of the International Brigades (Orwell 2003).

It is possible to identify the emergence of a public discourse on Francoist political repression. In particular, the theme of repressed memory surfaced during the 1990s in response to a wave of novels and memoirs written and disseminated within Spain (Cercas 2003, Chacón 2004), which undoubtedly laid the groundwork for the foundation of ARMH. Scholars working in the field of Spanish literary theory and analysis have been at the forefront of identifying the more covert or subtle treatments of trauma, loss, and memory that can be discerned in the cinema and literature produced both during and after Franco (Ferrán 2007; Kovács 1991; Resina 2000). The significance of this first wave of publications for the current exhumations is most clearly illustrated by the fact that the founder of ARMH, Emilio Silva, a journalist and freelance writer, professes that his initial investigations into his Republican grandfather's death were conceived as research for a novel about the Civil War, but prompted instead a search for the grandfather's physical remains that culminated in his exhumation (Silva and Macías 2003).

Nonetheless, this emergent debate was limited in terms of popular engagement and breadth of audience when compared with the volume of media coverage, internet activity, parliamentary debate, and new legislation provoked by the exhumation of Republican mass graves since 2000. Exhumation has marked a clear step change in the scale and tone of the public debate on Republican memory, moving it from the commitment of a few individual authors and commentators in the 1990s to a concerted memory campaign with mass grassroots participation. In effect, the exhumation of Emilio Silva's grandfather, the founding act of the ARMH campaign, was a pivotal moment in that it represented a transition from invoking the dead verbally or textually to materialising them physically. This shift in material register from the textual documentation of experiences to the exposure of bodies and objects in the mass graves has engendered a radical reconfiguration of Spanish memory politics.

MEMORY, MATERIALITY, AND MASS GRAVES

My theoretical approach to these exhumations draws on several authors. Following Parker Pearson (1982), I examine the dead and their traces as part of the material culture of the living, used to make representations about the past, present, and future. In line with the ideas of Verdery (1999), my starting point is that exhumation achieves not only a transformation in the condition and position of a set of human remains, but also a broader spatial and temporal reconfiguration that produces significant changes in a community's prevailing memory politics. The changing treatment of the dead, including the war dead, and specifically the placing of their bodies and the funerary and memorial architecture surrounding them, can be a manifestation of important societal change of the kind identified by Tarlow (1997, 1999) and Laqueur (1994, 1996) in the wake of World War I.

New forms of collective identity or new communities, coalesced and mobilised around the dead, can themselves become a force for societal change, according to Marres's and, more broadly, Latour's idea of the creation of distinct "publics" as interested parties drawn together around "causes" (Latour 2002; Marres 2002). The process of creation of publics is here complicated by the potential of exhumation and identification to activate biological networks of common ancestry amongst the descendants of the dead, and to elicit among the living varying degrees of sympathy or solidarity with the Leftist ideologies that bound together this category of Republican dead. These two bases for collective identity crosscut the formation of a new public united by a shared interest in the cause or "problem" posed by the remains of Republican dead in unmarked graves, and by the unacknowledged crimes that led to their deaths.

The characterisation of human remains as the material culture of the living is prevalent in current archaeological theory. This is important for an analysis of the interactions between the living and the dead, but can detract from an appreciation of the powerful material and aesthetic properties and affordances of the dead and their associated objects. The precise physical form and appearance of human remains vary, for example in their levels of preservation and decay and in the degree to which the remains are recognisably human or dramatically altered by death and burial. These particular affordances actively shape the responses and representations that can be made by the living when encountering the dead. While recognising the analytical complexity of human remains as material culture—due to their ambivalent status as once-human/still-human and to their being a physical index of death—this analysis follows Domanska (2005, 2006) in her characterisation of human remains as traces of the past amongst many other material traces. The representational and associative properties of photographs, mementoes, and intimate possessions of the dead can be just as nuanced and emotionally potent as the physical remains of the dead themselves, as some of the responses noted in this study will attest.

The analysis of memory in this study has foregrounded the potential importance for archaeology of considering imagined and remembered objects as a further trace from the past that must be analysed in conjunction with the bodies and objects rematerialised through exhumation or excavation. An attention to the material culture surrounding the exhumation also reveals the extent to which the exhumed bodies and objects are contextualised within an existing suite of related objects, particularly photographs, but also letters, documents, and other mementoes, creating new assemblages. The opening of the grave and the exposure of human remains activates new affordances even in familiar things such as photographs and mementoes, by bringing them into a new conjunction with the remains of the dead. The material indices of the dead that exist prior to exhumation are significant in shaping how the rematerialised human remains will be received and experienced, a point that resonates with Sant Cassia's work on mourning and exhumation amongst Greek Cypriots (2007).

Some studies of exhumation have been outcome-oriented in that they focus on the eventual relocation of the body and on the forms of political resolution and emotional closure achieved through the unearthing and ultimate reburial of the dead. However, human remains and their associated objects change materially and visually in important ways throughout this process: from concealed-but-imagined bodies underground, to exposed, comingled, and entangled corpses in the grave, to the clean remains processed in a laboratory or labelled and photographed in a scientific report. A breakdown of the exhumation into its progressive stages allows an analysis of these material changes. As an exhumation progresses, bodies and objects come to the attention of different audiences and their different physical properties are foregrounded. During exhumation, the dead are brought into new assemblages with people and things, shaping the particular representations of the past that can be made at different junctures in the investigative and commemorative process.

The literature on memory that I have drawn on most heavily is a body of work on "postmemory" (Hirsch 1996; Hirsch and Spitzer 2006) and on the "received" or "vicarious" past (Young 1997, 1998), terms devised to describe the form of memory and mourning that developed amongst the children of Holocaust survivors born after the war who have no firsthand memory of the people, places, and cultures that were lost, and whose childhood is nevertheless saturated by an awareness of that loss. They inherit a sense of that which was lost, yet are distanced from their parents by the impossibility of recalling the loss firsthand. For the children of Holocaust survivors, the condition of postmemory is made painful by the feeling that, despite their efforts, the depth of their parents' grief cannot be fully shared or assuaged. The significance of this work to the Spanish context is that the long delay between the Civil War and the current exhumations means that many of the surviving children of the dead were small infants at the time of their fathers' deaths, or were even born posthumously. Their firsthand memories of their fathers may be fragmentary, but their lives have been shaped by the repressed mourning of the female relatives who raised them: the wives, mothers, and sisters of the murdered men. The memory of this female mourning recurs in my informants' accounts, expressed as vicarious mourning. The body of work on postmemory is of relevance to this discussion in that it is strongly concerned with the materialisation of the past through photographs, letters, mementoes, and a range of material practices designed to "build" the past in order to mourn it more effectively. It is useful to situate the exhumation of human remains within these other materialisations of the past.

The replication and dissemination of these encounters with the dead through the news media and the internet have magnified the impact of exhumation, creating ruptures on both the local and national scale. The exhumation opens a new discursive space in which representations of the past can be made. The bodies and objects exposed, and the new scientific and commemorative practices surrounding the graves, afford new types of representation of the past. This work undertakes a detailed analysis of the interaction between the exhumation of mass graves in two small rural communities in Castile-León. It examines the existing forms of memory and representations of the past, and the new representations that emerge in the discursive spaces opened during the extended process of exhumation, scientific analysis, reburial, and commemoration.

My intention is to look at the exhumation, identification, and reburial sequence as a series of transformations in the way the past—both the dead and the violent events surrounding their deaths—is materialised, considering these materialisations as a progressive series of shifts between different material registers. Examples of material registers that will be analysed include portrait photographs of the dead, anonymous human remains, identified individual remains, photographs of human remains, personal possessions of the dead, and the monoliths and commemorative sites ultimately constructed after exhumation and reburial. I will examine each of the shifts in register discernible in the sequence of materialisations that constitutes the exhumation process as a fault line, or the opening of a discursive space. These are moments of opportunity in which particular representations of the traumatic past are made and contested. I will consider the multiple representations of the dead along an analytical axis of individual and affective representations versus collective and political representations.

The exhumations discussed in this book occurred outside of a designated jural framework for the presentation of evidence, and there is no process approximating a Truth and Reconciliation hearing or a tribunal, so the rationale for exhumation cannot be to attain a juridical determination, in the strict sense, of the cause and circumstances of death. There is a legal context surrounding most exhumations, including the notification of a magistrate or local authorities of the intent to exhume, or to gain physical access to the gravesite. These are procedural aspects that have, in part, been codified under the Law of Memory, but this legislation was not yet in place at the time of the exhumations under discussion here. It should be noted that the operating protocol of the Foro por la Memoria includes the notification of a judge and local police, and at some sites, supporters of the Foro have lobbied the local authorities to undertake a criminal investigation into the killings (Foro por la Memoria and Conde 2008, 136).

Instead of pursuing a legal outcome, the primary rationale for these exhumations lies in the perception of an enduring bond between the living and the dead, which causes the location and condition of these bodies to have some bearing on those living in the present. This bond could be represented as primarily collective or political, located in some ideological continuity or lineage connecting the dead to the present. The rationale for exhumation would be to achieve some temporal or spatial reconfiguration, in some way altering the conditions of this living collective by moving their dead. However, the prevailing pact of silence implies that this kind of explicitly political representation of the dead, and of an ideological bond between the living and the dead, will be widely perceived as negative. The act of materialising the dead through exhumation, and the perceived neutrality or objectivity associated with the act of materialisation, help to circumvent or counter this negative perception.

The condition of atomisation engendered in Republican families under Franco's dictatorship and the state of postmemory produced by the nearly seventy years between the Civil War and the exhumation render these affective and familial bonds stretched and difficult. The material affordances of the bodies and objects materialised during exhumation, and particularly in the practices of scientific human identification, enable ARMH and the expert practitioners to foster affective bonds and familial sentiments. Encounters with the bodies and objects from the grave engender a range of emotions, including a sense of identification and connection, a sense of ownership, knowledge of, and familial relatedness with the dead, and sentiments of empathy, pathos, and mourning. In this way, the unearthing of bodies can potentially overcome the stretched or broken relationship between the living and the dead produced by the atomisation under dictatorship, the pact of silence, and the state of postmemory.

As outlined in the preamble, the meaning of exhumation has undergone a process of convergence through which a dominant understanding has emerged with regard to the use of exhumation in both the investigation and the memorialisation of conflict and human rights abuse. However, a comparative look at the analyses of exhumation conducted by Verdery (1999), Kwon (2008), Crossland (2000, 2002), and Sant Cassia (2007) highlights the importance of the unique political, cultural, and temporal context in each case. The first parameter specific to Spain is the highly effective repression of any verbal expressions of memory in both written and oral form, characterised as the pact of silence, the pact of forgetting, or the pact of amnesia. These characterisations of the prevailing climate surrounding the representation of the past are widely acknowledged across the political spectrum, and the terms are used routinely in discourses about society and politics in contemporary Spain. The pact of silence is not an enforced condition resulting from political repression. It is a pact, meaning it is both a self- and mutually enforced condition of censorship across the political spectrum. Particular value is attributed to mutual tolerance and consensus-building across the political spectrum on both the macro and micro levels as safeguards against a return of Spain's recent history of political extremism and polarisation. This climate is so pervasive that it can be described as the hegemony of consensus. Political representations of the recent past and of the Civil War dead are experienced as inherently threatening and destabilising to this climate of mutual tolerance and coexistence. Those who make explicitly political or ideological representations of the Civil War risk being perceived as rancorous and inflammatory.

The contemporary Historic Memory campaign is a *de facto* Republican memory campaign, as the Francoist representations of the past constituted the dominant representations in Spain thus far. A Republican memory campaign is by definition political or ideological, as "Republican" indicates a collective identity based on a shared ideology and a shared experience of defeat in the Civil War. It entails the representation of the past as experienced by one side of the war, a clear transgression of the pact of silence and the hegemony of consensus. The fact that the majority of participants in the Republican memory campaign refer to it exclusively as a "Historic Memory" campaign rather than a Republican memory campaign is a semantic marker of the degree to which it transgresses the pact of silence.

This lends the materiality of bodies and objects exhumed from mass graves a particular power or potency to circumvent and ultimately undermine the prevailing prohibitions on the representation of the Republican past. As identified by Klinenberg (2001), the materiality of the bodies and objects exhumed from mass graves enable representations of the past to be made without apparent authorship or mediation, thus conferring them a form of political neutrality and objectivity. Furthermore, the ARMH campaign is aware of the precedents of exhumations around the world and of the mostly benign associations, and positive public perception, that have accrued to these precedents. This symbolic capital is employed strategically or instrumentally by the ARMH campaigners in their transformation of Spanish memory politics.

In addition to the materiality of the exhumed bodies and objects, the forensic paradigm entails a focus upon individual cases and the practice of individuating remains through scientific identification. This enables the campaign to foreground individual and affective representations of the dead. Of course, affective and familial sentiments for the dead form part of the complex and varied rationales behind these exhumations, but as widely held or natural human sentiments they are very hard for potential critics to challenge without appearing to lack humanity or common feelings. This further deflects the potential charge, levelled by opponents and critics, of politicising the past, and helps dispel the destabilising and threatening connotations that come with revisiting the recent past in Spain.

My hypothesis contends that the sustained repression experienced by Republican families engendered a condition of atomisation, dismantling memory communities and creating a hostile memory environment. This presents particular challenges for a Republican memory campaign. Collective and political representations of the dead were not permitted in this environment. Moreover, the condition of atomisation and the breakdown of the intergenerational transmission of memory about the dead also inhibited any detailed representations of the dead as individuals, or the fostering of affective bonds between the living and the dead, particularly amongst the surviving children of Republicans who were small infants when their relatives were killed. The prohibitions on mourning and the psychic state identified by some authors on the Spanish Civil War as "inner exile" (Richards 2002) suggests that not only the public acts of mourning, but also the sentiments of mourning were effectively repressed. The time span of nearly seventy years between exhumation and reburial has produced a particular demographic effect. The generational passing of the contemporaries of the war dead such as their partners and siblings, but also of the older offspring of the dead who still possessed some firsthand knowledge and memory of the Civil War, has resulted in a condition that may be characterised as postmemory (Hirsch 1996).

The children of the dead who participated most actively in the exhumation process in my field sites were in their seventies and eighties. The majority had little memory or knowledge of their dead father, either firsthand or transmitted by older relatives, yet they had been brought up in households that had been irrevocably changed by these killings. They were raised by surviving female relatives who were the bereaved partners, sisters, and mothers of those killed. The condition of postmemory identified amongst the children of Holocaust survivors describes this state of having one's own biography conditioned by the loss of people, places, or cultures that one cannot personally recall. As a primary rationale for the ARMH exhumations is located in sentiments of loss and mourning, the condition of postmemory and the complexity or even ambivalence surrounding the affective bonds between the living and the dead present a potential challenge or stumbling block to the campaign.

The materialisation of the dead through exhumation, particularly the individuating practices of scientific human identification, allows both ARMH and the expert practitioners to make a particular representation of the dead, not only to potential critics of the campaign but also to the relatives of the dead themselves, which privileges their individual identity and emphasises the uniqueness of their antemorten existence, which in turn fosters affective bonds between the living and dead and elicits sentiments of pathos and mourning, thus overcoming the possible ambivalence and resistance outlined above. However, the appearance of multiple remains, their intimate physical proximity, and their display of common features such as visible injury patterns, also enable collective representations of the dead to be made, thus opening up the spaces for contestation that will be examined throughout this discussion.

The tension between the individual and collective identity of the dead is due to the documented existence of shared political beliefs and connected political biographies among the dead found in the mass graves in my field sites. This tension is rendered more complex as many of those engaged in the Republican memory campaign are aligned to varying degrees with the left-wing politics that characterised the original Republican movement. Certainly the majority of participants in the Republican memory campaign would identify themselves as opponents to Franco's ideology, and thus they identify themselves with the Republican victims of Francoism as a collective.

My fieldwork reveals some paradoxes in the different sides of the campaign, in that, despite privileging affective or individual relationships with the past, the discourse and practice of the exhumations campaign reveal that ARMH is concerned with the formation or transformation of collectives in the present. Such campaign seeks to create a stronger collective identity amongst the families of repressed Republicans, spreading an awareness of Spain's leftist heritage as a rallying point for the contemporary Left and as a model for political action in the present. The attention and fascination that the exhumation of mass graves commands over public discourse and the media enable ARMH to disseminate an awareness of the brutality of Francoist repression. By raising public awareness of Francoist atrocities, ARMH engenders a wider critique of the dictatorship and the compromised transition to democracy, ultimately achieving a hegemonic shift toward the Left. The representations of bodies and objects that flow from the exhumations allow the campaign to forge and disseminate particular material representations of the past without having to formulate them verbally, making a direct contestation by Franco's supporters much more difficult than in a conventional verbal historical debate.

Following the work of Crossland (2000, 2002), I aim to show that the exhumation and reburial process in Spain is not a unitary process, and that the participants themselves are not a homogenous or unified group. This discussion does not concentrate on the political opponents to the Republican exhumation, but looks instead at three constituencies: ARMH campaigners; relatives of the dead, elderly surviving Republicans, and other sympathetic community members resident in my field sites; and expert practitioners within the investigative process, namely archaeologists and forensic scientists. These three broad constituencies are ostensibly united by common goals in undertaking the exhumation, yet my fieldwork suggests that they may be widely divergent in terms of the expectations, motivations, and goals underlying their participation. Their experience of the exhumation process, and the representations they make of the bodies, objects, and images encountered during this series of shifts in material register will vary accordingly. In my ethnography I will attempt to identify some of the key features that inform the divergent perspectives of these different constituencies. In addition to considering significant oppositions such as urban/rural or expert/layman, I will take account of age and generational experiences, particularly in terms of condition of postmemory.

Variations in the political or ideological convictions held by informants in these communities have, in part, been shaped by individual experiences of political repression and atomisation, especially amongst the elderly relatives of the dead who lived through the most repressive era of the dictatorship. Further points of divergence or tension between these three constituencies emerged in relation to the conceptualisation of death, mourning, human remains, and local notions of family honour and shame. I will analyse the local memory idioms through which the past is represented by the relatives of the dead and my elderly informants. These existing memory idioms, which predate the Republican memory campaign, reveal the challenges inherent in making any representation of the dead, political or affective, in the context of severe political repression.

The different meanings of a single exhumation will be discussed by paying close attention to the responses engendered by encounters with the bodies and objects at different stages of the exhumation. The representations made by my informants as a consequence of such encounters are particularly revealing of the tensions between the dual impulses to individualise and collectivise the dead. I will consider the qualities and affordances of the bodies and objects exhumed and recognise the potential agency of the remains. This entails an appreciation of how the affordances of bodies and objects can shape the meaning of exhumation for those participating in it, challenging their expectations or preconceptions of the dead. An example of this can be seen in how the emotional and political responses of the expert practitioners sometimes challenge the notion of professional detachment. I aim to demonstrate that the power of these bodies and objects lie in particular material affordances that may be isolated and analysed, and yet may still be polysemous or promiscuous in their meanings for different people. My intention is to undermine a static interpretation of this assemblage of material culture, and emphasise that the exhumation and reburial process by its nature engenders constant physical transformations of the same material objects, progressively changing what is revealed, the level of detail, the perspective, and the framing.

The concept of assemblage is important to my material analysis, as divergent representations may emerge from the same process of materialisation if this is brought into an assemblage with other material indices of the dead. This is particularly true of the intense layering of multiple materialisations of the dead that occurs at specific junctures, such as the reburial ceremony. The bringing of different material indices of the dead into new relationships is considered as a key activity of forensic practice, in particular the matching of ante- and postmortem data to achieve positive identifications of anonymous bodies. Expanding the concept of assemblage, my intention is to situate the exhumed bodies and objects within a broader material context in my field sites, and to consider them in relation to the objects evoked by memory and the objects and images that constitute mementoes of the dead, including physical locales and structures within the two villages that relate to Republican memory.

Finally, I will endeavour to assess the outcome of the exhumation and reburial process for the relatives of the dead and community members within the two villages, and assess these results against the goals of both the ARMH campaigners who orchestrate the exhumation and the expert practitioners who implement it. I will assess the impact of the exhumations on the affective and political representations of the dead in my field sites, noting in particular the emergence of new collective identities amongst the living that coalesce around the exhumation process and a shared bond with the dead. I will consider how these small-scale, village-level changes can be understood as part of a cataclysmic rupture produced in Spanish memory politics: the nationwide "mass grave phenomena."

CONSTITUENCIES AND INFORMANTS

To assess more precisely the different understandings, representations, and expectations surrounding exhumation, it is worth considering in greater detail the three broadly defined constituencies that I have identified in the course of my fieldwork: the relatives of the dead, the ARMH campaigners, and the archaeological or forensic practitioners. Although these categories are simplifications, they are necessary analytical tools to ensure that this discussion is sensitive to the multiple meanings of the same process. For elderly relatives and survivors from the 1930s and 1940s, the desired outcome of exhumation refers not only to their personal relationship with the dead, but also to their experience of marginalisation in a particular locale, and their own identity and family status within the context of the immediate community. For this constituency, the context in which the exhumations occur is a history of sustained repression and intimidation. Some have experienced the death of a parent, the prohibition of public mourning, the victimisation of their surviving female relatives, and the appropriation of material property resulting in destitution. All of the above repressive techniques draw their efficacy from culturally (and generationally) specific constructs of honour and shame, and particularly from a notion of family honour that emphasises filial duty, gender norms, and the material self-reliance of the family unit (Gilmore 1980, 1987). The significance of the exhumation and reburial of the dead for their relatives must be understood in the light of these experiences and within this geographical and cultural context.

After the cataclysmic violence of the Civil War, the relatives of the dead were subjected to constant surveillance and arbitrary punishment (Casanova 2002), engendering in a wide section of the population a form of self-monitoring and self-censorship in verbal communication that resulted in a severe breakdown in the transmission of memory (Cenarro 2002; Richards 1998) and in the production of culturally specific idioms to encode memory, as I will argue in chapter 2. This was accompanied by an internalisation of grief (Fidalgo 1939) and by the silencing of political debate, which induced a condition of atomisation amongst many surviving Republicans and their families that endured throughout the dictatorship into the present, despite the transition to democracy (Aguilar 2002). This constituency's experience of the exhumation process and the opportunities it affords for the expression of memory—both the factual testimony prompted by the investigation process and the emotional expression elicited by commemorative acts—must be understood in the light of this history of atomisation, as I will discuss in chapters 1 and 2.

Of the second constituency, the ARMH campaigners, some though not all may have had a Republican family member who was repressed under Franco, and may have initially approached the organisation to investigate their immediate family's history before taking a more active organisational role. In this respect there is a degree of overlap with the first constituency; however, the majority of volunteers who participate actively in the ARMH campaign are generationally equivalent to the children and grandchildren of the elderly survivors and relatives. They have not experienced the full force of political violence or the process of atomisation firsthand, though they may well understand their impact on the transmission of memory within families. Also, memory campaigners who are urban dwellers, well educated, or professionals are further removed from the logic underpinning the repression that occurred in small rural communities. The great majority of those active on behalf of ARMH are informed by a broadly leftist ideology, loosely aligned to, or to the left of, the mainstream *Partido Socialista Obrero Español* (PSOE).

Those assisting with the memory campaign are politically engaged and are more likely than the relatives of the dead to interpret the Civil War and the dictatorship in explicitly political terms as a war between ideologies or social classes, in which the ruling classes, the church, and the military joined forces to maintain their hold on power and resources. Some of them are committed atheists and express fiercely anticlerical views. Significantly, many of my informants who were active within ARMH were very well informed about the history of the Spanish Left, Republicanism, and the social and economic reforms made in the 1930s. As I will explore in chapters 1 and 2, this was a clear point of divergence from the elderly generation. Many of my elderly informants found the political activity of that period, and particularly of their own parents, to be a highly dangerous and disturbing topic. Although not all my informants explicitly offered Republicanism as a model or template for the future of Spain, many found personal inspiration in a Republican "spirit" or ethos that clearly formed the basis of their sense of identification with the dead. A few could be said to idolise the Republic and the Republicans, and felt a powerful sense of connection with this past. I heard frequent unfavourable comparisons between the apathy and materialism of contemporary Spanish society and the radicalism and idealism of the 1930s. The ARMH campaigners were highly diverse, but a fraction of them could be characterised as supporting the exhumations as part of a critique on both Francoism and the current climate of centrist political consensus. They participated in the exhumations with a view to achieving a hegemonic shift to the Left in popular political discourse.

The archaeologists and forensic practitioners form a third constituency, though this is an extremely porous category, as some of the expert practitioners who choose to volunteer in the exhumation and identification of Republican bodies are motivated by a history of political repression within their own families. The fact that all technical expertise in my field sites (and most of Spain) is offered on a completely voluntary basis, with some workers even taking unpaid leave from their "day job" to assist in the exhumations, reveals that members of this constituency cannot be labelled as "professionals" in a narrow sense, and are bound to have complex motivations for their participation. A considerable proportion volunteer their expertise out of ideological sympathy with the campaign, and go on to play a wider role in the ARMH campaign. They attend commemorative events and draw in an ever widening network of colleagues and peers, thus strengthening the campaign. This constituency seeks a particular set of outcomes evaluated on the basis of technical performance and the technically measurable success of the exhumation. This constituency has almost sole control over the laboratory analysis stage, which largely excludes the relatives of the dead.

The primary lens through which archaeologists and forensic practitioners view the bodies and objects is evidential, aimed at reconstructing the death event and identifying anonymous remains. Their representation of bodies and objects frequently dominates the exhumation and reburial, but also comes into conflict with the representations made by campaigners and relatives. As I will argue in chapter 3, the expert practitioners' experience of the remains is itself fluid, and technical representations of the dead conditioned by disciplinary training are often mediated by memory, family history, sentiment, and ideology. This constituency plays a significant role in emphasising the primacy of the individual in the work of the ARMH campaign, due to the paradigm of individual human identification they bring to the investigation. Expert practitioners also make frequent representations of their work through the media, technical reports, and academic publications. They have significant control over the perceived outcome of the exhumation for the relatives of the dead, in that their professional judgement will determine both the official narrative of the deaths produced by the exhumation and the attribution of identity to the bodies. They are, nonetheless, in a position of dependency on the local community for verbal testimony and material evidence, such as photographs or DNA reference samples, that will aid in their reconstructions of the past. They are also incomers, dependent on the hospitality of the local community, becoming socially integrated and emotionally involved with it; therefore, the power relations between expert and layman are not clearly defined or static.

My approach to the interview varied according to the informant. I conducted semistructured interviews and extended life histories with my older informants, who were primarily the children of the murdered Republicans. They either lived locally or had returned for the exhumation or as part of their habitual summer visit. Other elderly informants could be classed as the surviving contemporaries of the dead men, who were on the cusp of adulthood when the war started. They still resided in the two villages and had witnessed or experienced the most severe phases of Francoist repression. My approach to negotiating the intense emotions elicited by this subject matter was to let the informant lead the encounter as much as possible. Above all, I found the recording of life histories to be the most satisfactory approach not just in terms of the information collected, but also in terms of the degree of control retained by my informants. The order of the narrative, the point from which difficult themes were broached, and their presentation to me were chosen by my informants, and I felt that the speaker was in control of the ebb and flow of difficult emotions; anger, grief, fear, and anxiety. As will be explored in detail in chapter 2, the absence of a predetermined structure during my encounters with elderly informants allowed certain discernible patterns or idioms to emerge in the narration of loss.

My informants were skilled orators (and dramatists, often assuming several characters and reenacting key scenes of their lives), and this form of storytelling was much more in tune with their social repertoire than any question-and-answer format. The telling of life histories required so many digressions and diversions—into national and local history, family history, political opinions, religious beliefs, local geography, and explanations of work, tools, practices, customs, and food—that the themes I had intended to address with interview questions were covered much more extensively and spontaneously as part of these narratives. Paradoxically, despite the levels of fear and anxiety experienced by my informants in speaking about their experiences of repression, their life histories uncovered another strong cultural pull, related to the prizing of articulate narratives and animated orators. Kenny (1966) undertook a traditional village ethnography in this region and was struck by the eloquence and love of language he encountered. I noted in both villages a great pleasure in entertaining others by holding forth passionately or wittily on a theme, or by recasting an event from one's personal experience, dramatically or humorously, for the amusement of others.

Speaking in a crowd or at a social gathering in these villages seemed to me to fall explicitly into the category of performance. These performances were formalised into vignettes, riddles, "*chistes*" (involving shaggy dog stories, usually sexual), and reported conversations (conflicts or misunderstandings reproduced with gusto, using accents and expressive gestures), which all got a warm response from the listeners. Good speakers were described as the bringers of life and animation. They would be begged to perform, and to reperform every time a new listener joined any small gathering. Several of the elderly men who gave me their life histories could hold the floor for two or three hours without further questions and interruptions from me. Elderly female informants were generally more circumspect about speaking extensively and much more concerned with whether their account was "useful" to me, although their opinions were expressed no less forcefully. The atmosphere in one meeting with an informant could move from pleasure during a well-performed vignette, to tension over the breaching of taboos, to a cathartic outburst of anger. In most of my encounters with elderly locals or relatives of the dead, the imposition of a strict structure on the dialogue seemed contrary to my research goals. It was hard to reconcile this verbal culture with the dominant theme of silence, and clearly, containment, discretion, and judgement over what could or could not be said were also important qualities of people's accounts.

The ARMH coordinators with a longer history of involvement in campaign decision-making were very familiar with the media attention attracted by their work, and thus were becoming used to being observed and interviewed. They were confident when representing themselves and their campaign. The main challenge was to elicit opinions that were something more than a restating of ARMH campaign rhetoric and public relations. I would characterise ARMH as an organisation that carries on simultaneously an internal and an external discourse, one for the supporters and another for their critics or the undecided. The advantage of conducting participant observation in the very intimate and intensely social setting of the exhumations was the possibility to observe this insider's discourse at close quarters, and to use it to balance the outsider's discourse that was presented in my initial interviews with ARMH representatives. Over time, I managed to obtain interviews that were more critical, more analytical, and more candid. This was through repeated exposure to the same small group of individuals, with each return visit to my field sites over a four-year period demonstrating my commitment to understanding their campaign. Above all, the growing candour and reflexivity of this small sample of informants reflects the growing confidence and maturity of the campaign, which evolved dramatically during the course of my research.

At the beginning of ARMH in 2000, when its members were uncertain about the response their campaign would receive and wary of attacks from their political opponents, there was a defensive, closed quality to ARMH's rhetoric and self-representation. Over time, bolstered by the momentum of public support and the engagement of politicians and the media, ARMH has reached a position of strength that permits its members a more reflexive attitude and a critical discussion over the future evolution of the campaign. Several ARMH supporters who had become involved for ideological reasons and were already dynamic members of the community, some with experience in local politics, were well used to representing their opinions in a public setting, and made confident and articulate interviewees. A proportion of the ARMH supporters I encountered in my field sites had Republican relatives buried in those graves or in other graves in the Burgos region. These informants brought dual identities, shaped by their activism and their family history. Their negotiation of these two identities, particularly their explanation of how one fed into the other, made for complex interviews.

The archaeologists and forensic practitioners involved in the exhumations had an academic background, and therefore the majority of them were familiar with the concept of ethnographic fieldwork and data. They had expectations of a highly structured interview and appeared comfortable with the question-and-answer format, intellectually interested in the process, and enthusiastic over the opportunity to articulate their opinions. I encountered several challenges in interviewing these practitioners, be they archaeologists, historians, or forensic scientists. Treating me as a peer, my informants sought a two-way conversation to elicit my opinions and my "findings" from other interviews. It was difficult not to express my views in a way that would influence my informants without overly controlling the exchange and asserting my role as questioner.

In the course of these interviews, informants moved between their personal and professional identities, often explicitly making this distinction in the course of their answers. I tried to address the "person" in this dichotomy by asking informants to speak extensively about family history, family politics, personal politics, and the motivations behind their involvement in exhumation. I also encouraged detailed discussions of the thoughts and emotions elicited by each stage of the exhumation process, as they encountered human remains and possessions of the dead, heard testimonies, and formed social relationships with the relatives of the dead and other community members.

The perceived tensions between the personal and professional identity made some archaeologists and forensic scientists resistant to the exploration of their personal sentiments, as objectivity, detachment, and "distance" are constructed and maintained as prerequisites for effective work in these disciplines. Conversely, several informants entered into a very frank discussion of their emotional response to the exhumation as a welcomed release of sentiments that found no expression during the working day, since discussions at the gravesite were predominantly technical. My informants' negotiation of these identities over the course of our interviews helped me to clarify the hegemony of these disciplines not simply as areas of praxis, but as normative ways of thinking about the past, the dead, their possessions, and their social identity. An awareness of these disciplinary hegemonies helped me think through the precise significance of the application of archaeological and forensic techniques to Spain's encounter with its repressive past.

ARMH is extremely challenging to define in terms of a social movement. It is amorphous, having both a national framework with a clear leadership and an informal grassroots quality, due to the hundreds of local groupings it has inspired rather than directly founded. Any analysis of its discourse risks generalisations and misrepresentations of its members. The majority of local memory networks are affiliated in some way with the national network, though some exist explicitly in reaction against or in direct competition to ARMH, divided by ideological differences on the purpose of recuperating memory, on what constitutes memory, and on the role of human remains in this process. These grounds for division will be outlined in chapter 1 and returned to throughout this discussion. The groups and individuals currently active in the commemoration of the Spanish Left are as disparate and complex as the Left itself during the Spanish Civil War, divided along ideological, regional, and urban/rural lines. And as during the Civil War, the divergence amongst these leftist groups risks distracting from the fiercer ideological opposition coming from those on the political Right who savagely criticise the current exhumations in the media, the parliament, and less formal channels—including defamatory claims and even threats of violence against those participating in the exhumation, or, as I observed in my pilot study, threats of desecration against gravesites and human remains.

A critical analysis of ARMH's discourse and practice has to be placed in the context of the bureaucratic and financial obstacles the organisation currently faces and the historical weight of the systematic repression of Republican memory that it seeks to overturn. Any critique that exposes paradoxes in the campaign rationale, characterises either their discourse or practice as strategic, or questions the achievement of their stated goals is not intended as a negative evaluation of the Republican memory campaign's impact on my field sites or on Spanish memory politics and society. It is not intended to question the necessity of such a campaign, a necessity that is evident given Spain's history of political repression. The tireless volunteering of resources and energy by those active in the campaign must be reiterated, as well as the organisation's remarkable transparency in permitting researchers to have access to moments of decision making and debate that exposed problematic points of divergence amongst campaigners. My observations were of an internally democratic and genuinely grassroots organisation. All the individuals active in the campaign I encountered were notable for their thoughtful and impassioned engagement with the theme of Republican memory. Those within ARMH also supported my ethnographic engagement with the Foro por la Memoria campaign, even when the latter was launching heated public attacks on both ARMH's practices and its founders. In addition to making a balanced representation of ARMH, a further challenge of this work is to retain the specificity of the exhumations that took place in my field sites while reflecting the fact that they were quite self-consciously part of a wave of Republican memory experienced as a new national phenomena, and could not have occurred in isolation. The relatives of the dead are an equally diverse constituency, particularly varying in terms of age and therefore in the degree of political repression experienced firsthand and the degree of relatedness to the dead. The archaeologists and forensic practitioners have a shared disciplinary background, but their motivations for volunteering their expertise on the exhumations vary widely.

Field Sites and Fieldwork

I have situated my ethnography of two rural communities in Castile-León within the wider tradition of Spanish ethnography. Given the strength of regional identities in Spain, it is important to be cautious in any extrapolation of norms or traditions across different regions, for example Mediterranean Spain and its northern fringe. Yet Spanish ethnographies share some elements of political history. Although the Castile region is comparatively understudied compared to others, the work of Behar (1986) and Perez Diaz (1976) is of particular geographical relevance to my field sites. The ethnographic studies that resonate the most with the social and political questions I encountered in my field sites are those conducted by Gilmore (1980, 1987), who writes on class identity and antagonism in Andalucían village life; Narotzky and Smith (2002, 2006), who write on the influence of memories of war and dictatorship on identity formation and local politics in rural Spain; and Collier (1997), who writes on the ruptures between generations in contemporary Spanish society and the role of invented traditions in the new regional identities that have emerged post-Franco.

In the summer of 2003, I conducted a two-month pilot study. I established cooperative relationships with the coordinators of ARMH and participated in the exhumation of mass graves at three sites, one in Burgos, one in Extremadura, and one in Asturias. I gained significant insights into the degree of variability between exhumations, depending on their precise historical and regional context as well as the contemporary political and social dynamics in the surrounding community. Based on this pilot study I selected the village in Burgos, Villavieja, as my primary field site. I have not used the real names of my field sites in this work in order to protect the identities of my informants, and I did not include maps of the area for the same reason. Invented names are used to acknowledge the coherent and separate identity of each community and to enable comparisons. Informant names have been substituted with pseudonyms in recognition of the sensitivity of the material under discussion; this was agreed on with all informants prior to their participation.

The historical events surrounding the grave, the profile of the victims, and the biographical trajectories of their surviving relatives seemed highly representative of the Civil War violence in the province. The traditionally conservative character of the Burgos province, deemed a Francoist heartland, suggested that Republican memory had been heavily repressed. There had been no battle lines in the immediate vicinity, meaning that the mass graves in this part of Burgos unequivocally resulted from the massacre of civilians. Technically, the exhumation had run well, with grounds for optimism that the full process of identification and reburial would unfold as projected, enabling me to study it over time. Those volunteering on it had been expressive, reflective, and articulate, making for an encouraging beginning to fieldwork. On a practical level, the exhumation area was in immediate geographical proximity to the village, and this fostered a steady flow of visitors and observers that created a particularly intense dynamic around the grave, eliciting memories, comments, and testimonies. All those working on the exhumation were housed within the village with a high degree of contact with a cross-section of the community— unlike the other exhumations encountered in my pilot study, where the participants had lived in hostels as an insular group of incomers.

Significantly, the coordinators of the exhumation were mainly local. They appeared to have positive relationships and standing in the immediate villages, and some of the most dynamic protagonists of the exhumation were relatives of the dead. In the Burgos region, I had the sense of a local network of people in the process of mobilising. They shared their proposals for memory work with me—identifications of the recently exhumed bodies, reburials, commemorative acts, prospections for unmarked graves, creation of archives and oral histories, and future exhumations nearby—giving me confidence that their planned campaign of action would unfold in the region over the following two to three years, making practicable repeated visits to observe key events in the process.

During the pilot study in 2003, I spent a month in Villavieja, where I worked on the exhumation of twenty-two individuals, residents of villages and hamlets in the region, killed by Francoist militia in 1936. I met the relatives of the dead who had supported the exhumation and interviewed them on their motivations, opinions, and responses to the exhumation, as well as their broader life histories and family histories. I also carried out extensive interviews with all the archaeological and forensic practitioners who volunteered on the exhumation and with the ARMH representatives from both Madrid and the local campaign. Villavieja is approximately seventy kilometers from the city of Burgos, the provincial capital. It currently has 380 inhabitants, though the numbers fluctuate through the year and swell during summer, as many individuals who work full-time in Burgos city, Madrid, or one of the industrial areas of the north return in July and August. It is hard to assess the most up-to-date population figures because of an influx of seasonal eastern European labour that over the last five years has evolved into a permanent settlement of eastern European agricultural workers on the edge of the village. I have heard only positive commentaries on this demographic shift, specifically because the incomers consist of whole families, and this increases attendance at the local church and particularly at the village primary school, effectively keeping it open. These comments reflect the hope that incomers will reverse the trend of an "aging" or "dying" village that many of my informants comment on. The impression of an aging population is very strong. This is a closed, quiet, and conservative community with little animation or activity outside the municipal swimming pool, which is the hub of the village in July and August. The majority of informants say that Villavieja has existed since the beginning of the millennium, and the Romanesque and gothic architecture of the two central churches seems to confirm this. The occupied homes and streets are well maintained, but some spaces are in obvious disrepair, and some streets have been completely abandoned and consist only of ruined buildings. A couple of contiguous streets that are entirely abandoned are referred to as the *barrio pobre*, or working-class neighbourhood. The majority of Republican families who experienced repression resided here, and the Civil War violence in part explains this abandonment. The structures are so basic and small, relative to modern houses, that they are unsuitable for habitation or adaptation in the present.

Most informants ascribe the "dying" of the village to the absence of work, particularly work that young people are prepared to do. The main productive activity is horticulture or viticulture further afield. Villavieja falls within a well-known winemaking area and is surrounded by a number of vineyards, the quality of which is a source of pride and informs local identity. This history of wine production and appreciation is made highly visible by the massive network of underground wine cellars dug into the hill upon which the village is built, each family traditionally possessing a cellar, and each cellar necessitating a highly distinctive conical turret built of mud bricks for ventilation. They resemble huge ant nests and are scattered throughout the village (figure 1). The nearest administrative centre is Aranda del Duero, a medieval market town with 32,000 inhabitants, now on the *turismo rural* trail with a burgeoning strand of gastrotourism. Almost all bureaucratic transactions require a visit to Aranda or a larger village, as there are very limited shops or services in Villavieja—namely, two bars, two grocers selling dry goods, a bread delivery service, and a restaurant situated on the main road out of the village catering to travellers. Public transport links are limited to a few journeys a week. Throughout the period of my fieldwork, the elected mayor has been the candidate of the centre-left PSOE.

The investigation of the mass grave in Villavieja could not be separated from the parallel investigations conducted by ARMH campaigners

Figure 1. View of Villavieja showing network of tunnels and cellars.

and relatives of the dead in other communities throughout the province of Burgos. Through archive sources and oral history it was determined that some of the missing individuals from Villavieja had been buried in a large mass grave of forty-six individuals on the edge of a village called Las Campanas. Links were established between politically sympathetic individuals in Las Campanas and two of the key coordinators of the Villavieja exhumation, an expert on local history and grandson of two murdered Republicans from Villavieja itself, and an enthusiastic ARMH campaigner from Aranda del Duero. They quickly established that other relatives were visiting the suspected gravesite and enquiring into the feasibility of an exhumation. ARMH began making contact with interested relatives and commenced a detailed investigation of who had been buried in the grave. The large grave in Las Campanas contained several groups of individuals from distinct communities in the area. The strong and immediate support given to Franco's uprising by the authorities in the Burgos province put at the killers' disposal the existing repressive infrastructure, particularly the large prison in the city of Burgos, the smaller prison at Aranda, and a network of local police cells. Republicans would be grouped together, transported around the province, and incarcerated for some time prior to being killed. These roundups of prisoners came to be known as "*sacas*," a modus operandi that combined quasi-official detention with extrajudicial killings (Ríos et al. 2010). As a consequence, the narratives of the victims from these two villages had become intertwined. When the exhumation at Las Campanas was proposed, using the same core team of archaeologists and forensic specialists and many of the same ARMH coordinators of the Villavieja site, it appeared to be a logical continuation of my fieldwork, and I undertook participant observation on this gravesite in the summer of 2004. In addition, based on new evidence some of my informants from Villavieja decided to continue the search for their dead relatives in this new exhumation.

Las Campanas is thirty-five kilometers from Burgos and the same distance from Villavieja. It has 270 inhabitants, with a pattern of seasonal occupation similar to Villavieja's. Despite having a hundred fewer permanent inhabitants, it feels like a more substantial settlement due to the scale of the architecture, and in particular the presence of a complex of religious buildings on the apex of the gently sloping hill on which the village is built (figure 2). The monastery dominates the landscape both physically and aurally, ringing its bells for each service attended by the few surviving monks. It also contains an imposing town hall and a clock tower that now houses a new health centre. Young families and adolescents are visible in the village centre, especially in July and August, lending it a greater degree of animation and dynamism than Villavieja. Nobody talks about the village "dying." Although the

Figure 2.   View of Las Campanas street showing religious buildings.

provision of goods and services is just as limited (three bars, a butcher, and a baker), the bars are well attended and spill out onto the streets, some families drink and dine outside their homes, and promenading the village is a popular evening activity. As in Villavieja, the new swimming pool on the outskirts of the village is the main gathering point for all young families and adolescents as soon as it is warm enough for it to open. The nearest administrative centre is Lerma, historically a regional capital with a preserved baroque palace that attracts a steady flow of tourists. The importance of tourism to Lerma's economy means that from July to September the town holds a succession of markets, concerts, and themed festivals such as the annual "Fiesta Barroca" that are attended by village residents. There is a daily bus service to Lerma and Burgos. This proximity to Burgos makes urban life highly accessible, but are the pleasures of village life, particularly food gardening, keeping pigs and birds, freshwater fishing, and the home distillery, that dominate the time spent in the village: these activities constitute a large part of daily conversation and of the identities of village residents.

The village is surrounded on all sides by arable fields, but since farming became heavily mechanised, the fields employ a tiny fraction of the village, and nearly everyone of working age commutes daily to Burgos or Lerma or works during the week in Santander or Madrid. Wine is appreciated, but compared to Villavieja there are fewer important vineyards and wine production is discussed less. Some public spaces are in disrepair. It is a straggling and spread-out village and most occupied houses are modern, spacious, and expanding outward, compared to the cramped houses that line the older central streets. The unevenness of the roads, sometimes nothing more than dusty tracks, is a source of indignation and constant complaint. A proportion of old houses are abandoned and ruined, or given over to chickens and hay, which lends some parts of the village a forlorn appearance. Throughout my fieldwork the mayor has been the right-wing Partido Popular candidate. Historically, the mayor of Las Campanas is known locally as "Alcalde Cara Cruz," or "Mayor Heads or Tails," due to the fact that the adult population splits almost fifty-fifty between Left and Right during mayoral elections, and on one famous occasion an official from Burgos had to determine the election outcome by tossing a coin. Despite its tiny size, the abandoned houses, and the absence of any village-based economy, Las Campanas looked like a confident community undergoing a quiet renaissance rather than a decline, with my informants stressing that they commuted to and from the village by choice, because of the quality and particular type of life it afforded. A common phrase was "We have everything here," which was not a sentiment I encountered in Villavieja. Part of this impression of a dynamic community was due to an informally run village hall or club house, known as *peña*, that acted as a focal point for left-leaning and socially liberal villagers who organised cultural and festive events as an alternative to the traditional calendar of religious holidays. The resource of the club house and the social profile and commitment of this tight-knit group underpinned the ultimate success of the exhumation in Las Campanas.

The collaboration with those coordinating and participating in the exhumation was important not only to gain access to every aspect of the process, but also to ensure that I respected the aims of their investigative work while undertaking my own ethnography. They had clear investigative goals relating to the location and identification of the dead, and had to negotiate local concerns successfully to overcome resistance to exhumation. I needed a collaborative relationship with ARMH to make sure that in pursuing my research, I did not compromise or jeopardise the central goals of the exhumation. I also needed their help to explain to the informants my role and connection to the exhumation, although with research purposes that were separate and specific to me, as I felt that the maximum possible clarity over my status was an ethical imperative. The coordinators of the exhumation simultaneously introduced me to their network of contacts and established my separate aims. The exhumations raised extreme emotions, confronted traumatic memories, and contained the potential to reopen ideological divisions. The campaigners and exhumation coordinators were more experienced than I was in talking about the traumatic past, had developed strategies to negotiate these topics, and were immersed in the idiom necessary to broach them appropriately. I was unprepared for the reality of the pact of silence in a small rural community, and felt initially overwhelmed by the rawness of the emotions, particularly of fear and anxiety, that talking about the past elicited in my informants. Entering my field site as part of the exhumation and alongside the ARMH coordinators helped me to learn how to communicate appropriately and sensitively. The obvious counterbalance to this advantage is that, though I have attempted a critical analysis of ARMH in this book, throughout my fieldwork I have built a close and positive relationship with many ARMH members or individuals aligned with them, and have to acknowledge the degree to which ARMH members have shaped my understanding of my field sites.

There is clearly an element of contradiction between these close working relationships and the detachment necessary for an evaluation of the ideology and rhetoric of ARMH, which is an inherently political organisation. This is particularly true as its campaign rhetoric and its self-representation are multilayered and vary according to the context, with different discourses presented to those inside or outside of ARMH, to sympathisers, opponents, or the undecided. The contradictions surrounding my identity in the field and the potential impact of my relations with ARMH on the kind of ethnography I managed to produce were at their clearest during moments of divergence or tension between ARMH and the communities in which they operated over the running of the exhumation, its purpose, and the timetable of the exhumation-identification-reburial sequence. The exhumation process, despite local support and collaboration, is essentially a process of urban incomers—archaeologists, historians, forensic scientists, activists, and news media—arriving in a rural community, effecting a change, and leaving after a brief stay. This process brings with it its own set of misunderstandings, disagreements, and power relations around decision making. I managed with varying success to step outside of this dynamic by staying for longer periods in both of my field sites, and repeatedly returning to the villages alone over three years. In subsequent visits to these two communities, some informants shared their opinions, positive and negative, of ARMH as an organisation in a very open way, suggesting that they clearly distinguished between my ethnography and ARMH's exhumation.

To undertake participant observation, I worked as an archaeologist on the exhumations and lived communally with the volunteer archaeologists. The senior specialists were assigned private rooms and stayed as guests in houses in the village. The younger archaeologists and forensic anthropologists, who were either postgraduate students or newly qualified professionals, slept on the floor in a room of twenty, in a store room in Villavieja, and in the medical centre in Las Campanas. Chores such as shopping, cooking, and washing were communal in Villavieja, while in Las Campanas all meals were taken together in the *peña*, and the evenings were spent socialising in the village en masse. The exhumations were intensely social, despite the rigours of the working day, reflecting the fact that all participants were using their vacation time. The cramped conditions and pervading sense of shared purpose rapidly created close relationships amongst the volunteers. During both exhumations, the gravesite itself was a space of intense activity, constant interaction, and heightened emotion. I endeavoured to meet new visitors to the grave as soon as was practicable, so that my presence and my purpose could be drawn to their attention. It was important that my presence and purpose be explicit to those present, to overcome the potential voyeurism of observing people in such an emotionally charged space, particularly during their first encounter with exposed human remains. Being an English-speaking British visitor also underscored my separateness from representatives of ARMH. When approaching the subject of the Spanish Civil War, the status of being foreign and Anglo-Saxon creates specific complexities, some of which are considered reflexively by Congram and Steadman (2008). The fascination exerted by the International Brigades and the subsequent output by British and American historians have produced a particular Anglo-Saxon memory of the Civil War. There is an ambivalent undercurrent to the history of Anglo-Saxon involvement in Spain, which reflects the solidarity between the Spanish Left and its foreign supporters, but also reflects the potential charges of interference and the romanticisation and intellectual appropriation of the Civil War.

A range of people visited the gravesites: relatives of the dead; ARMH supporters; village residents motivated by curiosity or solidarity; journalists, photographers, and television crews; groups of school children; and police and officials. I used to introduce myself at the gravesite to explain my ethnography and ask permission to make further contact, in order to meet and conduct a recorded interview. On occasion, these initial exchanges became in-depth conversations, and I requested permission to seek a more private space in the vicinity of the grave and either record the conversation or begin a more structured interview. Initially, I strongly resisted the idea of recording interviews in the close proximity to the grave, worrying about the ethical implications of speaking to my informants in that charged environment. However, the ARMH coordinators systematically recorded a large volume of background information and oral history at the grave edge, and encouraged me to do the same. I came to realise that this was because the alternative—to make repeated visits to my informants' homes within the village proper—was a more fraught prospect for many elderly informants, especially in Villavieja, due to their preoccupations with surveillance, censure from village gossip, and norms surrounding the interior space of the home. I had the opportunity to visit the majority of these informants later in their homes and to revisit their responses over time.

On each exhumation, I found myself at the centre of a nexus of relationships that each day drew new people through word of mouth. By working in the gravesite, I was located at the hub of intense physical, social, and symbolic activity: the eliciting and recording of memory; commemorative acts; competing representations of the past; conflict and debate; and powerful displays of emotion. As most informants were encountered at the graveside, they form a self-selecting group, and a clear limitation of this study is that is does not incorporate the relatives of the dead, or community members, who rejected all involvement with the exhumation. A significant minority of relatives never engaged in the process, though many were drawn in during the later stages. For some, this was because an engagement with the past was too painful or too destabilising, and it would have been intrusive to insist that they participate in the ethnography. On the other hand, engaging those who had a strong political opposition to the exhumation seemed unduly provocative and contrary to the careful conduct of the exhumation coordinators, who never made reference to the political divisions within the immediate community. Nevertheless, amongst those who visited the gravesite there was a very broad spectrum of both affective responses and political positions, which will be explored in detail. In later fieldwork, I also visited the laboratories where the human remains and their associated possessions were analysed, to observe the bones and objects myself and to observe the archaeologists and forensic scientists in the laboratory setting. In addition to the exhumation itself, I observed a large number of both closed and public meetings, and events connected to the exhumations: press briefings, a book launch, lectures, and a conference devoted to the graves of Burgos that a significant proportion of my informants attended, some of them as speakers. As I will discuss in the final chapters, I also attended the commemorative ceremonies that marked the end of the exhumations, the celebratory parties, the all-night wake for the dead in Villavieja, and the mass funeral that accompanied the reburials in Las Campanas.

Chapter 1

REPUBLICAN IDENTITY AND SPANISH MEMORY POLITICS

INTRODUCTION

The aim of this chapter is to identify the existence of a Republican collective identity in the 1930s, in order to examine those components of the Republican memory campaign that identify with it and see the grassroots political activity that characterised the Republican period as an inspiration for present action. There is a clear divide between the campaign practice of ARMH, which emphasises affective familial bonds with the dead while drawing personal inspiration from the Republicans, and their rival campaign group and fierce critics, Foro por la Memoria, who conceive of an ideological bond with the dead and explicitly seek to resurrect Republican ideology in order to achieve a hegemonic shift to the Left in Spanish society. This chapter also discusses how the prewar Republican identity was successfully dismantled by Francoist violence, transforming any attempt to revive it into an ambivalent, complex, and emotionally charged experience for those who have lived under Franco. I will also analyse why violence, particularly the acts of marginalisation and humiliation perpetrated against Republican families, was highly effective in engendering a state of atomisation. This prevented the transmission of memory between generations and dismantled the basis for a strong collective memory amongst Republicans in my field site. The experiences of repression presented here cast light on why a political representation of the dead may be experienced as threatening and destabilising in these communities. I conclude by looking at how this overarching Republican narrative, moving from a vibrant collective identity to a condition of atomisation, and then to the individualist discourse of contemporary post-transition Spanish society, presents a specific set of challenges to the Republican memory campaign. This can be detected in the internal debates on the relative significance of the individual and the collective within the exhumation process.

REPUBLICAN IDENTITY PRE- AND POSTWAR

The villages of Villavieja and Las Campanas lie between the market town Aranda del Duero, the historic regional centre of Lerma, and the city of Burgos, capital of the Burgos province in the Castile-León region. The violence and oppression experienced by Republicans and their families in these villages has to be understood in the context of the war in Castile-León and of the traditional identity and political affiliations of Burgos as capital of the province and of the Old Castile region as a whole. Due to Burgos's self-perception and characterisation as a bastion of conservative social norms and devout Catholicism, the traditional political establishment and landowners of the city were natural sympathisers of the Francoist cause. A stereotypical characterisation would portray the region's identity as staid, civilised, refined, and "European," in contrast to the primitive and fiery South. In the Civil War, the South was perceived in pseudoracial terms as "tainted" by Moorish influences (Preston 2010). The area is seen historically as the cradle of the purest Castilian Spanish (a consciousness of being speakers of "received pronunciation" Spanish, and a belief in the aesthetic merits of Castilian Spanish were still apparent in these communities). This is the unifying state language in opposition to the regionally spoken vernacular languages that are associated with the more explicitly separatist regional identities further north in Spain. Burgos's central geographical position is equated with its status as the core or heart of "Spanishness."

A valuable document that emerged from this period is *Burgos Justice*, a contemporary account by district judge Ruiz Vilaplana (1938) that captures the prevailing relations between socioeconomic classes in the region of my fieldwork. His professional role led him to spend the days touring small peasant communities around Burgos, and the evenings in the upper-class social clubs known as *casinos*, in the company of landowners, fellow professionals, and minor aristocracy. This enabled him to observe the dissonance between two opposing perspectives on the same economic and social system. The communities around Burgos depended on farming, mainly arable crops. Small-scale farmers would rent the land from landowners, plant and harvest the crop, and then, due to their inability to organise their own markets, they would sell the grain back to the landowners, who could manipulate prices. My informants confirmed the level of overall economic and social control that came with landownership, and added that even those small farmers were fortunate in comparison to the day labourers who worked directly for the land-owners and who did not always receive payment in cash. Their job inse-curity forced them to conform to social norms of obedience, compliance, and piety (monitored by the local priest), or risk being blacklisted and becoming unemployable in the village. For labouring families that com-plied fully with these norms, quasi-feudal relationships developed over generations with the landowners, a situation similar to the one described by Narotzky and Smith (2006).

Accounts of the extreme level of social control maintained by the village authorities in both Villavieja and Las Campanas in the 1930s, primarily through the alliance between landowners and local clerics, were initially surprising to me. My informants told me of church-levied fines for all kinds of minor misdemeanours (particularly for working on one's private vegetable garden on the Sabbath, which was most work-ingmen's only day off). Working-class men also lost wages through the enforced "volunteering" of manual labour on church buildings and lands. Other techniques of control were: surveillance from the church steeple; limitation of the freedom of association by coded warnings not to "be seen with the wrong people"; village curfews during periods of shortage or strained labour relations to circumvent strikes or protests; and unofficial imprisonment in police cells below the town hall. These controls were quasi-legal, but within the self-contained environment of the village there were no higher authorities that could be appealed to. Remarkably, the trope of surveillance from the church steeple recurs in all my elderly informants' accounts of village life in the 1930s, and clearly reveals a strongly felt preoccupation. This was later conflated with unsubstantiated accounts of how Francoists (including even the priest himself) used the church as a vantage point from which to shoot villagers during the war. This was indeed documented for some villages, but I believe it may be an example of village myth (Corbin 1995) that nonetheless reveals a symbolic truth about the way the physical pres-ence of the church was perceived and experienced as omniscient and omnipotent. The dominant physical positioning of religious buildings in the village and the aural dominance of bells and celebrations are important factors contributing to the sense of surveillance that perme-ates these communities. The paradox of an armed priest is also a fre-quently invoked image amongst my elderly informants, perhaps because it is perceived as a moment in which religion's potential for coercion and violence is revealed.

The older generation of my informants were at that time small children or as yet unborn. Some children may have been able to understand the social conditions around them, particularly during a flashpoint such as a strike, something that a few informants recalled firsthand; however, their accounts of these conditions in the 1930s are for the most part picked up from their parents or older workmates and friends. The severity of these prewar conditions was described enthusiastically to me in vivid, evocative terms, detailing cramped conditions and recalling how people wore rags and subsisted on "bread and onions." There was no comparable common pool of knowledge about the organised resistance of the working-class communities in these villages in response to unjust conditions. Logically, there must have been a widely participated social and political movement throughout the 1930s, as by the time of the killings in 1937, both villages had a thriving *casa del pueblo* (workingmen's club and centre of cultural and political activity), and Villavieja had a left-wing mayor and an almost entirely socialist town council. Significantly, the same informants who vividly described the prewar material deprivation professed total ignorance over who had participated in village politics, or the forms it had taken. It is also highly significant that my elderly informants talked about these unimaginable levels of poverty in essentialist or depoliticised terms, stressing poor technology, ignorance, and a general "backwardness" in the countryside during the 1930s, rather than citing the distribution of resources identified by Ruiz Vilaplana (1938). As will be expanded upon in chapter 2, the insistence on uniform scarcity and deprivation has become an important device for excusing the actions of all sides during the Civil War and justifying the political upheaval of the 1930s, while at the same time removing the ideological underpinnings of Republicanism and effectively bracketing it off from the relative affluence of the present.

The absence of memory and the inability to vocalise one's own memories surrounding political activities will be explored in chapter 2. We can refer to the observations made in *Burgos Justice* to have a picture of what was happening in the area of my field sites at the time:

> Nuclei of trade unions and working men's associations were duly established in Miranda, Castrojeriz and Aranda and in the capital itself, while in the latter they even contrived to set up a Worker's Discussion Centre [...]. Burgos society, uncompromisingly reactionary, proceeded to launch its offensive against these experiments. The Church with its enormous influence over the big capitalists and industrial magnates set about persecuting members of the workers' associations [...]. But this organization of the lower classes was making headway, and was not to be stopped. In the people's *Ateneo* they arranged lectures which were given by eminent intellectuals uninhibited by the local atmosphere: the new spirit spread through the province, and political clubs were founded here and there. Then schools and libraries sprang up: and a people's choir even came into existence. (Ruiz Vilaplana 1938, 13)

These forms of political-cultural organisation mirror those recalled by informants in Mintz's classic ethnography *The Anarchists of Casas Viejas* (1982). Mintz conducted fieldwork in the 1960s, which means that his informants were of the generation that fought the Civil War and not their surviving children, as in my study. They were the neighbours and contemporaries of a group of anarchists massacred by the civil guard in 1933, and their firsthand accounts capture the almost messianic spirit of the Spanish workers involved in the labour movement in the 1930s, who felt on the cusp of a new reality. Interestingly, Mintz managed to obtain more frank and detailed accounts of participation in the radical politics of the 1930s than I ever heard during my fieldwork, or read about in other ethnographies. I think this is because the 1933 massacre at Casas Viejas is a famous and well-documented event, widely reported at the time. It is a matter of historical record, not shrouded in denial in the way Civil War massacres are, and therefore does not fall within the representational prohibitions of the pact of silence. The accounts and life histories in Mintz's ethnography give an insight into the daily life of those involved in the anarchist and socialist movements. They detail the significance of creating meeting places such as the *ateneo* (cultural centre) and the *casa del pueblo* to conduct public discussions. The significance of this new category of space cannot be overstated, since the working class had no equivalent of the traditional member clubs for the upper classes, the *casinos* (Gilmore 1980). The only other public spaces were the bar, which many labourers' wages could not stretch to, and the church, which was ideologically aligned to the ruling elites. The *casa del pueblo* was mainly a social space, but it also stressed the importance of literacy and access to newspapers and pamphlets. The main protagonists of the anarchist movement in Casas Viejas would travel considerable distances to meet like-minded representatives from other communities and return to disseminate news and opinions within their own communities. Their main aim was to situate the working class of each community within a wider regional and national network, in order to facilitate support in labour disputes and enable the transmission of ideas. This was of practical importance, for example when coordinating strikes, but also had a profound symbolic importance, as it infringed the insularity of villages and challenged the prevailing status quo within small communities. As will be explored in chapter 5 and in the conclusion, this has a clear resonance with the success of ARMH campaign in situating Republican families within a new nationwide network.

Mintz's informants also emphasise the wide range of norms and values challenged by anarchism and socialism in the 1930s. These challenges include publicly questioning the existence of God, new practices like abstention from alcohol and vegetarianism, and highly progressive views on family planning, the upbringing of children, gender roles, and marriage. A common theme in both Casas Viejas and my field sites was the reduction of the role of the Catholic Church in one's daily life by opting out of all religious rites of passage such as baptism and burial and pioneering secular alternatives. As I will show in chapter 5, the anticlerical dimension of Republicanism poses a problem to those formulating the new type of funerals and commemorative practices that accompany the reburial of the exhumed Republicans. These antagonistic movements had the same utopian vision shared by other revolutionary ideologies, and embraced the domestic and intimate realms, along with the public sphere, as spaces for political change (Buchli 2000). The spiritual and philosophical content of these ideologies meant that members of the politically active working-class were glossed simply as "*los que tienen ideas*," or "those who have ideas." This is an all-encompassing term that was used frequently in my field sites, but also recurs in ethnographic accounts of local politics throughout Spain (Mintz 1982; Narotzky and Smith 2002, 2006).

This diffuse form of politics is highly significant for memory politics in contemporary Spain and arguably presents a problem for ARMH, since many of the progressive goals of Republicanism now have come to be the accepted norm in contemporary Spanish society, particularly with regard to sexual behaviour and freedom of religious practice. This means that it is hard for anyone in the present to interpret those goals as manifestations of radical politics. It is hard to believe that in the 1930s, this departure from the social norms of the day was of sufficient gravity to render these people the target of political killings. This explains why many of the relatives of the dead, and even some supporters of the ARMH campaign, have trouble identifying these killings as politically motivated. When asked about the deaths in my field sites, my elderly informants' first reaction was to deny the existence of any political activity in the village. However, when asked specifically about their own relative, the majority of my informants offered the information "*No va a misa*" ("He didn't go to mass"). In the context of village life in the 1930s this was an inherently political act and an explicit challenge to existing hierarchies, but this scenario is either missed or remains unacknowledged by my informants. Holguín (2007) reflects on the difficulty of comprehending the intensely political character of daily life during this period, in which everyday actions were the site of "culture wars" long before the military conflict began.

I have been able to ascertain very little about the activities of Republicans in my field sites, but key informants from both villages had been gathering information for some years from both oral and archival sources, due to their own political affiliations and personal interest in local history. I was told in both sites that in the 1930s the leftists campaigned for a civil cemetery to be built in the region, and claimed the right to be buried in a secular ceremony without a priest. A story from my key informant in Villavieja, Julio, underscores the perceived radicalism of this demand: in the early 1930s a secular funeral was indeed conducted in another village within the Burgos province, and a small group of young people, both male and female, had journeyed to attend the ceremony in order to demonstrate their solidarity with the principle of secular rites of passage. On their journey back, they were ambushed by attackers who had concealed their identities, but were suspected of being young men from the elite families of Villavieja. The attackers shot one person dead and injured another. In Julio's story, which was first told him by his parents and then corroborated by others, there was particular consternation because a woman had been injured. The lack of an investigation into the attack was interpreted as an indicator of official complicity. This story suggests a backdrop of class antagonism at odds with the constant assertion from my elderly informants that there was "no politics" in the village.

Despite this evidence of social and political upheaval, it was a great shock when in the 1936 elections the province of Burgos came out with a leftist majority and elected a member of parliament, or Cortes, who was a small-scale farmer. This stunned the upper and middle classes, undermining a tenet of their conservative regional identity. This produced "an attitude of unrelenting hostility, there remained that solid phalanx of reaction which could never forgive. And which never forgave" (Ruiz Vilaplana 1938, 14). The parallel realities of working-class and middle/upper-class Burgos explain why this was simultaneously a place where Franco's forces were welcomed by conservative sympathisers at the onset of their military uprising, and where great violence and loss of life was experienced by the rural working-class population, despite the total absence of conventional warfare.

Upon the military uprising, the authorities in Burgos immediately aligned themselves with the Nationalist forces, who took control of the city within twenty-four hours:

> The rebel's main victories on July 19 were in the centre and north of the country. At Burgos, the old capital of Castile, a grave, reserved, conservative city, the rising triumphed without difficulty and with scarcely a shot fired. "The very stones are Nationalist here," the Condesa de Vallallano remarked proudly to Dr. Junod of the Red Cross in August. (Thomas 1990, 238)

Perhaps "the very stones" was a reference to the elaborate gothic cathedral that dominates the centre of Burgos and that provided a backdrop to the public events staged by Franco's wartime regime; or to the medieval castle and the monuments connected to El Cid, the mythic Spanish crusader whose story accorded so well with Franco's own ideology and self-mythologising. The fact that Burgos went over to the Nationalists "with scarcely a shot fired" is highly significant for a consideration of the atrocities perpetrated against the Republicans in Old Castile. The dead of both sides during the period from 1936 to 1939 are popularly perceived as "war dead" and grouped together as deaths resulting from combat; yet in the region of Castile-León the Republican deaths were unambiguously the result of social cleansing operations against unarmed civilians. It is also significant for local identity and memory that Burgos was a resolutely "Francoist city" during the war and the dictatorship, making the current exhumations potentially more threatening and destabilising to the local population.

During the war and in its immediate aftermath, the Nationalists invested energy and resources in the creation of an extremely negative characterisation of Republicans and Republicanism that was disseminated through propaganda and recurred in Francoist rhetoric. Sevillano (2007, 44) provides a vivid account of how members of Franco's propaganda division would systematically mutilate and defile the remains of war causalities (from both sides) so that the photographs could be circulated by the press as evidence of "Red" barbarities. It is worth briefly analysing this negative Republican identity to understand the levels of atomisation produced in surviving Republicans and the ambivalence felt in reclaiming the Republican identity of the dead. So much of the postwar Nationalist rhetoric seems designed to neutralise the Republican identity and render it useless as a basis for collective action in the future. This is because there are two challenges inherent in founding a regime on civil war, rather than a foreign war or a war of independence: first, the enemies live within the new state, and even if a significant proportion of them are killed or exiled, their children, relatives, friends, and neighbours will be subjects of the new regime. A second feature of civil war is the problematic sameness of the two opposing sides: in the case of Spain, there were no clear-cut ethnic, cultural, or geographical boundaries to be drawn between the opposing sides. Despite the strong and distinctive identities possessed by the autonomous regions within Spain's borders, allegiances within the Civil War did not follow exactly the same lines. (Although it should be noted that Franco aggressively pursued an agenda of national unity, and the Basque and Catalan languages and culture were subject to repressive measures early in his regime.)

This situation required a concerted process of "othering" the defeated Republicans in order to maintain a distinct and recognisable enemy against which a divided population could be unified. Much of the rhetoric of the new regime reframed the war as an operation of national cleansing rather than a genuine civil conflict between Spaniards:

> An ideological community coalesced around a state narration of triumph, aiming to inoculate society against forgetting or deviations. In this interpretation, Spain was incarnated as a quasi-person, a unique and permanent being, whose "organic continuity" reached back to the Catholic *reconquista* of Spain from the Moors and Jews culminating in the fifteenth century. The "spirit of 1936" depended on perpetuating the story of the unvarying constants of Spain's being... According to the Francoist view, there had never been a traditional Spain (bad) and a progressive Spain (good), as liberals claimed, but simply the "eternal Spain" and the "anti-Spain." This was the simple totalitarian duality portrayed in many school texts of the postwar era. It is not surprising that many Spanish children grew up believing that *la guerra de España* had been fought by Spaniards against foreigners. (Richards 2002, 100)

Richards identifies the "othering" implications of the term "anti-Spain," with its similarity to the idea of the anti-Christ—another term that recurred in my fieldwork to characterise the Republicans. But more than this, the anti-Spain is by definition foreign, and this characterisation of Republicans as alien and inimical to Spanish identity was elaborated upon by the postwar regime through terms such as the "Masonic-Bolshevik-Jewish" axis, a trio of foreign or imported identities (Graham 2004, 320). The ultimate aim of this logic was to invent a racial other within Spain, drawing on the historical theme of the Moorish and Jewish presence in medieval Spain. Preston (2004b, 2010) has shown convincingly that the Francoist project was conceived of "as a race war, not simply a class war" (2004b, 299), closely aligned to the ideology of Nazi Germany in the same period. He analyses the Francoist rhetoric with respect to the working classes, citing terms such as "slave stock," "subhuman," and "vermin" (ibid., 286). This rhetoric drew on the history of the Reconquista of Spain, in which the Catholic monarchs had expelled the Jewish and Muslim population. However, in the Francoist version, the expulsion had not been completed, and these races had gone on to form the proletariat of modern Spain. The proletarian class was biologically inferior and racially susceptible to the "Oriental" doctrine of Marxism, a reference to Marx's Jewish descent (ibid., 294). I believe this process of racial othering can be discerned in the Right's usage of the term *Rojos* or "Reds" as a collective noun for Republicans, with its structural equivalence to "Blacks" in Spanish colonial discourse. This blanket label, devoid of any specific ideological content, also masked the political realities underpinning the Republican cause. The place and function of the word *Rojo* in the Francoist regime's discourse has been theorised perceptively by

Sevillano (2007, 178), who finds similarities with the role of classificatory terms under German National Socialism. Through repetition, their use came to shape the kind of thoughts and utterances that could be formulated. This discourse was also fed by nostalgia for Spain's conquest of the indigenous peoples of Latin America and by the ongoing colonial brutality in Spanish-administered Morocco: "The attitude of the Nationalists toward the Left and to the rural and industrial working classes made sense only in terms of the postcolonial mentality [...]. The landowners viewed the landless peasants and the industrial proletariat as a racially inferior, subject colonial race. When they talked about the Left, they did so in pathological terms" (Preston 2004b, 285).

According to this discourse, Republicanism was a pathogen in the bodies of its supporters and, in turn, individual Republicans were pathogens in the body of Spain. This had a clear impact on Republican memory, as the children of murdered Republicans were inculcated with the idea that their parents were dangerous, infectious, and alien to Spain (Ryan 2009). Preston (2004b) links this rhetoric to a recurring wartime trope depicting Spain as a body (more specifically a female body) and Franco as a surgeon excising a tumour or an infection. Other authors have noted the characterisation of Spain as a woman in relationship to the masculine figure of Franco (Larubia-Prado 2000). Since Republicanism was contagious, the killings of Republicans were an act of containment, necessary to preserve the "body of Spain." This imbued those deaths with the logic of a scientific necessity. Moreover, since this infection was carried in the blood as an inherited disorder, to profess one's Republican parentage was to implicate oneself as a carrier of the pathogen, and this effectively engendered shame in the children of the dead. It can be argued that this discourse of biological transmission was an attempt to modernise deeply held preoccupations within Spanish culture, for example with original sin, family feuds, guilt, and revenge. Yet, this discourse was not a mere rhetorical device but was carried over into the scientific practice of the new regime. Both Richards (2001) and Vinyes (2002, 54) have identified the use of the emerging discipline of psychiatry to diagnose and treat "Red psychosis" and hysteria in Republican women. Bandrés and Llavona (1996) document the psychiatric testing that occurred in Spanish concentration camps according to a strongly eugenicist agenda that conflated morality, racial purity, and national "spirit." The biological paradigm even extended to the examination of the bodies of Republican prisoners to locate the physical site of their aberrance.

The biological essentialism of this rhetoric in terms of both race and disease is highly important to understand the potential ambivalence surrounding the exhumation process, since its whole premise is the reclaiming of a biological descent from the dead and the expression of family bonds. The parallels between the Francoist and ARMH discourses on inheritance become significant in relation to the ambivalence and resistance I observed around the genetic identification of the dead, particularly amongst elderly relatives. Perhaps for the older generation the investigation of biological descent from murdered Republicans was fraught with the weight of Francoist rhetoric on the biological transmission of subversive characteristics. The notions of Red contagion and genetic inheritance contain within them an anxiety about resurgence, retribution, and the revenge of the next generation.

The other metaphors that surface repeatedly have to do with cleansing or *limpieza,* and characterise the Republicans as scum or swine (*canalla*). Religious metaphors of cleansing and spiritual purification are also part of the Nationalist propaganda, including references to expiation and baptism, which represent a state of total cleansing. The cleansing power of spilt blood is a recurring trope noted by Rodrigo (2008, 57). A parallel to this is the organic metaphor of plants and regrowth that casts the Republicans as weeds whose unchecked growth is choking Spain. The spreading Republican ideas are presented as dangerous seeds, and Franco's rhetoric calls for this growth to be "pulled out by the roots" and "then the ground sowed with salt" to prevent the seeds from growing back (Rodrigo 2008, 49).

The preoccupation with total cleansing and "uprooting" expresses the fear of a Republican resurgence in future generations. It is therefore highly significant the use of organic or agricultural metaphors in my informants' analyses of the exhumation process, among both the relatives of the dead and the ARMH campaigners. The fact that both these groups employ plant or agricultural metaphors suggests a shared understanding among both victims and perpetrators of the possibility of cyclical resurgence, and that the condition of defeat can be characterised as one of dormancy or potentiality. The Nationalists' urge to "pull out by the roots" also explains a great deal of the logic of violence underpinning the events in my field sites. It was not sufficient to "pull out" or kill an individual Republican: the "roots" of Republicanism located in the family unit and in the community's collective identity also had to be dismantled or neutralised. Because the intimate, the domestic, and the local had hitherto been a space for the expression of Republican identity, it followed that Franco's regime sought to control these spaces as forcefully as it controlled the public realm.

POLITICAL VIOLENCE, ATOMISATION, AND MEMORY

It is worth considering in some detail my elderly informants' accounts of what happened in my field sites, in order to understand the mechanisms

by which Republican families and community identities were dismantled and the long-lasting impact of these traumatic experiences on the
transmission of memory. Graham (2004) helps situate my informants'
accounts within the context of what was happening throughout Spain,
and identifies multiple instances of the same goal of "breaking" the
enemy—in particular, the strategy of bringing violence into public
spaces, forcing the masses to become participants, witnesses, or victims,
and exacerbating the shame and humiliation of the victims by making
their suffering public:

> Why was there such a need to humiliate or to break the enemy, publicly
> or otherwise? All these forms of violence [...] were functioning as rituals
> through which social and political control could be reenacted. And sig-
> nificant here too is the manner in which the enemy so often met his or her
> death at rebel hands: at the start of the civil war, the mass public execu-
> tions followed by the exhibition of corpses in the streets; the mass burn-
> ing of bodies, the quasi-*auto da fe* of a socialist deputy in the Plaza Mayor
> of Salamanca in July 1936, or the fact that executions in the centre-north
> of the rebel zone often took place on established saints and feasts days;
> or the uncanny mixture of terror and fiesta (executions followed by vil-
> lage fetes and dances, both of which the local population was obliged to
> attend). This violence served to exorcize the underlying fear of loss of
> control. (Graham 2004, 318)

Burgos became the capital of Franco's wartime government, the *junta*,
from 1936 until the fall of Madrid in 1938. "Franco gave his first public
speech from a balcony on the town hall in Burgos on the subject of the
future of Spain: the ballot box would be eliminated in favour of 'a better way of expressing the popular will'" (Thomas 1990, 424). From this
point onward, the region in which my field sites lie was effectively run as
a microdictatorship, a precursor of the harsh postwar regime that would
eventually exist throughout Spain. The early victory of Nationalists in
my field sites allowed them to inherit a relatively intact and undamaged
bureaucratic infrastructure, the resources of police, army, and civil guard
(with their files and records on individuals), and the large Burgos jail to
house opponents of the regime. Nationalists were also comparatively
secure from a military point of view, and therefore free to pursue the
limpieza or social cleansing project, which the regime called at this juncture "cleaning up behind the lines." Psychologically, the close proximity
of Franco's powerbase gave morale, confidence, and a sense of impunity
to his supporters in the surrounding towns and villages.

Ruiz Vilaplana describes his experience of that time and the surreal
atmosphere created by the paradox between the superficial normality
of his role as a magistrate under the *junta* and the growing number of

extrajudicial killings, farcical trials, arbitrary imprisonments, and decrees and edicts that defied any legal principle. When he lodged a formal protest about the number of exposed corpses he had to register in the Burgos region that month, his Francoist interlocutor did not understand that he was objecting to the extrajudicial killings themselves, but believed he was objecting to the extra bureaucratic work (and physical mess) caused by the exposition of the bodies: "'We're just having the usual clean-up behind the lines' he said. 'Naturally, there are bound to be a few excesses. But all the same... this sort of thing must stop. From tomorrow on I shall see that things are done differently, and above all, corpses must always be properly buried'" (Ruiz Vilaplana 1938, 40). When Red Cross representatives monitoring the Civil War visited the area of my field sites, they found evidence of this matter-of-fact acceptance of the necessity of political killings. Passing the town of Aranda del Duero, their Francoist guide remarked, "That's Red Aranda. I'm afraid we had to put the whole town into prison and execute very many people" (Thomas 1990, 258).

In analysing my informant's accounts of this period of mass violence, it is useful to understand specific acts in the light of dominant cultural norms and values, in order to identify the sensitive areas that were targeted by the regime. For example, the opposition between interior and exterior is conceptually very significant in organising behaviour. This division is a structuring principle of village life and reverberates in other pairs of oppositions—private and public, concealed and revealed, denied and acknowledged. The opposition of interior and exterior and public and private dominates the ethnographies of Spanish village life (Barrett 1974; Collier 1997; Gilmore 1980, 1987). The carnival tradition documented by Gilmore (1987) receives its cathartic quality from the subversion of private and public, as the most intimate personal details and scurrilous gossip are inserted into simple songs that are performed publicly and that allow everyone to join in. Gilmore's descriptions of the threatening and wounding power of carnival resonate with Graham's notion of "the uncanny mix of terror and fiesta" (2004, 318). I argue that the underlying logic of violence in my field sites revolved around the subversion of the categories of interior and exterior, and public and private.

This helps explain the relatives' responses to the exhumation process, and particularly their preoccupation with the public representations of the bodies, the performance of public acts of commemoration, and the creation of public memorials. My informants' accounts of violence also make clear that there were also other victims, particularly Republican women targeted by gender-specific forms of violence that are not investigated or acknowledged at all within the exhumation process, due to its exclusive focus on the body of the male victim. This category of violence is written out of exhumation and reburial. I argue that this negation of the full breadth of violence and trauma experienced in my field sites was acknowledged or sensed by some of my informants, particularly relatives and elderly locals, with ambivalence and unease. This could be detected in their attempt to foreground both their own suffering as children and young people under Franco, and that of the wives and mothers of the dead men.

A significant form of psychic violence inflicted on Republican families was the total prohibition on mourning and commemoration: "In order to survive, the vanquished had to renounce their past experiences and identity. The Francoist coalition's triumphalism pervaded the whole public space. There was no room for preserving the memories of the vanquished, for recognizing their personal and political trajectories or endowing them with any value or significance" (Cenarro 2002, 170). The prohibition on burial, funeral rites, and mourning subverted the categories of interior and exterior, private and public. Collier (1997), Gilmore (1980) in Andalucía, and Pina-Cabral (1986) in Portugal emphasise the social significance of public and highly structured mourning. It is vitally important not only to mourn, but to be seen to mourn. Although mourning practices are particularly elaborated in Andalucía, a very different ethnographic context from Burgos, my informants' accounts suggest some commonalities, particularly concerning the significance of visiting and tending to the grave. Until recently, the material culture of mourning in Spain, especially in small communities, was conspicuous. Burials amongst the poor might be simple, but the mourning process was highly structured, in particular the female mourning for male relatives. There was a highly elaborated code of conduct prescribing subtle gradients of mourning, which would diminish in severity over the years. The strictures placed on women during traditional mourning practices is seen by contemporary critics as burdensome and patriarchal (Collier 1997), but for some widows to follow this code was a continuation of their emotional relationship with the dead, structuring their grief. In a patriarchal society, a highly codified widowhood gave a lone female a clear social role, as those norms dictated not only how she should behave but also how the rest of the community should assist and support her (Gilmore 1980).

Highly public mourning by widows, manifested primarily by wearing black, assiduously tending the deceased's grave, and modestly avoiding other activities in the public realm were considered a barometer of the "depth" or authenticity of feeling within the marriage. For children, mourning was a public expression of filial duty, an assertion of legitimate paternity and inheritance rights (Collier 1997). Deep mourning accrued honour to the dead man and his family, whereas insufficient mourning brought shame and raised questions of fidelity and legitimacy.

The prohibition on public mourning and the absence of a body or grave meant that a process that was normally social and performative became internalised. In this cultural context, the failure to observe any of the customary mourning practices could be expected to engender feelings of shame and a lasting guilt toward the dead (Fidalgo 1939).

Another example of the subversion of interior/exterior or private/public was the systematic use of gendered or sexual violence against women. The following two accounts of gendered or sexual violence in my fieldwork are consistent with other stories told by my informants and recorded in ethnographies and oral histories in other regions of Spain (Gilmore 1980; Graham 1995a). These descriptions are vital to understand the impact of fear and humiliation on Republican memory. The primary act of gendered violence was the procession of Republican women around the village streets, naked and with their heads shaved, which would pass the majority of homes and culminate in a public space, usually the main square outside the town hall. The careful planning of these events was demonstrated by the fact that, according to multiple accounts, there was a planned route and a brass band; the barber was coopted to cut the women's hair; and official permission for both public gathering and public nudity was sought from the town hall.

These processions were akin to the public revelry at a carnival, and had parallels with the meticulous planning that went into the more sombre annual processions of religious statues. During the procession the women would be stripped, and there are also reports of different kinds of physical purging or poisoning with castor oil and household chemicals, as well as sexual molestation and sexual insults. The head shaving and the enforced nakedness were an attack on symbols of femininity, but also served to exacerbate the exposed condition of Republican women. This logic of exposure is particularly underscored by the practice of purging and poisoning to induce vomiting and excretion in public, which symbolically opened up these women's physical interiors, turning them inside out and bringing the most private acts into the public. It was a very literal form of obscenity in that things that should not be seen were viewed by an entire community:

> I remember the people when they rounded up all the women who had suffered some murder in their family. They cut their hair and they took them around the village to sing the *Cara al Sol* [Face the Sun, the Francoist anthem] and I hid myself in a big jar so that they wouldn't see me because I thought they were going to kill me too. In my maternal grandfather's house all the *falangistorros* [pejorative for Francoists], those who played the trumpet [a brass band accompanied these head shaving processions], were gathered together and to my mother, they neither cut her hair nor

made her parade around. The women of the village insulted them, laughing at them. This I have lived. (Maria, Villavieja)

When I entered military service as a new conscript in this village, there was a lady, the wife of one of the murderers, who said "There's a communist conscript" because her husband helped to kill my father. After the killing, to a great number of women, they cut their hair to zero [shaved their heads], and the husband of this lady dedicated himself to parading the women around the village so that they would be seen. They shaved the heads of a great number of women. The only woman that was saved was my mother, but a son of a bitch gave her ammonia to drink. And in order to bring the can closer to her mouth, to make her swallow it, they grabbed her by her [sexual] parts saying, "This woman is crazy! This woman is crazy!" And shouted at the barber at gunpoint that he should cut their hair. She didn't swallow, but she took it into her mouth. Sons of bitches, they are Nazis, Nazis. Today, for all the bad hatred you have for a person, you don't do this, because today there is justice. There are judges who judge. (Luis, Villavieja)

In Villavieja there were reportedly two or three processions. In Las Campanas there was at least one. They were accompanied by carnival music, and in Villavieja there was a particular song associated with these events. All my elderly informants could hum the tune and some remembered the chorus: "¡Sin pelo, sin pelo, se vende por el estraperlo!" ("Without hair, without hair, it is sold on the black market!"). These parades made reference to an existing tradition of processions, and the history of these displays of humiliated women must be born in mind when interpreting the formulation of new commemorative acts by ARMH, during which the human remains of exhumed Republicans are brought from the main square to the village cemetery in a winding route that encompasses most of the village (see chapter 5).

It is highly significant that of the nine accounts that raise the subject of gendered violence in Villavieja, all contain a variation on the phrase "My mother (or female relative) was the only woman who was saved" (from the head-shaving procession). There are references to some kind of eleventh-hour reprieve or alternative punishments (as can be found in the two examples above). Yet it is impossible that all nine people's mothers or grandmothers were "the only woman saved." The level of shame associated with these events seems undiminished after nearly seventy years. Several informants in Villavieja obliquely implied that Nana (fourteen when her father died) had been forcibly carried around the village. However, none of them stated it directly; rather, when the subject of gendered violence was raised, several informants asked if I had met Nana and observed, "That family was treated badly." In an extended, unstructured interview Nana did not touch upon the subject of gendered violence, which was unusual for a female informant, of any age, in either Villavieja or Las Campanas.

Slightly younger women and women born after the war brought up the subject in hushed tones with a mixture of horror, fear, anger, disbelief, and fascination that something so far beyond familiar social norms had occurred in their village. Strikingly, a large proportion of middle-aged and younger women whom I met during fieldwork, even those with whom I had quite casual conversations, checked that I was aware of the abuse of women in these villages and throughout Spain, and wanted to direct my attention toward it. I think these incidents exert a particular fascination for several reasons: they expose the lie that violence during this period was born of political expediency or necessity, and that its targets were "legitimate" or followed the "rules" of war; they expose the frailty of the social norms and values that govern daily life and regulate relationships between close neighbours in a small community; they touch upon existing female fears of male violence in the present day; and they represent an enduring taboo that thus far has not been challenged by the ARMH campaign and does not find a space for expression in the exhumation process. I never heard any informant explicitly formulate this critique of ARMH, but I repeatedly sensed an impulse amongst my informants to reinsert the female figures of wives and mothers into the narrative. Although the great majority of this generation of women are now dead and were therefore absent from the exhumations, their presence was frequently evoked by my informants, particularly at the graveside, as I will consider here and in chapter 2.

The most disturbing aspect for me was that on three different occasions, a male informant interrupted a female informant's account of gendered violence. The male informant tried to change the subject back to "serious things." In two occasions, gendered violence was described laughingly by men from Republican families as *tonterías* (nonsense) and "women's things." I found this dismissive laughter profoundly disturbing and surprising, until I interpreted it as indicative of a level of shame and denial that made a conversation between women about gendered violence unbearable to the men. The male attempts to shut down these conversations were an indicator of acute sensitivity rather than insensitivity. The complex symbiotic relationship between male and female honour in rural Spain helps explain the degree to which the humiliation of these women would emasculate their surviving male relatives. In this cultural context, the male failure to protect these female victims would be categorised as an equal humiliation. The processions were an extremely effective way to communicate to recently bereaved Republican women that they now lacked any rights or any protection within the traditional social framework and could not rely on the established norms that governed gender relations. On the other hand, they communicated to surviving Republican men that they were not really men anymore, in any meaningful sense.

In my interpretation of these moments, male laughter was a distancing mechanism, and the characterisation of sexual violence as "women's things" (despite being perpetrated by men) was a disavowal of the symbiotic relationship between masculine and feminine honour, bracketing it off into the feminine realm so that these events would not stand as a reproach to the men's failure to prevent (and avenge) sexual or gender dishonour. My invocation of honour in this discussion is based partly on the treatments of honour in Spanish society in Mitchell (1988) and Gilmore (1980, 1987), but the applicability of the concept is not unproblematic (Herzfeld 1980; Lever 1986). In an ethnographic study of rural Spain, Lever identifies honour as an ideal amongst the socially dominant groups that may be resisted or subverted by others, depending on gender and class. However, her critique refers to the significance of honour in day-to-day relationships and transactions, not to its significance in the context of an extraordinary act of collective obscenity. The ritualised acts of exposure experienced in these villages make reference to shared norms and taboos, and constitute acts of targeted psychic, as well as physical, violence. The enduring silences produced throughout Spain, which persist even within the Republican memory campaign, are indicators of the efficacy of this violence.

There were also less extreme acts of violence that engendered guilt and shame. The mass appropriation and theft of Republican families' property that will be discussed in chapter 2 arguably follows the same logic of subverting the public and private. Informants recall the trauma of having household goods as diverse as food, furniture, and clothes turned out into the street, picked over, and taken away by strangers. Sometimes the very structure of the building was robbed, leaving parts of the house exposed.

> The Falangists came to the houses to ask for money, they took the clothes, the rabbits, the hens, the barrels of wine. Why? Because they wanted to do it, they are criminals. Here, there are still two criminals in this village. (Nana, Villavieja)

The logic of theft, particularly of the pathetic and desultory goods belonging to the poorest families, should not be interpreted solely in terms of material value. Gilmore (1987) describes in great detail the efforts made by the families in his field site to keep their neighbours ignorant about their (lack of) wealth and possessions, and retain privacy about the material conditions of their home. Gilmore's ethnographic work emphasises the link between material self-sufficiency of the family unit and family honour. The loss of the breadwinner and all other material resources removed from these households any possibility of self-sufficiency. It also compelled the women in these families to seek formal full-time employment instead of the more socially acceptable patchwork of domestic work, piecework at home, and the occasional "help" to the neighbours with seasonal work. While women in Spain's northern fringe traditionally had greater financial autonomy, the association between women and the private realm on the one hand, and between men and public space on the other, strongly pervades ethnographies of Mediterranean and central Spanish villages, even those conducted in the 1960s and 1970s (Barrett 1974). The woman's place in the home was the ideal if not the reality in these villages. Casanova (2002, 27) reports cases of the surviving female members of Republican families turning to prostitution to support themselves and their dependents. Although there was no reference to this in my field sites, the need to work full-time, often far away from home, stigmatised Republican women and set their families apart. Republican women's physical labour has been routinely exploited for decades, as they cleaned public buildings such as police stations on a "voluntary" basis. A significant proportion of my elderly informants made repeated reference to their mothers' work, the long hours and long commutes. The account below combines several of the themes discussed above. For example, the small incidents of stigmatisation are expressed in the idiom of infection, "as if we were the plague." My informant also touches upon unexpressed or incomplete mourning, and mentions her mother's working day. Most significantly, she characterises the condition of being fatherless as "like a sin," and describes the resulting feelings of guilt and shame as "the anguish of that sin."

> There are things that stay with you. There are so many things that now I don't remember, so many things about children's fights, insults, "for this or that they killed your father," as if we were the plague. When they informed us that he was dead, my mother put me in black and I went to school in the morning and the teacher entered, Miss Emilia, she was a substitute teacher, and asked me for whom I was in mourning and I could not answer. The only thing I could do was start to cry. It's that there was nothing more to say than the fact that we had been left without a father, and it was them that had killed him. But we couldn't say it. I couldn't do that because it was like a sin and it is the anguish of that sin we have lived with, because all the other children had their fathers and we didn't. My mother went to work very early and came back late at night. Sometimes I stood watching the children who had fathers and I didn't.

> I stood watching them when they shared out sweets, I don't even like
> sweet things, but they didn't give them to me because I was his daugh-
> ter... (Maria, Villavieja)

In her experience as an oral historian in Aragon, Cenarro (2002)
observed the tendency of shame or guilt to fill the vacuum left by the
absence of transmitted memory, compounding the process of atomisation. This sense of shame or guilt itself perpetuates silence and makes the
next generation complicit in its maintenance. Its internalisation removes
the need for surveillance or enforcement as people come to fear what will
be revealed if they break the silence:

> Since his mother had decided to impose silence about these events (the
> informant) had begun to have doubts about his father's and uncles' back-
> grounds [...]. Although he expressed the need to know more about them,
> he explicitly declared his fear of discovering an uncomfortable truth. He
> wondered whether his father and uncle had been assassinated for having
> done something wrong. Otherwise none of this would have happened.
> Obviously, the silence and ignorance of his family's past had produced a
> deep sense of guilt. (Cenarro 2002, 180)

A common aspect of most of my interviews with informants who had
lived through the postwar years and the height of dictatorship during
the 1940s and 1950s was the pervasive quality of the silence surrounding Francoist violence and their own Republican family's experience of
bereavement. Open-ended questions such as "Tell me about the village
in the years after the war" prompted descriptions of an absolute and
impenetrable silence. There was a category of unspeakable things and
unsayable thoughts. The impossibility of verbal communication was
always cited in response to the question "Have you ever thought about
exhuming your relative before?" The exhumation would have logically
entailed an unthinkable kind of communication and was therefore itself
unthinkable. Evocative watchwords, almost proverbs, emerged in my
interviews that had the singsong quality of parental sayings remembered
from childhood: "*En la calle, cállate!*" (In the street, you shut up!) or
"*Somos mas guapos con la boca cerrada*" (We are prettier with our
mouths shut), which is a variation on "*Con la boca cerrada estás más
guapo*" (You were prettier with your mouth shut), a putdown or rebuke
to someone who has just said something thoughtless or inappropriate.
Descriptions of the postwar years by all my elderly informants were
accompanied at some point by the physical gesture of zipping the mouth
closed, and the sound of a zipper.

The "street" features as the epitome of the public, the observable,
and the audible in my informants' accounts. The significance of the street

as a space of fear and vigilance, where everyone's utterances and conduct are open to external surveillance and require internal monitoring
or self-policing, will be discussed in relation to the very public occupation of the village streets during the reburial ceremonies that conclude
the exhumation process. The street was often contrasted to the home, at
least superficially, using phrases such "with the doors closed," "amongst
ourselves," or euphemistic tautologies about sympathetic Republican
individuals and families, "You could talk with those with whom you
could talk." This last phrase is revealing in that this tautology depends
on mutual recognition of some kind of collective identity that is implied
but not named explicitly as a Republican identity. Some studies have
noted a strong and active transmission of politicised memory, but they
mainly pertain to the political struggles of the early 1930s (Mintz 1982)
or the years of the Republic (Bunk 2002), rather than the painful events
of the war and postwar years. Both Moreno Gómez (2002, 197) and
Mir (2002, 139) document examples of organised armed resistance that
continued after Franco's victory, but this option was not open to everyone. Everyday forms of resistance and of a surviving collective identity
amongst those repressed are noted in two revealing studies (Cabana
Iglesia 2010; Cenarro 2002), but they require a sensitive reading of subtle
manifestations of noncompliance with the rules of Francoist institutions.
Vinyes (2002, 170) notes that strikes and protests took place amongst
Republican prisoners. Narotzky and Smith's work on contemporary
political identity in Spain (2006) reveals the transmission of a sense of
leftist political affiliation along with an inherited sense of one's social
class and status within the community. Although a similar consciousness
manifested itself subtly in some discussions with elderly informants, it
was rarely associated with the brutal class violence that these communities had experienced during the Civil War and after. The most coherent
and explicit expression of identity was framed as an opposition:

> In the street, you couldn't tell this, never, it always had to stay hidden.
> And still in this village there are the twisted ones, who still think like
> before, like fascists, here there are plenty of fascists, half of the village.
> (Celia, Villavieja)

Despite my informants' juxtaposition of "behind closed doors" and "in
the street," and despite the examples of resistance noted by other authors,
it is debatable how much free communication was permissible inside the
home in these communities. Many of these homes were now female-
only, and the social outlets for unrelated Republican men or women
to be together were very limited. There was no freedom of association
even in a private home. My informant, Santiago, recalled making the
mistake of inviting five or six young men to his home for a snack after a

spontaneous five-a-side football match in the early 1940s. Each one of the young men who had been seen going to his home was subsequently arrested and badly beaten for holding a "seditious gathering." There was a constant fear of being overheard by one's own children, whose lack of political understanding made the "closed doors" porous. This impact of totalitarianism on family dynamics has been identified by Arendt (1985), and the potential for children to inadvertently betray their own families and trigger political repression has been documented by Buchli (2000). These fears created atomisation within the family home:

> The silence that surrounded children's lives in the 1940s is often recalled as something stubbornly intangible. Some people speak of growing up with a profound, though inexplicable, sense of instability during the early Franco decades, when the year 1936 acted as a barrier within the family, widening the generation gap. The Spanish reality was contemplated as a provisional situation, and many children conveyed an unfathomable but pervasive sense of frustration and anguish. (Richards 2002, 100)

The dictatorship was experienced by some Republicans as a "life in parenthesis" (Richards 2002), an indefinite hiatus in the trajectory of their lives. It is not surprising that parents undertaking this kind of "inner exile" (Cenarro 2002) could generate an intangible anxiety inside their homes. Children would sense the shadow of parental secrets, and learn not to ask questions. Underscoring this point was my discovery that a high proportion of the young volunteers for the ARMH exhumations, particularly the archaeologists and those recording oral histories from the elderly, described this activity as being in part a substitute for talking to their own parents and grandparents about their experiences of war and dictatorship. They deemed this "impossible" within the prevailing dynamic of their family. It was too threatening to delicate intergenerational relationships, and entailed the risk that some of these left-wing volunteers would discover something unpalatable about their grandparents' political allegiances. Thus, it was safer to collect the life histories of other people's grandparents.

An informant whose father was briefly held in the Villavieja police cells (under the town hall) and then released, and whose paternal uncle was killed in the massacres, describes the extent of his communication with his father on the subject of the Francoist repression:

> He never spoke to us because he was afraid, he died before he spoke, he hardly spoke at all on this subject because we were small and children tell everything. Children and idiots speak the truth. He spoke once, when we were older, he was working for the people from around here, working "for the face" [working for free, as part of the informal exploitation of

labour from Republican families] without wage, and he just shut up and kept working. He died in '77 and Franco died in '75; the first elections were in June '77. He said to us that the *falangistas* [Francoists] were very bad, always, they were renegades. Then this epoch arrived [the democratic transition] and he had an anxiety attack, as if to say, "They'll take me and they'll bump me off." He couldn't speak, and he shut up. (Pedro, Villavieja)

The phrase "children and idiots speak the truth" seems poignant and telling in this context. It acknowledges a failing on the part of the child (the speaker himself) for being unreliable and akin to an idiot. But this failing lies in speaking "the truth," implicitly pointing out that this is what the adult world is withholding from him.

In a significant and disturbing adjunct to this, my key informant Julio told me that his own father had once told him that Pedro's father was famous amongst the older Republican men in the village for assisting informally as sexton and volunteer grave digger in the village cemetery. This was generally interpreted as "good works," or working to maintain a good reputation. However, this man revealed to his inner circle of friends that it gave him great satisfaction to outlive the Francoists of his generation in the village, and this satisfaction was compounded by putting them in the ground, as if to physically verify that they were dead. Laughing, Julio told me that Pedro's father used to linger at the end of a burial service of an old Francoist and, once alone, he would stomp around on the surface of the newly covered grave, compacting the earth. Julio mentioned there was a saying about "dancing on your grave." Julio was fascinated by the idea that Pedro's father had "danced" on the graves without anyone knowing. He was also very satisfied when I added that dancing on a grave was a figure of speech in English, too. He commented, "It's universal." Then Julio proceeded to recount the story to Pedro, who appeared shocked and disturbed by this insight into his late father's state of mind, and clearly did not wish to discuss the topic further either with me or Julio. I believe Pedro was frightened that recounting this story might lead to its wider circulation within the village, posthumously damaging his father's reputation and thus the status of his family and their relationships with Francoist families. I think this preoccupation with outliving the local Francoists revealed by Julio's anecdote lends an additional emotional significance to Pedro's account that his father entered a state of anxiety around the death of Franco and the transition to democracy, and in fact died at the time of the first democratic elections.

In these communities fear is rarely spoken about as a personal emotion or reaction, but is rather framed as a blanket presence, a condition of life that, like unemployment or disease, exists outside of individuals or even groups. In statements such as *"Hay mucho miedo"* (there is much fear) or *"La gente tiene miedo"* (people are afraid), fear is a generalised abstraction related to, but distinct from, the moments of fear experienced in reaction to a specific threat. In addition to these references, however, I encountered many manifestations of real, present-oriented fear in the course of the exhumations and the interviews. A man in his late seventies, who lived in a village two-hour walk away and had known an individual who was presumed to be buried in the second grave at Villavieja, slipped out of his village at first light to walk through the fields to the grave. When we arrived at eight in the morning, he was waiting for us. He believed he would become the target of hostility if he left later or took public transport, as others would know his destination and deduce his intention to come to the grave. He talked to the archaeologists, speculating about who was in the grave, examined the work, seemed satisfied with his trip, and started to walk back. We were very concerned about the physical toll of his walking back in the heat, and he was eventually persuaded to accept a lift, on the condition that he be dropped off well outside his village.

This ambiguity surrounding the location of fear, oriented toward the present or remembered from the past, emerged in the ethnographic and oral history work conducted by Narotzky and Smith on the southeastern coast of Spain (2002). In order to enable a comparative study, the authors investigated the attitudes to political participation in the same rural community that Smith had studied following the transition to democracy in 1978. Certain observations on the mood and atmosphere pervading their ethnographic work accord exactly with my impressions:

> Some twenty years after Franco's death, we were interviewing elderly rural working women about the socialist sentiments and activities of their youth, when a silence fell upon us as though an angel had passed [...]. Then one of the women laughed nervously and, hospitably gathering the two anthropologists in with the working women, she said: "We'll all be in jail again soon anyway," and everybody laughed as we returned to our earlier conversation. (Narotzky and Smith 2002, 200)

This encounter is ostensibly focussed on memories or reminiscences of activities that were once repressed but are now permitted. Yet the fear this still evokes in the present is palpable as the "angel" passing. It does refer not simply to the memory of having once been afraid but also to the risks associated with the present act of talking aloud and transmitting transgressive memories. It is a fear of the future based on past experiences, the probability of further oppression yet to come—"We'll all be in jail again soon."

In order to make the initial contact with potential informants and find out a convenient time for me to visit, my key informant led me to several homes of the surviving children of murdered Republicans. These first meetings, in the middle of the morning, were often extremely brief, publicly visible, and full of social niceties and little talk about the exhumation. A later time and date would be confirmed for me to visit alone and spend some hours in the house. The first week of meetings I thought these informants took shorter than average siestas, until I realised that the time was set at mid-siesta precisely to allow me to arrive unseen, a little before the rest of the village woke up. This also made it hard for neighbours to judge how much time I spent in someone's home. With some informants in Villavieja, the curtains and shutters would be checked repeatedly to ensure privacy. The tension would ebb and flow as people would become absorbed in their narrative for sustained periods and then suddenly realise that they were talking aloud—the "angel" would pass—and the room would become charged with a sense of clandestine activity and the fear of being discovered. Once I was instructed to hold my tape recorder under the tablecloth every time we heard footsteps outside, despite the fact that we were sitting in the dark, behind shutters, invisible to the street. In another house I had my tape recorder shoved down the back of the sofa when the baker's van came.

On one occasion, at the second grave of Villavieja, a middle-aged man approached us and initiated a conversation regarding what his parents had told him about who was in the grave. He agreed to step into a clearing and talk at greater length to an archaeologist, in case he had useful information to aid the identification of the bodies in the grave, and he consented to my request to record the conversation. Then he saw some distance away that some neighbours of his, a right-wing family, had arrived by car to view the grave. A slight atmosphere of tension surrounded their approach to the grave, as they arrived in an expensive car and were dressed and groomed in the rigid style of *pijos*, a Spanish term for snob that equates well to the British "Sloane Ranger." Most participants in the exhumation are alert to these subtle signifiers of class and political allegiance, and this family did not fit the "profile" of ARMH supporters. Our informant entered a state of extreme distress and started to talk inarticulately about having his family home daubed with graffiti or damaged if that particular right-wing family had seen him. It was a disturbing and temporally confused story, making it impossible to unpick whether his family home had indeed been defaced in the past, whether it was his fear for the future, or both. We attempted to diffuse the situation as much as possible, walking further out of sight of the right-wing family, and gave him the tape of his memories to destroy there and then.

After destroying the tape he recovered his composure, thanked us for the conversation, and wished us luck with the exhumation.

The above accounts and observations all support Graham's identification of a systematic "breaking" of the enemy with types of violence that inspired fear but also inculcated intimate feelings of guilt and shame, creating barriers to communication between members of communities that had once shared a powerful collective identity, and even between members of the same family (Graham 2004). Being part of Republican communities and families was stigmatised, dismantling the basis for collective identities and collective memory and successfully engendering a widespread condition of atomisation that persists in the present. Echoing the paradoxical condition of "inner exile" described by oral historians working in Spain, one of my informants powerfully articulated her experience of repressed emotions and social erasure as a kind of "living death": "What I feel most is that they have killed me for all my life" (Maria, Villavieja).

As outlined in the introduction, the transition to democracy at the end of the 1970s was predicated on a pact of silence and did not address any of these experiences or provide any public space or process in which they could be expressed or acknowledged. The pact of silence, while ostensibly a two-way pact, was inherently one-sided in that it disproportionately affected Republican families who had already been silenced for over forty years. The nature of the democratic transition created a culture of impunity in many small rural communities, allowing psychological intimidation and the threat of physical violence against Republican families to continue unchecked. Nestor, one of my informants in Villavieja, who had endured two bouts of imprisonment and torture in the 1930s and 1940s, had lost two male relatives in the massacres, and had experienced a lifetime of rearrests, bureaucratic harassment, and physical intimidation, was nevertheless an irrepressible character, who spoke articulately about his experience and retained a spirit of defiance. He recounted how he continued to be singled out for intimidation despite the transition to democracy:

> Nowadays there is no fear. Well, yes, there is still fear, there are people who still have it, those who had their father killed and don't even dare to say it. When the democracy came, in '77, I went into the village and we went to the bar and there was someone there who was a civil guard, standing with another person at the counter, and he said loudly to his companion, "I know that one already." They were talking about me. So I drew up close to him and I said, "What do you know about me, you who have sowed (scattered) crosses (headstones) through the countryside, like you did? You who have made the countryside so full of crosses?" He shut his mouth and we left to go to sleep and I was sleeping and they knocked

on the door, and I climbed out on the balcony and there he was with a pistol in his hand. He's dead now, but he was a civil guard in '77, so you can see… why here people still have fear. It's that they sowed terror in such a way that was dreadful. (Nestor, Villavieja)

It is worth noting that Nestor's clear analysis of his experiences and his assertive and outspoken accounts were particular to his character, and I encountered different responses to comparable life experiences. In Nestor's case, his perspective on the past appeared to be in part shaped by a visibly affectionate and supportive marriage. Nestor's wife, Mar, was also from a local Republican family, and despite being much more agitated than her husband about participating in the interview, she constantly chipped in to Nestor's narrative, expressing pride and admiration for him and horror at some of his experiences. She also encouraged him to include certain narratives and reminded him of others.

My most extensive and detailed interviews and life histories in Villavieja came from three other comparable couples who shared a family history of repression prior to their marriage. The strength of collective memory within the marital home enabled a less inhibited form of communication and a fuller recollection. Herrmann (2003) documents the same findings in her collection of life histories. Significantly, Mar made repeated reference to the fact that her children and grandchildren lived outside the village and all were *muy bien-colocado*, meaning well positioned socially and economically. I believe the success of their descendants gave Nestor and Mar a form of social capital that made them more defiant and confident in their critique of the village, as they were no longer dependent on its power structures.

The atmosphere of intimidation endured throughout the 1970s and 1980s in Las Campanas. My key informant in Las Campanas, Eulalio, was in his forties. He came from a known left-wing family and was active in local politics. He described the experience of mortal fear on the day of the abortive military coup in 1981. He was working his land outside the village and heard about the coup on his car radio as he ate lunch. He telephoned his wife and they agreed that it was not safe to return to the village, and decided he would drive to his brother-in-law to collect food and clothes before crossing Spain's northern border into France. He slept in his car in the woodland and upon waking up he heard that the coup had failed. Later that week, he went into one of the village bars, and upon entering he was heckled by a Francoist neighbour who said, "Congratulations, you were number one on the list!" referring to the list of those who would have been killed if the coup had succeeded. Eulalio mockingly acknowledged the honour and the comment was laughed off. "It was a joke but it was a true one," Eulalio commented, encapsulating the paradox of peacefully coexisting with neighbours who would like to kill you, and would act on the first opportunity to do so.

This uneasy form of coexistence continues to the present day, and a tangible undercurrent of tension and even threat of violence ran throughout my fieldwork. During my initial pilot study, I participated in the exhumation of a mass grave in Valdediós, Oviedo, to the north of my eventual field sites, during which archaeologists would receive telephone calls threatening to harm investigators and desecrate the grave. At Valdediós, an incoherent handmade plaque was left over the grave accusing the dead of being communist agents. Another volunteer archaeologist in Albuquerque had the word "Red" written on the door of his university office, and after I participated in the ARMH internet forum with a posting that explained the aims of my research, I was sent a series of obscene emails which expressed loyalty to Franco and far-right political views. The emails warned me not to "interfere" and accused in graphic terms all the archaeologists of engaging in necrophilia.

FRANCOIST MEMORY POLITICS

The adoption of exhumation and reburial as the primary structuring activity of the Republican memory campaign must be situated in the context of the postwar memory regime instigated by Franco. The state orchestrated an outpouring of the victorious side's experiences of war in the form of a unique nationwide enquiry, the *Causa General (Informativa de los hechos delictivos y otros aspectos de la vida en la zona roja desde el 18 de julio hasta la liberación)* (General Proceedings [Report on criminal events and other aspects of life in the Red zone from 18 July until the liberation]). This was a survey of all those killed while fighting for Franco. It provided the newly constructed Francoist state apparatus with a mechanism to reach out to every community in Spain and assert its new bureaucratic and organisational authority. From a Francoist perspective the *Causa General* created a definitive account of the war, building a narrative of liberation in terms of a purging crusade against the Republicans, characterised as the anti-Spain: "*The Causa General* is the most striking peculiarity of the Spanish case because, although it was supposed to have a merely informative function, it was in fact a state instrument for encouraging denunciation and consequently a means for officially sanctioning the social division of postwar Spain" (Cenarro 2002, 170). On a practical level, the *Causa General* formed the basis for the administering of pensions and economic support to those widowed or invalided in the Nationalist cause. It also enabled the commencement of the mass gathering of the human remains of the Nationalist war dead on a nationwide scale. The gathering was accompanied by the construction of a massive centralised mausoleum, the Valle de los Caídos (Valley of the Fallen) outside Madrid. The construction of this huge monumental complex, partly hewn out of the surrounding hillside and including a crucifix visible for miles in all directions, was achieved using the forced labour of twelve thousand Republican prisoners of war. Thousands of bodies of the Francoist war dead were exhumed and transported across Spain to be incorporated within this monument. Franco's own mausoleum is now situated at the centre of this complex and continues to be an important symbolic centre for his supporters, a site of both religious services for the dead and political rallies (Valis 2007, 426). A comparable programme of mass exhumation and reburial occurred as part of the construction of the Paracuellos de Jarama cemetery for the victims of the Republican-orchestrated "Paracuellos massacre" (Rodrigo 2008, 200).

Every community across Spain, from the small villages to the neighbourhoods of large cities, has a material echo of this central monument in the form of a standardised plaque bearing the inscription "Fallen for God and for Spain" and listing the names of all the community members, military and civilian, who died in the Civil War in support of Franco. This plaque is normally located on the side of a church or on the wall of a key public building. In addition to this public representation of individual deaths, the nomenclature of streets and public buildings was changed in the aftermath of the Civil War to commemorate Franco's military leaders and the dates and places of important victories. The main square of Villavieja was called Plaza de Generalissimo Francisco Franco. In addition to the standardised plaques, many communities, even tiny villages, erected statuaries to celebrate Franco and his generals. The same martial emphasis could be found in the new calendar of public holidays and other commemorative dates, along with the associated public acts of mourning that Aguilar and Humlebaek (2002) have described as the "Francoist litany," as they both mirrored and appropriated religious festivities (for a list of these new public holidays see Preston 1989). Representations of the past in state schools and universities were also tightly controlled (Claret Miranda 2006). Francoist ideology and the official narrative of the Civil War were learnt through a new curriculum of "civics" that consisted of the rote learning of questions and responses in a kind of political catechism (Pinto 2004).

IDENTITY POLITICS WITHIN THE REPUBLICAN MEMORY CAMPAIGN

To discuss the tensions between individual and collective memory and individual and collective identities within the Republican memory campaign, it is worth starting with Narotzky and Smith's analysis of the lasting impact of the Francoist rhetoric on the "Reds," the biological transmission of Republicanism, and the broader process of atomisation and dismantling of a Republican collective memory: "People are limited to private, personal and particular memories of the past, and to political filiations through lineages, all of which render ahistorical and essential the realities of political identity production" (Narotzky and Smith 2002, 190). This highlights the potential opposition between "personal and particular" narratives and "historical" understandings that contextualise those narratives within larger-scale events. Significantly, Narotzky and Smith's ethnographic material predates the "mass grave phenomenon," but it foreshadows the key debates that would arise within the Republican memory campaign surrounding the role of exhumation and human remains in the "recuperation" of memory.

It is worth considering in some detail three extended passages in which informants involved in the Republican memory campaign reflect on these tensions in highly revealing ways. These extracts (from two interviews and an internet blog) provide a rich source for an analysis of the different positions within the campaign. The first extract is from the cofounder of ARMH, Emilio Silva, whom I interviewed at length on several occasions. He has permitted me to quote his words using his real name, as he has written and commented publicly on his role and is recognisable from the discussion below. This interview was conducted in 2005, when the exhumations were already extremely high profile in terms of the florescence of affiliated groups across Spain, media attention, internet activity, and political debate. Of key interest in this interview is Silva's repeated emphasis on the relatives of the dead as the primary beneficiaries of ARMH's search for the bodies of their missing relatives. In addition, he reflects on the significance of the official name chosen by his campaign group, particularly the absence of the word "Republican."

Silva acknowledges the "media effect" of human remains, considering in highly positive terms the number of individuals who are drawn into an enquiry into their family's past by the extensive media coverage, rather than reflecting on why the media are drawn to the exposure of human remains. Significantly, he refers to these new participants as "grandchildren," privileging their familial relation to the past, rather than as "public" or "young people." This implies a highly individualised memory, yet Silva also problematises the campaign's paradigm of physical/bodily investigation into the past by identifying an opposition between "the bones" and "the history" (which it should be noted could also be translated from Spanish as "the story"). His reflection on the symbolic and emotional significance of "the bones" depicts them as more important than "the history," but the precise relationship between the two remains ambiguous in Silva's formulation. Finally, Silva suggests another opposition, parallel to the opposition of "bones" and "histories," between "to see" and "to know." Bones are seen and histories are known. Silva implicitly privileges the visibility of human remains over the knowledge of history by offering the example of the children of murdered Republicans who have grown up in exile. They have been raised outside of the "pact of silence" and therefore may know their family history, but some still return to Spain to experience the exhumations firsthand, "to see":

The association is a collective that principally groups the families of those who disappeared in the Spanish Civil War and some affiliated people who help those families and who are themselves concerned with the problem of the disappeared. We created the Association for the Recuperation of Historical Memory in December 2000 and registered this name with the Ministry of the Interior, which means it has effect in the whole state. I don't remember how we chose this name. Other possible names had something to do with memory, but without the word "recuperation." We thought for a long time that it had to have something to do with Republicans, but in the end we decided not to put that. But it's an association whose basic objectives are to help families search for their own disappeared.

I believe there is a lot of difference between those who are relatives [of the dead] and those who are not. It's a question of sensibility, for me the relatives are the most important thing in this. The media impact this has had, the media effect, that one had a positive effect, because now many people are getting involved, many people have started to search, we receive lots of emails now from the grandchildren who begin to search for the history of their grandfathers. Not only their bones now, but their histories. I don't know which of these two, the bones or the histories, is more important to people. I imagine it depends on each family situation, what they know already or not. I believe that the bones are a symbolic thing, very basic and very important. It's a cultural question, we've been performing burials for thousands of years. This is a very primal history. For me it did not always have this significance: when I began to first think of my grandfather's body, I rarely visited cemeteries. Sometimes I went to the one in my village because there are many people with my surname, it's like that's where my roots are. But some months ago my mother died and now I give it so much more importance, now every weekend I go to my village where she is buried. Now I think this [the bones] is the most important, but the two things are both very important, it's important also to know what happened. I think the ones who come from abroad, the children of exiles, they know what happened, but they need to see it. This is very important, to know and to see. There is a movement of people who want to know. (Emilio Silva, Madrid)

It is useful to consider these passages along with an extract from an interview with a senior forensic expert practitioner, one of the most preeminent in Spain, whose constant assistance in ARMH's exhumations has been critical to their success. He is a high-profile supporter of ARMH's campaign, lending it gravitas and authority. He is highly reflexive in his own practice of exhumation and identification, speaking widely in the media and at gatherings of both experts and laypeople on the significance of this work. Unlike Emilio Silva, he explicitly addresses the link between the "media effect" and the exposure of human remains:

> The exhumations are serving to socialise and to recuperate the forgotten, something that before came to us only from oral sources, testimony, and archive. The oral sources were not sufficiently attractive to the wider public, which seldom knew the results of the investigations, if not from some newspaper report or a little book that the public wasn't interested in. The archives can generate books, and perhaps that gives more to society because those books sell now, or they can make songs or plays as well, but all these things are confined to the realm of experts, whereas, without exception, the mass graves draw in the interest of a whole cross-section of our society. Because it's the proof of the reality of a crime. It's a thing that is very demonstrative of a real act. When you read a book, you have to think whether the author is lying or not, but it's irrefutable when we view a photo of a mass grave in a newspaper and immediately come to the conclusion that it's certain and it's serious. For this reason some people, politicians, and groups try to take advantage of the repercussions of mass graves in our society.
>
> The whole human race all over the world is impressed by the confrontation with death. This occurs in archaeology: if some Roman skeletons appear, this has more attraction for the general public than if some ceramics appear, because you are looking at individuals, they're not objects, and therefore it's a more human reality. (Gabriel, Burgos Province)

In this extract Gabriel explains the importance of exhumation and human remains to the Republican memory campaign focussing exclusively on the reality effect and the mistrust of other historical representations. Given his disciplinary training as a forensic practitioner, this emphasis on proof is perhaps unsurprising, but it is also a perspective that privileges the individual and the particular in the encounter with the past. Gabriel does not privilege familial relationships at all: the individual and particular is important because it is "demonstrative of a real act" and it triggers empathetic engagement, "because you are looking at individuals... it's a more human reality."

In the light of these two extracts from key participants in ARMH, it is important to look at a severe critique posted on an internet site run by a rival Republican memory group, Foro por la Memoria, under the auspices of the Spanish Communist Party. The more recently formed Foro criticises in particular ARMH's privileging of individual over collective memory. (The manifestation of this opposition within the Foro's campaign practice is analysed in Herrmann 2010.) The central points of this debate can be found in the following comment by the Foro founder and president Jose Maria Pedreño:

> ARMH don't even pretend, within their objectives, to resurrect the Historic Memory of the anti-Franco struggle and the repression, only the bodies of their relatives to give them a "dignified burial." Their work goes no further than this and they work without any kind of ideological reference.
>
> They treat as private matters those that were political murders. That's to say, for them the important thing are the "bones of the grandfather" and to take them to the cemetery without further consideration. Foro has always considered these as political murders and one has to treat them from all points of view, including the human aspect of returning the body to the family, but without forgetting the social and collective memory of this country. The militants not only had families, but also comrades and companions and an intense social life, a life of struggle. When they died as a result of their struggle, those were social deaths, not particular deaths. They transformed themselves into the dead of us all. (Pedreño 2004)

As part of this lengthy online critique, Pedreño also touches on the opposition between "the bones" and "the history," or in his own formulation, between the body and the mind of the dead. His point is that these people were turned into "bodies" by their oppressors in order to silence their minds: "a whole people murdered physically in order that they be castrated ideologically." To resurrect their bodies without resurrecting their ideologies is to perpetuate the goals of the oppressors. Pedreño's rhetoric is explicitly situated in a far-left discourse, most notably when he calls those who participate in ARMH's exhumations "neoliberals of memory" and warns against the "privatisation of our Left heritage." Pedreño argues that the goal must be to learn from the dead: "their way of thinking, their struggle, their lives, how the social and political life of this epoch developed, the lessons that we can take back, an analysis of historical processes that we can bring to light, the comprehension of how the present was constructed" (Pedreño 2004).

A senior member of the Foro whom I interviewed at length in Madrid, Mariano, described the process by which he became involved in the Republican memory campaign and chose to involve himself with the

Foro rather than ARMH: "I realised that this was something necessary if we wished to construct the Left of the twenty-first century in my country." In the discourse of Pedreño and other Foro supporters, the dead no longer belong solely to particular families but belong to the political Left as a collective; and not only as part of their collective past, but as a present- or future-oriented model of political action. This apparent polarisation between the Foro and ARMH is by no means as extreme as it may appear from the extracts above. The complicating factor is that ARMH's significant success in attracting both media and political attention resides in the degree to which the campaign modifies and manages its public discourse and public representation to make it palatable to the climate of centrist, consensus-oriented debate that is prevalent within the press, the political establishment, and public opinion (Desfor Edles 1998). Above all, ARMH understands that a focus on familial relations, sentiments, and the "dignity" or decency of burial traditions is almost impossible for the political Right to publicly contest without appearing rancorous or inhumane. The discourse amongst individual ARMH campaigners during interviews or internal discussions was much closer in content to Pedreño's stance on collective memory, though gentler in tone. An example can be seen in Emilio Silva's clarification on what he meant by his frequent phrase "dignify the dead," which Pedreño had simplified in his critique as constituting only a "dignified burial":

> We have to find them and we have to do everything possible to dignify the memories of the Republicans who were murdered during the Civil War. This means trying to publish books, hold conferences, or try to have the press disseminate the ideas of these people. Any type of actions that can give a public dignity to these people. Not that these families ever lost their dignity, but it was private, behind closed doors, without bringing the story of their families outside the house. In some way this has produced for a long time a public silence around these people and this has allowed the Francoist version [of memory] that was established over forty years to endure and that has never been contested. (Emilio Silva, Madrid)

Here Silva appears to be talking explicitly of fostering or disseminating a Republican collective memory because he wishes to publicly contest "the Francoist version" of the past. In reference to the extent of media coverage the exhumations generate, he adds that this could be used "to have the press disseminate the ideas of these people," which would seem to accord exactly with Pedreño's goals. It is highly revealing that in the first line of this extract Silva appears to conflate bodies and memory so completely that the subject of this sentence becomes unclear: "We have to find *them*... and dignify the *memories*," suggesting how deeply entwined the two things have become in ARMH's campaign. Pedreño's stated goal of learning from the dead rather than simply "dignifying" them, which he expresses as "the lessons we can take back," is also echoed in the more private reflections or speculations of forensic expert Gabriel, who in our interview strongly regretted the lack of a legal structure or legal hearings in which the physical evidence of the mass graves could be presented and interrogated as proof of the past. This is instructive, in that Gabriel retains his forensic focus on individual bodies and "cases," yet believes that, given a proper forum, individual cases could be drawn together into an overarching narrative of the past, thus reconciling the demands of individual and collective memory. This echoes Wilson's concerns about the TRC in South Africa (2001), namely that case-by-case investigations do not always cohere into a historical understanding:

> I'm not saying that we have to prosecute the Francoists, or those who committed murders, who now are old people themselves, but with these international laws, you could bring these cases for the clarification of the truth, going down the path of the truth commissions, [and] that later might have pedagogic value for the whole country, to reinforce democratic ideals, to recognise the mistakes we incurred, but for sure this will never happen in Spain. (Gabriel, Burgos)

This is a much milder and less partisan understanding of the lessons of the past, concerning the reinforcement of "democratic ideals" rather than "the formation of the Left in the twenty-first century." It is conciliatory in tone, rejecting the idea of prosecuting the perpetrators, but also realistic or pragmatic in its ambition, in that Gabriel suggests that a truth commission could never happen in Spain. Despite these differences in tone, the last two extracts from Emilio Silva and Gabriel show a strong awareness of, and concern with, the fostering and dissemination of some form of Republican memory, and this exists in a state of tension (as exposed by Pedreño's critique) with their primary mode of operating, the exhumation and reburial of individual human remains at the behest of the relatives of the dead. The groundbreaking and popular book *Las Fosas de Franco* published by Silva and Macías in 2003 exemplifies this mode of operation, as it presents detailed individual cases of Republican death and repression, region by region, yet the individual narratives presented could resonate with a very wide readership. This book, which could be characterised as "in memory of Republicans" rather than an ideologically informed "Republican memory," nevertheless fostered an awareness and public acknowledgement of how widespread these experiences had been throughout Spain, arguably the first step toward any kind of "collective" memory.

Conclusion

In this chapter I have described the Republican political and social identity that coalesced around a broad spectrum of leftist ideologies amongst the working-class and progressive middle-class in prewar Spain. I discussed the systematic dismantling of this identity and its negative characterisation within the Francoist rhetoric, and highlighted an enduring preoccupation with the transmission and resurgence of a Republican collective identity revealed by the use of biological and organic metaphors. I examined the experience of violence and systematic political repression within my field sites, particularly the significance of the concepts of honour and shame in the production of a condition of atomisation. The breakdown that occurred in the intergenerational transmission of memory, including the political memory of the Republican collective identity and the intimate memory of the dead men as individuals, has rendered both political and affective representations of the dead complex and problematic for the living, a theme that will be developed further in the next chapter.

The reflections of key actors working within two rival groups revealed the challenges surrounding the representation of the dead within the Republican memory campaign. The two positions can be simplified as follows: ARMH places a primary emphasis on the affective bond between the living and the dead, and stresses the necessity of enacting this bond through exhumation and reburial. In contrast, Foro por la Memoria places a primary emphasis on the ideological bond between the living and the dead, and stresses the necessity of making a political representation of the dead that is not so dependent on the act of exhumation and reburial. Significantly, the two ARMH workers emphasise the affordances of human remains: to command popular fascination and media attention; to convey reality and dispel suspicions of mediation or authorship; and to structure affective bonds between the living and the dead. All these themes will be analysed in detail in chapter 3 with regard to the representations of the bodies and objects that emerge during the exhumations.

Chapter 2

MEMORY IDIOMS AND THE REPRESENTATION OF REPUBLICAN LOSS WITHIN THE CONFINES OF A FRANCOIST DISCOURSE ON THE PAST

INTRODUCTION

This chapter examines the way in which my informants, primarily the surviving children of those killed in 1937 in my first field site of Villavieja, talk about the killing of their fathers and the subsequent repression experienced by their families, exemplifying the kind of atomised memory that I outlined in chapter 1. I look in detail at certain memory idioms—narrative tropes, themes, and stock phrases that recurred in my interviews and in more informal communications—to understand the mechanisms by which memories of loss and political repression are articulated in an environment dominated for over forty years by an official version of the past formulated and enforced by a repressive regime.

Above all, this official discourse explicitly assigns all guilt and responsibility for the political violence between 1936 and 1939 to the dead Republicans and their families. My informants have been saturated with these discourses for most of their adult lives, and I analyse the negotiation that takes places between their firsthand memory, the memory transmitted within their families, and the official history that they have not only passively absorbed but were aggressively inculcated with. These personal and public memories are diametrically opposed, especially over the relative morality of victim and perpetrator and the perceived "necessity" of these deaths. It is possible to find ways of remembering that mediate some of these inherent contradictions, creating a workable or liveable memory that makes coexistence with one's oppressors possible.

Particular ways of remembering can claim the exceptionality of one's individual loss, thus distinguishing personal stories from official historical narratives and avoiding contradictions between the two. These memory idioms can expiate the guilt attached to these families by Francoist discourse, and offer a coded resistance or alternative to this dominant discourse without provoking further political repression.

It is important to address the possible forms taken by local memory in the villages investigated by ARMH in order to critique the unproblematic characterisation of individual memory inherent in the group's official name. "Association for the Recovery of Historical Memory" posits memory as a neutral and natural resource existing within individuals, or held collectively in a community, that only needs to be "recovered" or harvested, so that it may then be disseminated. Within ARMH's campaign, the opportunity for memory to be recovered lies with the materialisation of human remains through exhumation. The investigation underpinning the exhumation includes extensive interviews with the relatives of the dead and surviving Republicans, and the dramatic physical rupture of exposing concealed human remains also disrupts the normative prohibitions on memory that have dominated these communities. This resource of memory is characterised as something hidden or buried that only needs to be "brought to light." The challenge lies in the struggle to elicit verbalisations of memory, rather than in the complexities and ambiguities of the memory itself. A direct analogy with the physical "bringing to light" of corpses through exhumation is frequent in ARMH's public discourse: the frozen potentiality of a seed is an image that recurs within the campaign, as if memories had been in stasis during the dictatorship and were finally ready to flower. In reality, memories of the Republican experience have been in a constant, albeit imbalanced, exchange with the official state discourse for over sixty-five years. The memory idioms encountered in my field sites illustrate the divergence between the local idiomatic representations of the past and the affective and political representations of the dead made by ARMH campaigners and the expert practitioners coordinating the investigations. This divergence may be experienced as potentially threatening and destabilising by some participants in the exhumations process, and may provoke responses of ambivalence and resistance from the relatives of the dead.

A week-long summer school of workshops and meetings was held in Burgos in July 2005 for researchers, campaigners, relatives, and surviving Republicans to compare notes on the current state of the investigations into the Republican experience in the region. It was a mixed, informal, and animated gathering that facilitated the sharing of information and experiences. A panel of oral historians commented that if one phrase was emblematic of their interviews with the children of dead Republicans, it was "My father was NOT a communist! He was a very good man"— even in the paradoxical case cited by one historian in which one of the surviving memento of the dead man that the family possessed was his Communist Party membership card. The anecdote drew a laugh of recognition from many colleagues in the room who had encountered identical or comparable phrases from their own informants. The laughter, however, was followed by a sigh of resignation over the pervasive quality of a Francoist logic that had made being communist and "a good man" so incompatible as to be a self-evident contradiction.

This emblematic phrase drew recognition from those in the meeting because it encapsulated the gap between the interviewer/investigator and the informant, and the often radically different premises under which they were engaging in the "recovery" process. Generally speaking, the majority of those active in the Republican memory campaign belong to the post-transition generation, and are situated on a broadly left-wing spectrum in their personal politics and principles. The campaigners share an understanding of Republicanism as an era of political engagement, resistance, and socially progressive ideas, and seek to recover a memory of those individuals who "died for their ideas." Paradoxically, some of those who can supply firsthand memories—surviving children and eyewitnesses—are particularly conditioned by the Francoist discourse and engage with the memory campaign as an exceptional case, to free the dead of the perceived stigma of the ideas they died for and thus rehabilitate them as "good men."

An archaeologist, Juanma, who collaborated as an expert practitioner on the exhumations in my field sites, and who works full time on the investigation of Republican graves, left the meeting in Burgos dejected and angrily commented, "We'll have to change our name because there's no memory to recover. It doesn't exist in Spain. It will have to be created." It appeared a strange comment from a person who had spent the last three years recording, filming, and writing up firsthand testimonies of the political violence that had created the mass graves. If data such as names, dates, and places had not been held in living memory, he would not have been able to perform his job. When I asked why he had left the meeting so abruptly, he said that the discussion had suddenly depressed him. I attributed his frustration to a realisation of the atomised quality of the memory he had encountered in his work, and to the absence of any *Republican* memory or collective Republican narrative, which in his opinion would have had to be created. This assertion did not in any way refer to fabrications. Rather, it referred to the construction or assemblage of a historical narrative from the raw materials of individual memory.

Theft, Poverty, and Material Envy in the Representation of Republican Victimhood

In ARMH's practice there is an integral relationship between the collection of oral history/testimony in a community and the exhumation of individuals from that community, either as a preliminary to a planned exhumation or with the explicit intention to gather background information for a possible exhumation in the future. A certain proportion of the interview questions asked by ARMH at my field sites could be classed as forensic in that they directly borrowed from the questionnaires used in the exhumation and identification of bodies from mass graves around the world. Although in-depth interviews into family and community histories and personal reflections on the past were recorded as part of the investigative process, some of the questions can be characterised as the collection of antemortem data in order to match known information on the dead with the evidence that emerges from the grave, to identify the human remains, and to reconstruct the events surrounding the death.

A key piece of information to enable the identification of a skeleton is a description of the probable clothing and of any personal artefacts likely to be found by the archaeologist on a particular body. I observed or participated in a number of interviews or less formal discussions in which there seemed to be some confusion about these clothes and possessions. The informant would describe a piece of clothing or an object, specifically a suit, a belt, a wallet, or a watch, and the expert practitioners or ARMH coordinators would take note of these details, understanding them as antemortem data that could be matched with the objects found in the grave. When the object had been described and its qualities expanded upon, it would emerge that while it had certainly belonged to the dead person, just as certainly it had been stolen at the time of death and therefore could not possibly appear in the grave during the exhumation. The theft was widely known about because the killers would wear or use the object upon returning from the killings. I initially took this as an example of the mismatch in expectations and assumptions between scientists and informants, with the investigators so deeply entrenched in the logic of their working practice that they failed to explain it at the outset of the interview. Furthermore, I took it as an illustration of the power relations between the investigator and the informant, which rendered the informant eager to furnish an example of the uniquely individuating object that the investigator appeared to be seeking.

> If it's possible to identify them, yes, then I want them to be identified. My uncle had some pocket watch, I know, a present, but they robbed him after they killed him. With my granddad, when they killed him, they took the money he was carrying but I don't know if he carried any special object. (Amparo, Villavieja)

I became interested in the clarity and precision of the memories my informants had of these stolen objects, and in the enthusiasm with which they recounted the theft to the interviewer. There were interesting parallels between the way the investigators invested any unique object with a talismanic status due to its power to individuate a skeleton, and the way informants too seemed to invest unique objects with talismanic properties, but for reasons that were less immediately apparent. These thefts were a major topic of conversation in the discussions the inhabitants of Villavieja would have at the grave edge during the exhumation. Different visitors, even middle-aged individuals who had no firsthand memory of the deaths and otherwise professed their ignorance over what had happened, could chime in and confirm the theft of a specific object, strongly suggesting that the theft of objects was a safer theme in the intergenerational transmission of memory. People became animated and highly indignant in tone when recalling these thefts:

> Another old man whom they killed some days after, this man had a corduroy suit, and they took it off him to put another one, and another [man] from my village had a new belt for his trousers, they took it off him, and there was one man from Fuentes [the hamlet outside Villavieja] who was using it until very recently. Look at the *fainas* [burdens/unpleasantness] we go through. (Tina, Villavieja)

I noted a discussion of a particular corduroy suit in which the participants agreed that it had been an expensive, fashionable, newly purchased suit that was so distinctive that it was immediately recognisable when the killer returned wearing it. In the course of this discussion no direct memories were elicited of the life history of the original owner of the suit, despite the fact that the remains of his body were in close proximity. Knowledge of the perpetrator's identity was claimed by all those present, but his actual name was never used in the discussion, a form of self-censorship that I observed in almost every discussion on the past throughout my fieldwork, and that investigators reported too. Perpetrators' names remained an absolute taboo, regardless of the speaker or the context. Unfortunately, I did not record many of these conversations at the time, except by accident, because of my own preconceptions. They seemed not only bafflingly inconsequential and surreal, but also distasteful to my sensibilities on the relative importance of human beings and material possessions. At this point in the exhumation, I was managing my own responses to the newly exposed human remains, and the reminiscences of thefts seemed a petty or misplaced concern when compared with the overwhelming evidence of violent death that was being gradually exposed at the gravesite.

Reviewing the fieldnotes I took during my first attempts at interviews, I noted that my initial discussions felt like wrestling matches, with me trying to talk about death and the informant trying to talk about theft. After a while, communicating with more people in Villavieja, I encountered certain stock phrases that made me regret my failure to engage with these conversations. The most vituperative comments I heard in condemnation of the Francoists were "*fascistas-ladrones*" (fascists-thieves) or "*fascistas-criminales*" (fascists-criminals). I was struck by the absence of "*fascistas-asesinos*," or of a characterisation of the Francoists primarily as murderers or killers. I never heard this articulated verbally; the only expression of "*asesinos*" that I encountered was in an impressively large piece of graffiti stretched across the side of a storehouse on the roadside leading in and out of the village, reminiscent of a billboard in its scale and location, which read "Fascists—murderers of half my village." No one could recall the exact date it had appeared and no one would explicitly tell me its author, but some village residents hinted that it could have been my key informant's father who had painted it on his own property as a double bluff. Informants also recalled that two unsuccessful attempts had been made by Francoist youth groups to scrub it off, and the inscription was now left to weather away naturally, fading into the stone wall.

Fascistas-ladrones specifically refers to the thefts that accompanied these killings, and I think *fascistas-criminales* is an extension of this, which asserts that the Francoists acted as "common criminals" rather than as the highly organised perpetrators of an ideologically motivated violence supported by the Francoist bureaucracy and sanctioned by the military. The absence of any widely held characterisation of fascists as murderers potentially problematises ARMH's investigative process in Villavieja. This process is constructed around, and structured by, the act of exhumation, privileging the recovery of human remains and the scientific reconstruction of identity, bodily trauma, and cause of death. The attempt to reconstruct the exact sequence of abduction, violence, death, and burial, closely mirroring a forensic investigation into a mass fatality, privileges the killings as the defining act of oppression in the village.

The characterisation of the Francoists as thieves or common criminals could be described as the expression of a depoliticised, atomised memory. Republicans and their families during the war years experienced theft twice: first, the robbery of personal items and clothes from individuals at the time of their death; second, the robbery or looting of domestic property and the imposition of *multas* (quasi-official fines collected in money or goods) to the homes of recently killed Republican men. More systematic financial penalties were imposed after the war as part of the highly punitive and retroactive legislation developed under

Franco's regime to punish "political crimes," known as the Ley de Responsabilidades Políticas (Political Responsibilities Act) (Ryan 2009). By focussing on the transgressive act of robbing the dead or the soon-to-be-dead, Republican families can assert the immorality and self-interest of the perpetrators without explicitly contradicting the Francoist discourse that insists upon the essential necessity of these deaths for the purification and salvation of Spain.

The portable, wearable quality of these items compounds the transgression because their previous intimacy with the dead implies some taint of morbidity or impurity, but above all because they can displayed by the perpetrators. In addition, Stallybrass and Jones (2001) demonstrate how intimate pieces of clothing such as gloves and shoes, which take on the form of the wearer's body over time, come to powerfully represent the person. The same power accrues to certain items of jewellery that are never normally removed, as well as to spectacles, as their removal from the person speaks of some catastrophic rupture in the normal routine. The specific way these objects are used, and the way they materially change with use, render them inalienable. The power of these objects to represent an individual means that their continued "life" after the death of their owners engenders a sense of dissonance or eeriness. A similar feeling is produced by the watches of the dead, due to the presence of moving parts that makes them analogous to the heart, and to the fact that the watch quantifies a particular individual's time, i.e. his or her life. That life has now stopped, yet the watch continues impartially to measure time, a troubling paradox which plays on a wealth of associations between the measurement of time and human mortality.

The strength of memories of stolen and reused objects hints at a particular kind of trauma, which is not a simple bereavement but a simultaneous realisation of one's utter powerlessness in the new status quo. The murders were not clandestine but open and flagrant, to the degree that the killers could return to the village wearing the suit, watch, or belt of their victims as a kind of advertisement of their participation in the killings. They could function as trophies, eliciting and structuring the killers' accounts of these deaths. This effectively communicated the new prevailing power relations to the bereaved families, and sent the message that the perpetrators apparently had no fear of community censure, opprobrium, or future redress for their crimes. The account given by Ana of the abduction of her uncles when she was eight years old illustrates how material objects can encode a certain reading of the deaths:

> They have disappeared, Teodoro, Braulio, and Primitivo, they were all three brothers of my mother, my maternal uncles. I saw it all with my

own eyes, what happened to my uncles. They were kept prisoners in the cell in Fuentes [hamlet of Villavieja], and at dawn they put them on a lorry to take them I-don't-know-where, but we knew that they were going to kill them. I climbed up into the lorry and they asked me to get down: "If not, you go with them," they told me. We were informed that they went to Burgos. We didn't know anything else, we found out later when we saw people wearing their clothes. The ones who took them away were wearing their clothes. It was some bosses from the village, but they ordered some people to kill them for a crust of bread, and one of my uncles wore a gold signet ring, very good, because he'd been in France, and they cut off his finger to remove it. All that, we know. (Ana, Villavieja)

Evoking the stolen clothes, the crust of bread, and the gold ring, this narrative implies a certain economy of the objects that surround these deaths. The theft of clothes makes the killers into common criminals. The crust of bread that prompted the killings may refer to actual food, although the expression *"un cacho de pan"* is frequently used figuratively for trifling amounts of money or goods of little value. It is a useful metaphor in this case, as bread communicates real material need or hunger and thus partially absolves the killers, or at least diminishes their free will. Moral responsibility is located with the "bosses," and physical responsibility is located with those they could pay to kill for a crust of bread. Divided in this way, guilt appears dispersed or diffused. The detail of the gold ring and the severed finger convey the morbidity or depravity of the perpetrators without explicitly condemning them. The illustration is left to speak for itself in this account. The explanation for these deaths is shifted away from the political realm and made material instead of ideological.

This allows some complex shifts in this narrative. First, by linking the death to the killer's covetous desire for a particular object possessed by the victim, an exception can be made for the morality surrounding that particular individual's death. The logic is that while some victims were *necessarily* killed for being "Reds" or part of the "anti-Spain," one's own relative was *opportunistically* killed for his suit, watch, or money. This explains why we are told that the ring was very good and came all the way from France. The properties of the ring, its inherent desirability, attribute a degree of agency to it, in that it feeds into a chain of events that leads to its wearer being killed and having his finger cut off. In this way the guilt or agency is diffused a step further, shared between the boss, the hired killer, and the coveted object, the ring itself. Second, the materialistic motive makes some space for an understanding of the killers, as material need humanises them and makes them also victims of external forces. The removal of ideology from the killings diminishes the inherent opposition and incompatibility of the two groups within the village, opening up the possibility of coexistence or enabling the speakers to reconcile themselves to it. Moreover, if we consider the rhetoric surrounding the biological transmission of Republicanism, conceived of as a heritable disease, this appears to be also a survival strategy for Republican families. For the relatives of the dead, to describe one's own particular bereavement as a materially rather than ideologically motivated killing was an act of self-preservation in order to downplay the Republican identity of the victims. However, this is a more instrumentalist reading; the affordances of these objects and their agency, particularly of the gold ring, will be returned to in greater detail.

The attribution of either material need or greed to the killers comes across very clearly in my informants' memories of the robbing and looting of their homes. The most commonly cited objects in these narratives of theft were furniture, clothing, stored food, animals, and alcohol, as outlined in chapter 1. The climate of material scarcity and competition is emphasised by two terms, *miseria* (poverty) and *envidia* (envy), used with notable frequency both in the interviews and in more informal communications. When people in my field site first found out what I was researching, the same words would be repeated emphatically to me as if they were a key piece of explanatory information, necessary to my proper understanding of the events in the village. It stood out to me that while not much information was offered voluntarily by the village inhabitants not directly involved or supporting the exhumation, as friendly as they might be, this advice was volunteered routinely as received wisdom. "*Hubo mucho miseria*" or "*era miseria*" ("there was a lot of poverty") was used as a gloss for the prewar conditions and served a dual explanatory purpose. The condition of material deprivation could explain, without directly alluding to it, the degree of working-class militancy in Villavieja in the 1930s in the form of unionisation, strikes, and political organisation around the *casa del pueblo* (working-class social and cultural centre) and in support of the Republican government. The emphasis on the widespread prewar poverty also provides a context of material desperation in which complicity with the Francoists—killing for a crust of bread and the chance to rob a body—becomes more human and more easily comprehensible. Barciela (2002, 339) notes that the inaccurate characterisation of the Second Republic as a period of economic underdevelopment was maintained by Francoist ideologues after the war.

The only informant in Villavieja with memories of the 1930s who could be drawn to explicitly address prewar conditions and relationships between the social classes was the most right-wing and upper-middle-class individual I spoke to, a woman in her early nineties called Fermina. Her husband had been a prominent Francoist, but since she had been widowed for a long time and had been active within the church and engaged in good works, she was classed by my other informants (the children of murdered Republicans) as a good person tainted by her Fascist husband. Although Fermina was willing to expand on the story, she equally described the prewar period mainly as a time of poverty, and summed up class conflict in terms of overall scarcity and competition:

> There was poverty. I think it's all very easy to understand that if a gentleman is very well off and has workers, then the boss probably accuses them of being useless and idlers, and the workers say the opposite, the boss is demanding, he exploits us, he gives us nothing. It is very easy to understand that each family, it talks of a thing, like the worker in that epoch said "we have rights" and really, they had no rights, there wasn't any social security, there weren't hospitals, there was only poverty. And the boss also complained because he didn't have many rights either, but at least he could pay his expenses. The workers fought for a better life. There was poverty and that was all, that was all, daughter. (Fermina, Villavieja)

Fermina implicitly naturalises conflict in this account with the phrase "It's all very easy to understand." In conjunction with poverty, the prewar and war years are characterised as a time of envy. When I asked my informants why their particular relative had been killed, trying to elicit some background information of the victim's political activities or affiliations, the response was always "*por nada... por envidias*" (for nothing... for envy), or "*envidia... nada mas*" (envy... nothing more). Envy moves beyond the simple material desperation, the willingness to kill for a crust of bread, to include the desire not only to procure an object but also to actively deprive someone else of it. In this way it introduces the element of spite: this is a very powerful idea in such a small community where every other inhabitant would have some awareness of each material object acquired and owned by a neighbour.

I had two interesting and moving encounters outside of recorded interviews when informants took me to specific sites to tell me in detail what had been stolen and the circumstances of their loss. I found the informants in both these occasions extremely sympathetic and likeable, and—in contrast to the recorded interviews, in which they had remained quite controlled and impassive—they exhibited more anger or regret at these particular incidents of theft. An elderly couple, Faustina and Federico, took me out into their market garden, ostensibly to admire it. Federico had inherited the house and the garden from his mother. The couple were both children of Republicans shot in Villavieja. Federico described how the garden had been looted by the Francoists after his father's murder. He took me to various patches and described what had been growing there in August 1936. He also indicated a tree that had been stripped of fruit. Some of the fruit and vegetables had not been ripe or ready to pick and he harbored a particular anger at this wasteful, senseless action on the part of the Francoists. I found this brief outburst of moral indignation extremely moving, because it highlighted things that he had left unsaid or unexpressed in our interview.

My key informant in Villavieja, Julio, was a local ARMH coordinator in his forties; both his maternal and paternal grandfathers were killed in 1936. We spent a lot of time walking around the village together and driving around the surroundings to look for graves. Near the end of my fieldwork, he took me to see the outline of some stone foundations and a pile of small stones on the edge of the village. His paternal grandfather was building a new house when he was murdered, and the Francoists had systematically dismantled the structure to rob the building materials. He described this as a bitter and disheartening moment for his family because the house was in an advanced state. This was not a firsthand memory (he would never personally see the house close to completion), but this sense was transmitted to him by his father. He was sad, quiet, and pensive, and said that he thought about what happened to his grandfather every time he passed by this spot. I found his experience of this site of material loss and memory even more striking as we were within walking distance of the execution site and mass grave thought to hold his other (maternal) grandfather. The wastefulness and destruction inherent in both these cases—the theft of the garden produce and the dismantled house—exhibit a degree of spite and communicate that such acts were not motivated by a logic of straightforward material gain, but by the logic of *envidia* that seeks to deprive others of the things they have.

In the summer of 2004, I participated in the excavation of two mass graves in Villavieja with a team partly consisting of archaeologists and archaeology students from Madrid. I then stayed on to conduct interviews in the weeks immediately after the exhumation. Meeting up with some archaeologists back in Madrid, I discussed my findings with Aldo, who was in his early twenties, highly politicised, historically well informed, and involved in the contemporary anarchist movement in Spain. I told him about the incidents of theft and the degree to which material envy appeared to be a motivation behind the violence in Villavieja. He was unimpressed by my interpretation and told me bluntly that *envidia* was a myth and "the big lie," and that the myth of *envidia* "made things easier for everyone." This dismissive statement resonated with the unease I had felt during those discussions of theft, material loss, and envy. I had instinctively found the concerted materialisation, and corresponding depoliticisation, of these narratives to be disturbing in that they threw into relief what could not be said, and were testament to the efficacy and power of Franco's memory regime.

I repeated Aldo's dismissive rejection of *envidia* to Mariano, a leader of the Communist Party's memory campaign group, the Foro por la Memoria, and a coordinator of numerous exhumations of Republican mass graves throughout Spain. He admitted that he had reflected for a long time on the narrative trope of *envidia*, which he also had encountered constantly during his own investigations. Unsurprisingly, his interpretation accorded closely with the preoccupations of the Foro por la Memoria with the individual and the collective in Spanish memory politics analysed at the end of chapter 1. In his analysis, the trope of *envidia* served to individualise the killings, undermining the collective identity of the dead and the ideological motives for their deaths. He suggested that the invocation of *envidia* by Republican families had once been a political expedient to distance themselves from Republicanism, and that this stratagem went on unchallenged in the present day because the explanation of *envidia* was less threatening to Spain's "individualistic" society than the recognition that these deaths were politically motivated:

> The politicisation has to follow when you bring out the reality of this story. It's necessary to talk about why the killings actually happened. I talk of politics as the translation of ideas into the concrete. Another thing that calls our attention in the villages is the great social richness that existed then [during the 1930s], the number of grassroots organisations, clubs, meeting houses, and they were very politicised, and everyone came together in these organisations. There was a great richness in the social fabric of Spain and this isn't talked about, they only talk of poverty and the priest. For envy, one doesn't take four people affiliated to the same trade union and kills them. That isn't for envy. It's more comfortable because it's the best way not to confront the fear, and it's the way we justify ourselves for not doing anything, for our own apathy. Spanish society is asleep; it's a civil society lacking articulation. Individualistic people who shut themselves in their houses…
>
> I was at a grave where they said "Oh, the envy, the envy, it was all envy." But one old man stepped away from them and told me, these were all from the Socialist Party, the others were from the Falange, all of them were in the *casa del pueblo* and they were unarmed, the others were in the *casino* and had guns. When they found out about the military uprising they came and killed them. There was a lot of politics here but nobody is informed, he told me. The fear has been planted so deep that it penetrated into the roots of the people, and generation after generation it is still there. (Mariano, Madrid)

The beginning of an interview with Mercedes from Villavieja illustrates how the politics or ideology behind a killing can be omitted from a narrative by privileging the motive of material envy. Mercedes's account seems to typify the kind of narrative that Mariano criticises and to support, at least partially, his analysis of the depoliticisation of memory:

> My father was the mayor of Fuentes [hamlet on the edge of Villavieja], he left six orphans and in addition the Falange put on a fine of 30,000 pesetas. My mother had to look for the money to pay it because otherwise they would have taken possession of everything. They seized our house and left us in the street. They already had plans to share all the goods between them. The guilty ones were two butchers because my father was a butcher, and for envy they denounced him… Look at how badly they treated my father… Later because of the envies and the material things, they kept them eight days prisoners there, they said that they were going to take them to Burgos and brought them here to kill them. (Mercedes, Villavieja)

At the heart of this narrative is the assertion: "My father was the mayor, but he was killed for being the butcher." In this telling, the man's political identity as mayor is overshadowed by his material status as a successful butcher. Mercedes's father was active in community politics and social life; he frequented the *casa del pueblo* and attended council meetings in Villavieja, building a sufficient profile to be elected mayor as the candidate of the Popular Front. The first grave we excavated contained all the Republicans elected for local office as mayors or councillors in Villavieja or the neighbouring hamlet of Fuentes. They were all killed on the same day, which appears to confer a very strong collective identity on the dead and points to the overwhelming causal factor motivating these killings. Mercedes at various times showed that she was aware of who the other people in the grave were, of the collective identity of the dead, but her narrative still resisted this collective identity as a causal explanation of the deaths. Instead, her focus on the house, the household goods, the 30,000 pesetas, and the murderous envy of the two rival butchers enabled her to individualise her father's death.

HIERARCHIES OF LOSS: PEOPLE AND THINGS

The analysis of the trope of *envidia* offered by individuals active in the Republican memory campaign shows that with their growing experience of exhumations and investigations throughout Spain comes an increasing awareness that Republican memory is not a neutral resource to be "brought to light" or recovered, but is rather inherently conditioned by the Francoist discourse on the past. Those engaged in the memory campaign, specifically those investing their energies in the exhumation and reburial of Republican bodies, have an obvious interest in challenging accounts of material loss and *envidia*. The construction of a Republican collective memory or overarching narrative will not be achieved if the investigations recover a history of thousands of Spaniards dying for *envidias* rather than for their ideas. The concern with increasing public awareness of the politics behind these killings and achieving a hegemonic shift to the Left in contemporary Spain is made explicit in the mission of the Foro por la Memoria, though it has a more ambiguous place in the campaign goals of ARMH.

The preoccupation with material loss in Republican memory idioms also exposes the degree to which the campaigners' concern with death and human remains is, to some degree, imposed upon the community as the sole focus of the campaign to recover Republican memory. The massacres in these villages are single, compressed episodes of extreme violence that are the primary focus of the current investigations into the traumatic past, but this focus risks excluding the raft of repressive measures sustained over many years that characterises the experience of many Republican families. It is in the interest of campaigners to present *envidia* simply as an example of "false consciousness" or "bad faith" (a myth, a big lie, a strategy to make things easy and comfortable), but I argue that the dismissal of *envidia* as false consciousness is in itself a politically motivated oversimplification that has to be resisted in order to understand both the nature of the oppression that took place in these villages and the forces that shaped the memory of these events.

It was striking to me that Mariano, an avowed Marxist and an active member of the Spanish Communist Party (PCE), was dismissive of the individual accounts of theft, material loss, and envy that he had encountered during exhumations in rural communities around Spain, and yet in the course of our extended interview repeatedly referred to the vast resources and infrastructure that had been stolen from the Communist Party and various trade unions immediately after the Civil War. This suggested that he understood the correlation between the material appropriation and power relations at the macro level of national politics, but not at the micro level of the village or the household. This exasperation with "the myth of *envidias*" is redolent of the points of disjuncture between narrator and interlocutor highlighted by Trinch (2003). Trinch points to the occasional emergence of diverging subjectivities that occurs when the female victims of spousal abuse offer a reading of their experiences that diverges from that of the victims' advocates. The response of the victims' rights advocates appears at moments to border on frustration and impatience with those whom they seek to empower and protect. Another powerful and persuasive admonishment to really listen to people before we try to "speak" for them or "empower" their voice is articulated by Das and exemplified in her work:

> When we use such imagery as breaking the silence, we may end by using our capacity to "unearth" hidden facts as a weapon. Even the idea that we should recover the narratives of violence becomes problematic when we realize that such narratives cannot be told unless we see the relation between pain and language that a culture has evolved. (Das 1997, 88)

In the case of my informants, this could be reformulated as the relation between pain, language, memory, and material objects that these communities have evolved until this point in time.

The concept of envy is inseparable from a broader set of ideas on social relationships and status and, perhaps more interestingly, culturally specific ideas on the visual register and the power of the gaze. Within this framework, material objects have their own particular affordances and powers: they are inseparably bound up with their owner's life history, drawing on ideas that associate the visual and material properties of an object with its ability to draw envy or luck and thus intervene in its owner's fate. This is dependent on a strongly visual understanding of the envy and ill will of others.

Examples drawn from other cultural contexts on the role of material possessions in the formation and expression of memories may furnish some insights into the role of objects in my informant's accounts of theft, loss, and envy. First, it is important to emphasise the mechanics of the repression that took place in my field sites. In chapter 1, I considered the symbolic and economic significance of the theft of household goods, particularly the inversion of the opposition between interior and exterior. Both violating the "inside" space of the home by picking over clothes, furniture, and food, and forcing the Republican women "outside" into the role of breadwinner engendered a sense of shame. However, accounts from my field sites show how the theft of possessions was part of a more systematic assault on these families' self-sufficiency. These families had to be made destitute in order to be then reincorporated into the new social order as recipients of charity. According to my informants, the stolen food and household goods were effectively recycled by the soup kitchens and welfare groups run by the Sección Femenina (the women's division of the Falange). Republican families would be offered back their own goods if they presented themselves as recipients of charity. This mechanism is described by Faustina. She told me that her family was repeatedly robbed "so that they could put on the show," meaning the provision of soup kitchens:

> There was much mistreatment of the people of the Left, the Falangists came round here with a rifle. Always taking away and robbing things

from the houses... There were social service canteens because the people were dying of hunger, and they went to a shop or a house and confiscated whatever they fancied, everything, chickpeas, lentils, flour, bread, or whatever was there to give people to eat so that they could put on the show. For them everything was fine, for them Franco was a Superman; for me, I wish to God he'd never been born, the hour his mother begot him... But I don't enter into these matters. (Faustina, Villavieja)

Near the end of summer 2004, I was shown some archive materials from the town hall in Villavieja that had been collected as part of the investigation surrounding the exhumation. The most chilling document for me was a register of newly created widows and orphans in the immediate aftermath of the killings, to be passed on to the local Francoist women so that they might provide for charitable support. This list was written at a time of systematic looting of the homes and gendered/sexual violence against the female relatives of the dead. I found the list very moving because it included the names of some of my informants along with their ages in 1936. The list was written in copperplate writing, with little pen marks to indicate the women who were known to be pregnant. I found this meticulous list disturbing because it offered a counterpoint to the mass grave that we were exhuming at that time, which contained bodies and objects in disarray. Taken alone, the grave suggested that the violence had been spontaneous and frenzied, whereas this list of women and children spoke of systematic planning and of the banality of evil.

The ideological implications of receiving this charity and the relationship between material dependency and repressed memory for Republican families are eloquently described by Pilar Fidalgo in her memoir *A Young Mother in Franco's Prisons*:

> Widows and orphans still living and free had to hide their pain for fear of the killers. They begged clandestinely because whoever helped the widows and orphans of a Red exposed themselves to persecution. Only the Social Service that had been organized could alleviate material suffering, but even then in exchange for the imposition of moral suffering: obliging the orphans to sing the hymns of the murderers of their fathers, to wear the uniform of those who had executed them, and to curse the dead, and blaspheme their memory. (Fidalgo 1939, 31)

Likewise, Faustina concludes her account of her direct experience of Francoist charity as a young teenager with the phrase "This you carry inside always, I remember it constantly, those degrading times, I can't overcome it..." Here, Faustina's words suggest that there was something very powerful in that conflation of material and moral degradation, which caused her to internalise this experience in a way that has endured into the present, twenty-five years after the end of Franco's regime and sixty-five years after the end of the Civil War. Ryan (2009) argues that the pattern of violence and material deprivation followed by the charitable support, or even institutionalisation, of Republican widows and orphans was a systematic nationwide strategy to destroy Republican families and prevent their further functioning as a social unit.

My understanding of the situation in my field sites during this period is informed by the fine-grained economic histories of everyday living conditions undertaken by Richards (1995), the contemporary commentator Vázquez Montalbán (2003), and historian Graham (1995a, 1995b). Graham emphasises the link between the enumeration of material goods and female narratives of survival, and she also analyses the frequent references to staple material goods in the Spanish popular culture of the time to show how material survival was a collective preoccupation. Vázquez Montalbán has characterised the first half of Franco's rule as "the reign of material truths" (in implicit opposition to the struggle between ideological truths or metanarratives that dominated the 1930s), arguing that the postwar conditions of material deprivation were permitted by Franco's regime to achieve an "orchestrated depoliticization of social consciousness" (quoted in Graham 1995b, 240), as material scarcity rendered the population too busy with the task of physical survival to permit any political reflection or action. Graham develops this argument by pointing to the impact of "the reign of material truths" on memory: "The personal and collective aspirations of 'before' were self-repressed because the memory of what had been lost was a hindrance making unbearable all the petty acts of mediocrity and prostitution (literal or metaphorical) which survival inevitably entailed" (ibid., 241).

Looking at popular culture and oral history accounts, Graham identifies the correlate to the reality of "material truths" as a fantasy world of "material myths" in which the longed-for objects are fetishised and their properties conflated with other absences—the missing people, the epoch before the Civil War: "The space left by the self-repression of personal and collective memory was filled by an alternative mythology of things—white bread, olive oil, meat, 'the food from those days before the war,' soap, a good cut of cloth, housing" (ibid., 241). This identification of material myths accords very closely with the specificity of my informants' lists of stolen goods: chickpeas, lentils, barrels of wine, hens, rabbits.

It is possible to argue that the rupture created by familiar objects being stolen from home is precisely the kind of event that children would witness firsthand and strongly recall as adults. On the other hand, it is also possible to speculate that the fixation upon lost objects was transmitted from the mother over time through repeated references, reflecting her anxieties around material survival, as seen in the narratives studied by Cenarro (2002). Either way, I believe many of the references to material loss to be further examples of my informants' closeness to these absent women, which prioritised the maternal experience and created space for them within ARMH's exhumation process. In this, I have been influenced by the capacity of Das's ethnographic work to acknowledge the experience of women survivors of conflict as well as their traumatic memories of cataclysmic violence.

A consideration of the significance of *envidia* as a culturally specific concept also enables a closer understanding of the material affordances of particular objects. My analysis of the meaning of envy in these accounts is based on Gilmore (1987) and Mitchell (1988). These studies show to what extent the divide between urban and rural areas and the generation gap in Spain have led to a misapprehension of envy, which partially explains the dismissive comments of Aldo and Mariano. In his work on Portugal, Pina-Cabral (1986) identifies similar themes in his informants' accounts of cosmology, morality, and death. He emphatically warns against interpreting envy "by resorting to the English or the Portuguese bourgeois concept of envy as an emotion"; instead, it should be understood as

> a principle of evil, an uncontrollable and unpredictable force existing in society, a basic reason why humans cannot create the perfect society in this fallen world. In opposition to envy as an emotion, it does not exist purely within the person who experiences it, but rather as a relationship between the person who generates it and the person who suffers its effects. (ibid., 176)

And it could be added that this is indeed a three-way relationship between the person who envies, the envied person, and the material object that incites envy. It is also worth pointing to the sense of fatalism conveyed by the line "a basic reason why humans cannot create the perfect society": as we will see in further detail, this suggests that envy and acquisitiveness were bound to hinder the idealism and experiments with collectivism that characterised Republicanism. The emphasis on both personal self-improvement and the improvement of one's material circumstances that characterised leftist politics of this time was deeply threatening to the zero-sum game of the village economy, and could attract envy from working-class peers as well as threaten the ruling elites. Following the fatalistic logic of *envidia*, by standing out from the crowd, the murdered Republicans brought ill luck upon themselves.

Significantly, this conceptualisation of envy is primarily visual. Its power resides in the eye of the envious, is transmitted through the gaze, and is drawn by visual stimuli. In his Portuguese field sites, Pina-Cabral found that for his informants the word "envy" was almost interchangeable with the term "evil eye" (ibid., 180). The analysis of Spanish village culture undertaken by Gilmore (1987) is very powerful as he relates the importance of the visual register to the oppositions between interior and exterior and public and private, arguing that the strength of these oppositions can only be understood if the power of the gaze is recognised. His informants speak as if their apprehension of a person's character and motives could be inferred visually from his or her physiognomy and physical bearing. Even a glimpse of the interior of a home allows the viewer to grasp details about a family's intimate life, morality, honour, and finances. Gilmore notes an erotic preoccupation with spying or "peeping" amongst his male informants during the 1960s. It was almost an accepted recreation; and even today the etiquette around the gaze in these field sites, and rural Spain more broadly, is disconcerting to the outsider. Steady, openly appraising gazes in public spaces are acceptable, and should be submitted to confidently and returned, if one has nothing to hide. The number of idiomatic phrases I heard surrounding the eye underline its haptic and consuming quality—for example, in expressions such as "to eat with the eyes," "to make love with the eyes," and, as I heard once, "to steal with the eyes." Gilmore stresses the extent to which his informants conceived of sight as a form of consumption. Pina-Cabral (1986, 180) notes in his discussion of envy that he was warned by his informants that someone with a "strong" gaze could unwittingly tear a piece of clothing hung on a line, just by using the eyes.

The close relationship suggested here between the sight of an object and the consumption and destruction of both the object and its owner sheds light on why my informants would cite particular stolen objects as significant to the narrative of their relatives' deaths. Their causal or explanatory role was predicated on a culturally specific understanding of the power exerted by the gaze of others, and the power of the object to capture and hold this destructive gaze. Because of the way private spaces, especially domestic interiors, are conceived in my field sites (as well as in Gilmore's), a publicly visible object is halfway to being owned by someone else. In my fieldwork I noted a particularly fatalistic attitude or sense of hubris in relation to beauty and attractiveness (of both people and objects) and all visible markers of health and success. I was told on countless occasions that "many" Civil War deaths were the result of female beauty, with the victims targeted so that the perpetrators could gain sexual access to, or even marry, the victim's wife or daughters. In some of these accounts, the women's physical attributes were elaborated upon as the causal factor:

> There was a story I heard, a carpenter who had two daughters, two beauties. When the war came, the women were found dead in a field, naked as babies. They weren't just women but *mujeronas*. (Celia, Villavieja)

Mujeronas has no literal translation but means "the most womanly woman": nowadays it suggests an overweight woman, but the older woman speaking here meant voluptuous or striking women.

In both Pina-Cabral's and Gilmore's field sites (Gilmore 1987; Pina-Cabral 1986), the prosperous returning migrant is particularly susceptible to the evil eye. The exotic provenance of an object or other sign of material wealth, be it foreign or urban, draws the evil eye, perhaps because exotic objects upset the balance or homeostasis of the closed system of the village. Coming into possession of a sudden windfall, perceived as an "unearned" gain, is also particularly provocative to the evil eye. In this context, three objects in my informants' accounts become more significant; "a gold signet ring, very good, because he had been in France," "a watch he had that was a gift," and the corduroy suit, made of a fabric that was exotic at the time.

CRUCIFIED REPUBLICANS AND FRANCOIST JEWS: THE APPROPRIATION OF RELIGIOUS IMAGERY TO EXPRESS REPUBLICAN LOSS

To extend this discussion of Republican idioms of loss, it is important to look at a set of images and analogies recurrently invoked by my informants—or, more accurately, invoked by my informants' mothers but remembered and transmitted to me by my informants. This set of related images concerns the story of the crucifixion, of Christ's suffering and the Virgin Mary's bereavement, and associated tropes of sacrifice and betrayal. The narrative of Christ's betrayal and crucifixion is complex, and furnished a rich source of characters and events from which Republican families were able to draw analogies with their own experience. This set of images had a particular significance in a cultural and historical context in which religious conformity was integral to the Francoist state, and religious rhetoric central to Francoist representations of the Civil War.

Religious imagery was employed here in a social context in which religion was highly charged with political implications. For the majority of the Republican men killed in Villavieja, the accusation "*no va a misa*" (he doesn't go to mass) was cited alongside other radical or provocative behaviours within the process of denunciation and blacklisting that would culminate in their deaths. As detailed in chapter 1, the church as both a physical building and an institution was identified as a repressive presence in village life. Even in the prewar years, protests against organised religion were dangerous, as proven by the fatal shooting following a secular funeral described in chapter 1. Atheism—or more accurately, the rejection of the particular form of organised religion represented by the Spanish Catholic Church—was not universal amongst the Republicans killed in Villavieja or Las Campanas. In both these communities, and in other cases documented by Mintz (1982), anticlericalism seemed to be stronger amongst Republican men than Republican women. Even in households in which men were anticlerical, women could be devout Catholics, or at least regular attendees at mass. This may be explained in part by the much greater significance of church attendance to female sociality and the relative absence of alternative public spaces for women when compared to the male preserves of bars and *casas del pueblo*. Equally, gender norms and social status were much more closely associated with religious piety for women than for men (Collier 1986, 1997), perhaps explaining how these apparent contradictions in religious observance were reconciled within Republican households or between couples. This possible divergence in religiosity within a single Republican household becomes a complicating factor when attempting to devise appropriate commemorative and funereal practices in order to rebury the bodies exhumed from mass graves, as will be explored in chapter 5.

As some of the following accounts will show, it is consistently agreed across the village of Villavieja that at least one of the local priests was instrumental in denouncing those who would be shot in 1936. There are also vague but recurring allusions to nearby monasteries as Francoist strongholds and centres of religious fanaticism, and claims that, in unspecified ways, the monks exacerbated or inspired the killings. This meant that after 1936 women who were religiously observant became completely disenfranchised and alienated from the church because of its role in their husbands' deaths. Within the Francoist discourse, these women were collectively portrayed as atheists, subversives, and morally sick (Richards 2001; Vinyes 2002), and Republicans in general were portrayed as mortal enemies of the Church (Preston 2010). For religious women, this must have been a traumatic rupture in their relationship with the Church. Furthermore, the Francoist discourse on the necessity of *limpieza* was saturated with religious imagery and references to a crusade for Spain's soul, a second Reconquista (after the reconquest or the purging of Jews and Muslims from Spain under Ferdinand and Isabella), and most disturbingly, a second Inquisition (Preston 2010). Arguably, the hypocrisy of these claims of extreme piety and religiosity must have been very hard to endure, and by appropriating a religious imagery Republican families, and particularly women, could probably offer some resistance to the Francoist monopoly on "Christian values."

The employment of religious imagery clearly shows a subversion of the Francoist rhetoric and the appropriation of its power by Republican families. These accounts entail an explicit condemnation of the oppressors and the attribution of moral culpability. However, the theme of *envidia* and material loss cannot be separated from the use of religious analogies, as they are linked by conceptualisations of the figure of Judas and of the monetary transaction through which Jesus was betrayed. By invoking Judas's betrayal of Jesus, my informants communicate the conviction that their relatives were not simply betrayed but were sold, and that a material transaction of some kind surrounded their deaths. There are also parallels between the two tropes in the invocation of fatalism or inevitability, of people simply "playing their part."

Amparo was aged eighty, a daughter of the family that lost the greatest number of adult men, four from the same home—her two maternal uncles, her father, and her mother's brother-in-law, or Amparo's uncle by marriage—leaving an all-female household. During an interview, she became very angry and condemned the perpetrators in the following way:

> They were utter Jews, they could not do otherwise. From my family, it's the most that they took, four people, because they wanted to, like they did with everyone, they came and took them like they did with everyone, there isn't a reason, because they were some Jews, that's what they were. Some scum. (Amparo, Vilavieja)

I had never encountered casual anti-Semitic language in my field sites, and was initially surprised by this choice of imagery. When I asked my key informant in Villavieja why the killers were "total Jews," he seemed surprised that, first, I could not grasp why the Francoists were Jews (and just repeated it back to me), and second, that someone could consider this expression as in some way anti-Semitic. He explained briefly that this was a reference not to real Jews, but to the Jews from the bible, because "they sold people."

Paz, sister of Maria, related that she drew the idea that the church was strongly implicated in her father's death from her mother's sudden refusal to ever attend church again in her life. (She later emphasised this by underlining her mother's refusal to physically enter a church for any reason, to such an extent that this created problems for family rites of passage such as baptisms and marriages, and caused a painful quandary over her mother's own death and burial, as I will discuss in chapter 5.) She also described how her mother used the image of the betrayal of Jesus to reproach a neighbour over her husband's death:

> Something to do with the church, or with the monks at the monastery, they had something to do with the deaths because my mother never again wanted to step inside a church and she lived in a village that lived for the church and lived to go to mass [...]. There's another anecdote that I remember from when I was a little girl. My father must have been very well regarded, he must have done many good things, because I remember that

when I was little, these two (her brother and sister) were a little older and they were sent upstairs to bed and I, as I was a little girl, heard everything that was said and I remember that someone from the village came to ask for my mother's forgiveness for not having been there when they took them to shoot them; and so my mother said, yes, you did what they did to Jesus Christ, you denied him and you killed him, and you amongst all the people could have saved him, and so, amongst all, it is you who killed him. (Paz, Villavieja)

In this account it is clear that the informant's mother is alienated from the Church, yet employs the narrative of Jesus's betrayal and crucifixion to conceptualise her own husband's death. She explicitly compares her husband and the figure of Jesus, as a clear assertion of his moral worth and innocence. The casting of these Republican men as Jesus figures is also thought-provoking in the broader context of the New Testament in which Jesus challenges prevailing power structures, supports the underdog, and is portrayed as visionary and idealist.

A common feature in the accounts above is their fatalism, or the implied inevitability of the events narrated. The first story contains the statement "Jews, they couldn't do otherwise... there isn't a reason." The second testimony is more subtle, but in its rhetorical structure it appears to make reference to Jesus's predictions to his disciples over who among them will betray him. It appears to echo the paradoxical idea in Jesus's prophecy that those who love him the most are those who will commit the greatest betrayal. This rhetorical significance is further suggested by the way my informant emphasised that this was reported speech and stressed the precise formula employed by her mother. In this sense, the New Testament narrative is being employed for its mythic quality. It contains an eternal or cyclical story that was simply played out in this particular time and place in the village. In light of the preoccupation with the dormancy and resurgence of Republicanism identified in chapter 1, it is significant that the logical end to a narrative that casts the Republican dead in the role of Christ is one of eventual resurrection. However, none of the representations of the past I encountered in my field sites drew on an imagery of resurrection, so it is important not to stretch or overinterpret this aspect of the religious idiom.

My middle-class informant Fermina, the widow of a prominent Francoist, mentioned the sudden disappearance of the widowed Republican women from church services following the massacres, although she did not elaborate on the causal link. Speaking as a devout Catholic, she said she was unable to comment on the role of the priest in these deaths, and only observed that, thankfully, there was no cause for religious "fanaticism" anymore. She also recalled that one woman who had lost her only son in Villavieja in 1936 had stopped attending church but had continued to attend the annual procession of the Virgin statue around the village, and every year would come to watch the group of devout (mainly middle-class women) who dressed and attended to the Virgin (interestingly, the Virgin of the Sorrows) in the weeks surrounding the procession:

> It's some years ago already, a lady came to the Virgin of the Sorrows, which my mother dressed all her life, and now I dress her myself, [and] there was a lady, they had killed her son, I don't know why, she never talked about it with me. The Virgin wore a rather big rosary and the Christ [crucifix] had been lost, and I said "Look at that, what a pity that the Christ has been lost," and the lady got up, all those years she had come to see me dress the Virgin of the Sorrows, and she went and came back in a moment with her own rosary, and said to the Virgin, "Take it, this is for you, because neither you nor I did anything to cause them to kill our sons." This remains in my soul, "Neither you nor I were to blame." The suffering of a mother that has a son taken... it's too much. And then if it's true that God forgives everything, this is forgiven, but...
> (Fermina, Villavieja)

This example is thought-provoking because the bereaved Republican woman was effectively excluded from church life, yet still owned a rosary and, more importantly, still identified herself with the Virgin of the Sorrows. She came to watch higher-status middle-class Francoist women who interacted with the Virgin, effectively monopolising this form of religious devotion and claim to social status. When the statue of the Virgin lost her crucifix, she lost the material representation of her son, a metaphorical reenactment of her bereavement. This prompted a clearer expression of the Republican woman's identification or solidarity with the Virgin as another bereaved mother. It is particularly significant that in this narrative the bereaved woman spoke directly to the statue, instead of offering her rosary to any of the Francoist women responsible for dressing it: she bypassed them, thus resisting or undermining their monopoly over the Virgin. Although these women had an apparent intimacy with the statue, expressed by their washing and dressing it, she claimed a deeper, empathetic connection with Mary herself. She was distinguishing between organised religion as represented by this *hermandad* or sisterhood of middle-class women and her own beliefs. By addressing the Virgin directly and drawing an explicit comparison in front of the Francoist women, she was temporarily creating space for the expression of Republican mourning, which was highly transgressive at that time, especially as the women of the *hermandad* were likely to have close social or familial links to those responsible for her son's death.

Because she invoked the Virgin, who is above reproach, she placed herself above reproach or censure. The impact of the analogy between bereaved Republican women and the Virgin was highly effective: despite her familial and class loyalties, Fermina found the analogy haunting and disturbing—"This has stayed in my soul."

A further example of the power afforded by religious metaphors to contest or critique Francoism comes from a story Maria told about her mother. She recounted how one day a pair of women from the Sección Femenina had come into her house in Villavieja. They were selling badges or insignia inscribed with the Falange's symbol—the yoke and the arrows, derived from the symbol of unity under the Reyes Católicos, or Catholic Monarchs. The symbol was referred to by my informants as *las flechas*. When Maria's mother was encouraged to buy a little arrow insignia, she became violently angry and indignant. She shouted, "I have one of your arrows already. It's here in my heart. Your arrows pierced my side and I feel them every day." In my informant's account, her mother gestured at her imagined injuries and clawed at her body while pushing the women out of the house. The Sección Femenina women retreated in fear. My informant said that such vocal resistance was dangerous and foolhardy, but that she felt proud that her mother "had so much character." She added that there had been no retribution after this outburst because the Sección Femenina women had felt ashamed. Although this account does not include an explicit comparison to the figures of Jesus, Mary, or Judas, I believe it draws on iconographic Catholic representations of pierced hearts and of Jesus's pierced side. It subverts a Fascist symbol of strength and unity, revealing its violence, and provides an idiom in which a Republican woman can express her pain and challenge her oppressors directly.

It is worth considering in greater detail the claims made by Republican women through their identification with the Virgin Mary in this cultural and historical context. It is clearly a powerful appeal to the definitive model of normative feminine identity (Mitchell 1988) at a time in which the femininity of Republican or "Red" women was under attack both by Francoist rhetoric and by the gendered violence described in chapter 1. The obvious associations of the Virgin with chastity and modesty were even more significant in the light of the physical exposure and sexual harassment these women endured, and could be used to contest the sexual humiliation they experienced. However, the concept of *marianismo* (Collier 1986) is more elaborated than these simple associations with chastity and piety would suggest. In explaining normative behaviour for married women in Spanish villages, Collier identifies *marianismo* as a model of femininity that privileges the maternal above all else, so the woman is defined by her relation to a child rather than a male partner. *Marianismo* prizes the selfless and self-sacrificing woman who sublimates her individual identity or needs into those of her children and family. This ideal diverges from contemporary Spanish understanding of femininity in that *marianismo* ascribes a particular social and moral worth to neglecting the self, disregarding the body, refraining from material consumption, enduring hard physical labour, and withdrawing from the social and public sphere.

At first sight it may be difficult to reconcile the radical challenges posed to gender norms and power relations by the Republican movement with the apparent retreat into *marianismo* and religious analogies that followed the Civil War. Herrmann (2003) conducted a sensitive analysis of several life histories of Republican women who had been engaged in the vanguard of the movement, experiencing frontline combat, prison, torture, and exile. She detected powerful expressions of mourning not just for the people and places they had lost, but also for their defeated feminist ideology and their brief experience of new gender relations during the Republic. Herrmann describes both their lives and their styles of narration as "incomplete and fractured" in part by the dissonance between pre- and postwar gender norms and roles (2003, 13). Yet, the attributes of Mary privileged by *marianismo*, as outlined above, could resonate with the experience of recently bereaved Republican women facing marginalisation and deprivation, perhaps mediating this dissonance. This religious imagery also offered Republican women an irrefutable idiom in which to resist their characterisation under Franco. It enabled them to speak back to Francoist women and expose their hypocrisy by comparing their superficial claims to normative morality and piety with the Republican experience of real suffering.

UNREADINESS AND UNUSED TALISMANS AS REPRESENTATIONS OF INNOCENCE

When I attended the screening of an amateur documentary made by the teenage great-nephew of one of the dead in Las Campanas, I noted a recurring trope in the accounts given by the children of the dead who were speaking to the camera. It concerned their last "memory" or their last "visual impression" of their fathers. I put these words in quotation marks because it was impossible for the audience, and possibly the speakers themselves, to distinguish which of these lasting visual images were recalled directly and which had been described and retold in detail so many times that they were experienced as a visual memory, in the same way that detailed visual scenes "remembered" from infancy are in fact composites of, or elaborations upon, oft-viewed family photos. These images concerned the "unreadiness" of the father at the moment he was taken away to be killed. One informant told that his father had been taken while he was working in the fields, and had not been allowed to finish what he was doing. Two more referred to jackets, recalling that it was a cold night and one man had been bundled off the door with his jacket half on. In another narrative, the informant's mother had run to fetch a jacket for the departing father but his persecutors had not waited and he had been taken away without the jacket. In the most poignant narrative, the father was shaving over a basin and was not permitted to finish. Tracing a line down his own face for emphasis, the informant claimed to have an image of his father's half-shaved face etched into his mind, the half-shaved face echoing the trope of the half-worked field. The stories about the jackets and the shaving all end with the perpetrators' mocking reassurance, "*Donde se va, no hace falta,*" or "Where he's going, it doesn't matter."

These last images encode a particular understanding of the lost fathers and the circumstances of their death. The unreadiness is an assertion of innocence or blamelessness. If the fathers had really been engaged in the kind of criminal, deviant, or seditious behaviour portrayed in Francoist rhetoric, they surely would have been prepared or equipped to defend themselves. Instead, they went out into the cold without a jacket. These images depict a humble domestic or working life, specifically invoking mundane objects and practices that shift the suspicion of guilt away from the father. The vindictiveness of the perpetrators is implied in the chilling "*no hace falta,*" usually a reassuring phrase, and in the petty indignity of forcing the men to leave the house half-shaved. In one account of this "last moment," the father was holding the child when the killers arrived and they had to be separated, which is a clear image of parental love and involuntary parting. By emphasising physical unreadiness, these accounts imply that the narrators' male relatives had no inkling that they might be targeted, despite the military uprising and the fall of the regional capital Burgos to the Francoists. However, there is evidence to suggest that this was not the case. Fermina recounted an anecdote to me that she said came from her own father, a major landlord and employer of some of the men killed. According to this anecdote, several of the most politically active men had informed Fermina's father that they would not be able to report for work because they had to go into temporary hiding in anticipation of the roundups in Villavieja. Two men in hiding were discovered and were amongst the dead.

These tropes of physical unreadiness furnish further insights into why certain stolen objects were the focus of a particular indignation and seemed to elicit a sense of pathos in my informants, namely the unripe fruit that is picked regardless of whether it is ready to be eaten and the part-built house that is near completion but is dismantled. These unready objects have a clear parallel in the unready bodies, standing in as examples of biographical objects (Hoskins 1998) that implicitly comment on the unreadiness of their owners for death. They speak of a life interrupted, in a close analogy with Hoskins's example of a "green bottle" death, so called because a glass object once shattered can neither be repaired nor recycled (ibid., 161). The image of the green bottle is invoked by one of Hoskins's informants in a narrative about a young woman who dies unmarried and childless to underline the wastefulness and futility of her death. The images of premature interruption and unreadiness here echo the destruction of the near-finished house or the theft of the unripe fruit discussed at the beginning of this chapter.

The narratives above appeared in a film on the relatives of the dead in Las Campanas but resonated with the accounts given by my informants in Villavieja during a discussion of the last memory of their fathers:

> When they came to the house my father was standing by the door holding me in his arms. Two of them came in with rifles on their shoulders so my father put me down and went with them. Then they passed by the house again but my mother was not able to tell them that we had a piece of paper, a signed declaration from the Deputation of Burgos saying that our family was not to be touched. But the head of the local Falange told us, "You can save yourself the journey [to Burgos] because if we don't kill them this afternoon, we'll certainly kill them tomorrow." They were kept some hours overnight and then they brought them out the next day to shoot them. My uncle, my father's brother, was in a village very near here, he was over there working in the fields. He was halfway through the harvest in August and they picked him up, too. They took them both and killed them. (Luis, Villavieja)

In this account, guilt is further refuted or deflected by focussing the narrative on this piece of paper, this signed declaration that is supposed to function as a talisman, ensuring the protected status of the family, but tragically the talisman is never used or invoked. This account locates the injustice of the father's death in an administrative error rather than in a broader critique of the inherent injustice of the extrajudicial killing of civilians for ideological reasons. Of course, during this period and after the war, bureaucratic delays and misidentifications did occur in "mistaken" arrests and killings, as documented in Gómez Bravo's study of mass incarceration under Franco (2009). In the course of my fieldwork, I heard several accounts of a personal contact or "an understanding" with a representative of officialdom, be it an employer, a landlord, or someone in the military who could intercede; but for some reason this authority was not invoked successfully, or was invoked too late. The activation of these personal networks occurred particularly in the desperate period between the detainment of male relatives and the confirmation of their deaths. This period of time, during which it was still possible for the female relatives to intercede, was described as one of intense anxiety and figured vividly in my informants' accounts, echoing the narratives of South African women's desperate encounters with officialdom following the disappearance of male kin under apartheid (Ross 2001). This liminal period of uncertainty recurred in the narrative structure of the accounts of the deaths:

> They took him, they kept him prisoner for eight days. Then they told us they would transfer him to Burgos [to the gaol], but instead they brought him here to kill him. My mother found out that they had left the village, so she called the Civil Guard lieutenant in Burgos, who had been here, the one my brother had served with, but he said to her, "No, nobody has arrived here." So my mother took all us children and we went to talk to the local Civil Guard and he told us then that they were dead and that they were there. (Tina, Villavieja)

In Fermina's account of the men who went into hiding, the Republicans anticipated their persecution and informed their boss of their plight. The subtext of Fermina's story is that her father was so influential that people would ask him to intercede for them, though whether he refused to act or his intercession was ineffectual was not made explicit in the story. The memory idiom of an unused talisman must be situated in a cultural context that conceives of encounters with officialdom or authority as mediated through personal relationships, as identified by Barrett (1974). His ethnography of a Spanish village in the late 1960s identifies how personal networks may be activated to negotiate successfully the encounters with power. Graham's analysis (1995a) concerns the functioning of the Franco regime in the immediate postwar period, during which the rapid imposition of new legislation and the inconsistency of implementation were instruments of control to destabilise the population; Barrett's analysis of the 1960s spans the whole Francoist period. Both these studies identify how institutions and figures of authority were experienced with a degree of fatalism and were characterised as arbitrary and capricious.

Conclusion

An analysis of the existing memory idioms in my field sites illustrates representations of the dead that predate the exhumation process. This is the context in which the alternative representations of the dead that are generated throughout the exhumation process are received. There is a form of collective memory in these communities, in that both the experiences recounted and the tropes employed are shared amongst Republican families, but there is little expression of a consciously held collective identity, and some of the narratives seek to depoliticise and individualise the deaths of my informants' relatives, exempting them from the broader picture of political violence.

The condition of postmemory is indicated by the central place of female relatives in these narratives, primarily the wives and mothers of the Republican victims. They are a constant presence in discussions about the dead men, and this underscores the way memories and sentiments for those killed were mediated by these women. The bereaved women who raised my elderly informants are now dead, but they are identified as the bearers of memory, those who had maintained the strongest affective bonds with the dead men and expressed the strongest sentiments of mourning. These women's experience of suffering and their struggle for survival elicit vivid firsthand memories. The experience and agency of this generation of wives, sisters, and mothers has profoundly shaped the representations of the past, and of the dead, in these families. Yet a limitation of the exhumation process, with its central emphasis on male death rather than female survival, is that it is hard to incorporate or encompass this aspect of Republican experience. The fact that the generation who had the strongest memories and affective bond with the dead has now largely passed away is potentially problematic to the Republican memory campaign, as it entails an implicit criticism that this work has come too late. This undermines the construction of a redemptive narrative around the eventual recovery of these long-neglected bodies, and also implicitly challenges the familial and affective rationales for exhumation prioritised by ARMH.

Although Pedreño's and Aldo's casting of the memory idiom of *envidia* as some kind of false consciousness or a marker of political apathy is an oversimplification, it is true that the *envidia* idiom excises the ideology of both victim and perpetrator from these narratives. The prevalence of these narratives illustrates the potential resistance and ambivalence among the relatives of the dead in my field sites toward a political and collective representation of the dead during the exhumation, and the degree to which in a social context in which people are accustomed to these idioms, an explicitly political representation of the dead may be experienced as threatening and destabilising. On first sight, the accounts of death and repression in my field sites appear to make highly individualised representations of the dead and of the circumstances surrounding their deaths. There is remarkably little mention within these narratives of the similar experience of their neighbours—the other Republican families caught up in the same events—and this illustrates the depth of atomisation that was produced. The memory idiom of the unused talisman is an individualising representation of the dead, a claim of exceptional status. It suggests that even within the logic of Francoist violence, this particular death was a mistake. In contrast, the use of a religious memory idiom seems to offer a coded resistance to the justice, legitimacy, and morality of these killings.

The memory tropes of material envy and unused talismans distribute agency, and therefore culpability for the deaths, between the perpetrators of violence and the envied objects that are pivotal to these narratives. The culturally specific understanding of an object as containing or in some way activating the preordained fate of its owner will be explored in chapter 4, which analyses the fascination exerted by the material objects that are crucial in conferring individual identity on a set of human remains. The reservoir of both imagined and remembered objects identified in this chapter forms part of the interpretative context that mediates the encounters with the bodies and objects materialised during exhumation, as will be seen in chapter 4. The construction of imaginative assemblages linking remembered and imagined objects with the items that emerge from the grave will be discussed in chapters 3 and 4.

The striking recurrence of material objects in all these memory idioms is highly significant, since objects serve to structure representations of the past in a social and political context in which the act of representing the past is inherently fraught with the danger of saying the wrong thing. Descriptions of a material object recur throughout these narratives. This is shown by the illustration of the quality of a stolen object, its value and provenance, or the enumeration of foodstuffs stolen from the house, or the material gesture of offering of a rosary to a statue. Physical descriptions and appeals to materiality serve to detract from any apparent authorship or mediation on the part of the speaker. The breakdown in intergenerational transmission caused by the passing of the Civil War generation has engendered a condition of postmemory in many of the relatives of the dead, characterised by the use of material indices to build one's past. Physical descriptions and appeals to materiality in these narratives are both a search for, and an insistence upon, the tangible veracity of these representations of the past. This emerged clearly when Julio and Federico recounted their narratives of theft at the very sites where they had occurred, indicating the pile of stones and the trees, which were still visible. The emphasis on materiality in the construction of fraught representations of the past seen in these memory idioms prefigures the prominent role of the materialisations of the dead in the reburial ceremony in Las Campanas that will be discussed in chapter 5.

Chapter 3

MATERIALISATIONS OF THE DEAD BEFORE EXHUMATION

INTRODUCTION

Having identified the forms of idiomatic memory that recur in my informants' accounts of the past, the aim of this chapter is to look at the shifts in the register through which the dead are materialised prior to the exhumation process. This will allow us to evaluate the transformations that occur before, during, and after exhumation, and to appreciate the extent to which these shifts create opportunities to formulate and contest specific representations of the dead. I will begin by identifying the parameters unique to the Spanish context: here, a sixty-five- to seventy-year time lag and the passing of generations have resulted in an absence of memory, or a condition of postmemory, surrounding the life of the dead individuals, particularly an absence of physical or sensory memory. This is an important consideration since exhumation inherently privileges bodily knowledge and is an expression of a bodily connection between the living and the dead. This significance and the potential divergence between the existing memory and the memory "recovered" through the exhumation are highlighted by the way ARMH coordinators and expert practitioners endeavour to foster a sense of bodily and affective connection between the dead and their relatives prior to the rematerialisation of individual bodies in the form of exposed human remains.

I will look at how other potential indices of the dead, namely photographs and mementoes, have hitherto been used in a muted or censored way due to the state of atomisation that permeated the interiors of Republican homes under the dictatorship. This is important in order to identify how the opening of the grave appears to effect a transformation in the way photographs and mementoes are conceived of as materialisations of the dead, activating new forms of use and display that will be analysed in chapter 4. Specific to this context is the way in which the dead were materialised sixty-five years ago in acts of exemplary violence and collective obscenity that were characteristic features of the Spanish Civil War, meaning that the exhumation is in reality the second materialisation, or a rematerialisation of these human remains. I will examine the development of an imagined or structural distance, through the trope of "scattered" bodies, as a collective response to these traumatic encounters and the close physical proximity of the mass graves. I will explore the potential meanings of the plant and animal metaphors that recur in my informants' representations of the dead, to identify how the physical remains of the dead are conceptualised and, therefore, how their rematerialisation through exhumation is experienced.

The Unremembered Body

Due to the chronology of the war, dictatorship, and democratic transition in Spain, the exhumation processes that I studied occurred between sixty-five and seventy years after the deaths of those being exhumed. This is by no means unique: fortuitous discoveries or archaeological investigations are still uncovering material artefacts and human remains from World War I, which still elicit fascination and strong emotions amongst the relatives of the dead and the public at large (Pollard and Banks 2008; Saunders, N.J. 2002). Similarly, the dead on both sides of the American Civil War still exert an affective and imaginative hold over the living, even after a very long period of time. The exhumations described by Verdery (1999) of the victims of ethnic and partisan violence during World War II in former Yugoslavia took place over forty years after the deaths, yet still inflamed nationalist sentiments. However, the Spanish chronology is significant in that the exhumations in my field sites have not been undertaken within the kind of explicit collective frameworks seen in these other contexts, in which a shared national or ethnic identity binds the living and the dead. In other autonomous regions of Spain, particularly the Basque country and Catalonia, although divisions during the war were highly complex, after the conflict a pronounced cultural identity emerged that informed the resistance against the centralising Franco regime and now informs representations of the past, perhaps providing a ready point of connection with the dead (Muro 2009). However, as I discussed in the introduction and in chapter 1, the regional identity of central Spain (and its Civil War history) lends itself less readily to this.

As we have seen, ARMH aims to exhume remains on behalf of the relatives of the dead, privileging an affective and familial bond between the living and the dead. This supposes that the living and the dead are bound by a sense of relatedness and inherently personal connections both sentimental and biological in nature, either experienced firsthand or transmitted by the previous generation. In this context, the degree of overlap in the lifetimes of the living and the dead becomes particularly significant. The largest group of surviving children of Republicans, who are also the most vigorously engaged in the exhumation process, are in their seventies and thus were small infants when these men died. Their age will determine the type of relationship that they had developed with their fathers prior to death. Furthermore, as argued in the preceding two chapters, even the children of the dead who had firsthand memories of their fathers would not have access to a memory community in which those memories could be shared, acknowledged, verified, or elaborated upon.

Exhumation differs from other types of memory work in that it privileges the physical traces of the dead in the form of their human remains. This implicitly privileges the memory of the body above other memories, and memory of the body must be a firsthand, sensorial experience in life, unlike the words, deeds, possessions, or beliefs of the dead, which may be apprehended at second hand, even posthumously. Several commentators have identified the way in which, through the rematerialisation of the body, exhumation can, at least temporarily, reactivate the relationships based on bodily knowledge and the physical expression of an affective bond with the dead. Crossland reflects on the words of Berta Schubaroff, one of the mothers of the disappeared in Argentina, whose intimate engagement with her sons' remains provides a useful counterpoint to the exhumations in my field sites:

> She described her reaction on receiving his remains: "I became very moved because I had found my son. I began to kiss him, kiss all of his bones, touch him, and caress him" [...]. Significantly, this intimately embodied understanding of the dead contrasts with the disembodiment of the dead which underlies the idea of bodies as evidence. (Crossland 2000, 154)

Crossland's comment sets up an opposition between two of the primary rationales for undertaking an exhumation: the desire for a loved one's remains versus a forensic or jural investigation into the deaths. ARMH's exhumation campaign privileges the former; yet, the intimacy described above in the words of Berta Schubaroff is a reenactment of maternal care, and there is a very limited history of intimacy or bodily knowledge between the living and the dead in my field sites, so it cannot be reactivated when the bodies are rematerialised. During my participation in mass grave exhumations throughout Spain, I reflected on the points of contrast and similarity with my own observations of the postconflict exhumations in Kosovo in 2000. In Kosovo, the exhumations were periodically disrupted by relatives of the dead who felt compelled to touch, kiss, or address the dead verbally, all with a desperate intensity. For some, the desire for physical contact with the bodily substance of their loved ones was visceral and overwhelming, even with disarticulated body parts or fragments of clothing that had no resemblance to the person in life. Similar illustrations of "this intimately embodied understanding of the dead" have been noted in the context of other exhumations around the world, for example those investigating atrocities against indigenous communities in Guatemala (Sanford 2003).

This dynamic was largely absent from the exhumations I observed in Spain, even when the direct descendants were present, as if the seventy-year time span had broken the bodily connection. For the most part, the interaction I observed could be characterised as remote and restrained. In addition, the cases of physically demonstrative or intimate mourning I observed in Kosovo involved either a bereaved parent or a physical partner of the dead, rather than a child or grandchild as is the case in Spain. Apart from the different kind of mourning that comes with the death of a child, perceived as a disruption to the generational order, this contrast perhaps illustrates that the body of a partner or a child may be experienced viscerally as an extension of one's own body, with a strength that transcends death and decay. The connection between adults and the bodies of their parents or grandparents may be experienced in a subtly different way, based on the bodily basis for the relationship in life (see the use of clothing as bodily indices for a parent, a child, and a partner, respectively in Miller and Parrott 2007; Layne 2000; Ash 1996). In the exhumations I observed in my field sites and throughout Spain, the primary way in which relatives physically engaged with the dead was by assisting in nonexpert manual tasks. This work might include digging the topsoil, sieving the grave fill, or washing the soil from disarticulated remains. This was particularly true of the male relatives of the dead, who applied themselves to physical tasks around the gravesite with a degree of vigour and focus that suggested this manual labour was a form of emotional expression, and perhaps catharsis through exertion. It was a physical manifestation of care and affection for the human remains, but not a reenactment of physical gestures of affection from a remembered in-life intimacy. Of course, this restrained expression may be partly determined by the confusion of the bodies in the mass grave and the degree to which a set of human remains is recognisable, a question that will be returned to in the next chapter.

Figure 3. Flowers and note left at the mass grave in Las Campanas.

Some of the placards and notes that are left with flowers around the skeletons while the exhumation is underway express this state of mourning for a body unknown or unremembered (figure 3). "Your daughters don't remember your kisses but they never forgot you and they long for you." There are also recurring phrases that are variations on the formula "We shall never forget your *memory*," which is a form of remembrance that is one step removed from "We shall never forget *you*." This expression of longing for what one has never known resonates with Hirsch's examples of how postmemory is expressed (1996). In some of the first-hand memories of the moment at which their father was taken away seen in chapter 2, my informants emphasised the physical proximity or bond between the adult and the child:

> When they came to the house my father was standing by the door holding me in his arms. Two of them came in with rifles on their shoulders so my father put me down and went with them. (Luis, Villavieja)

Crossland (2000) has described the process by which bodies are constructed as forensic evidence as one of "disembodiment," in that the human body loses its integrity and becomes a sum of materials and tissues upon which are recorded the marks of certain acts such as injury and disease, which can be decoded to reconstruct an individual's death. However, this transformation into evidence is also a process of hyperembodiment that removes any personhood and socially meaningful identity from the discursive space occupied by the body, leaving space only for physical characteristics to be enumerated (Gere 1999). Crossland (2009a) explores how fine a line exists between postmortem scientific interventions on human remains that seem to reiterate the individuality and personhood of the dead, and those that reduce it to an object of study.

This also became clear in my field sites. That the father's body may be unknown or unremembered is brought into the foreground by the paradigm of human identification, which requires a close questioning to produce a minute physical description of the dead and to record any distinguishing features that might form the basis for a positive identification. In several interviews, when trying to describe the dead my informants seemed to fix their rapt attention on something in their mind's eye or their peripheral vision and shaped the air with their hands as if they could see something but not quite well or concretely enough to describe it verbally to another person, as if the paucity of factual content would result in the value of their memory becoming diminished under the gaze of another. The memory of their father was not tangible enough to translate into words, certainly not a detailed description of specific features that might aid in identification. My elderly informants combined: memory and postmemory, constructed or deduced from known facts and transmitted particularly from female relatives; sensory memory; and the product of years of imagination. It is also important to reflect on the particular sensory memory of a child, as it is of a different order from that of an adult. The physical scale of one's environment; the novelty of new stimuli; a different comprehension of events and repertoire of emotional responses; a different prioritisation in what is observed and retained: these are all considerations when interpreting childhood memories. The investigative process in my field sites repeatedly demanded that the elderly relatives of the dead translate their childhood memories into the adult realm. I suspect that for some of these informants, the attempt at verbal description was incommensurate with, and even destructive of, the particular kind of memory they had of their father, like smoke being dispersed. There was also a power relation to consider, as the inability to practically assist the expert practitioner could be experienced as failure, a sentiment noted amongst the Srebrenica families by Wagner (2008). I was made sensitive to these value judgements on memory by the number of informants, particularly women, who would enquire while giving their life histories as to whether their story was "useful" and whether it "helped."

In addition to the power relations between the incoming expert practitioners who posed the questions and the relatives of the dead and the elderly in the community who attempted to answer them, the absence of firsthand memory appeared to engender shame and embarrassment amongst my informants. My own questions about their knowledge of the dead were intentionally left open, to encompass transmitted knowledge as well as firsthand memories. Yet I was disturbed by the degree of discomfort they produced and by my informants' apologetic admission of "remembering very little," and I felt that they experienced this absence of knowledge as unnatural and stigmatising. This is in accordance with the informant's account in chapter 1 contrasting "those with fathers and those without," in which the paternal absence evokes "anguish" and above all a sense of "sin." This relates to the significance of deep and public mourning as an expression of a child's legitimacy and entitlement to patrimony. Memory as a duty is encompassed in the phrase "We are only truly dead if you forget us," a formula that recurs in discussions on the importance of exhumation, and which I observed once on a floral tribute left in the grave after the exhumation and again on a headstone in a neighbouring village cemetery. This implies that forgetting is a form of violence against the dead, which is a hard burden on those descendants who have not so much forgotten their dead, as never known them. For the children of the dead, failure to remember the parent can be experienced as "unnatural," a social stigma, and a personal failure of filial duty that betrays the dead parent.

Informants' physical descriptions of the dead are vague and generic, conflating physical and moral qualities. Typically, an informant might list: big—strong—a labourer—a working man—very hardworking. This transition from "a big man" to "a worker" is more of a deduction than a memory, as well as a moral statement countering the Francoists' allegation that working-class activism was akin to laziness and malingering. The commonly occurring assertion that one's father was tall or had a large stature may be the product of a child's sense of scale. Descriptions of the dead that appear to draw on visual characteristics are not always what they seem, as they are based on the individuating features of *moreno* or *pelirrojo* or *cojo* (dark-complexioned or red-haired or lame). These are generic terms routinely used to distinguish people in everyday conversation in a small village, said after their name or incorporated into their nickname, which in no way constitute the kind of privileged or intimate details of a firsthand memory of a loved one. I heard a conversation around the gravesite in Villavieja in which some elderly residents mentioned that one of the dead had been "strikingly ugly" and was widely famed for his unfortunate cast of features. In comparison with how the dead are conventionally eulogised, this conversation bordered on the disrespectful. The speakers at this moment were carried away by the enthusiasm of having summoned some knowledge of the dead, and enjoying the interested attention of others. The fame of ugliness was what had survived of him, rather than a memory of his face.

Locally Meaningful Identification

In Villavieja I observed a peculiar adaptation of the paradigm of forensic human identification—the privileging of a detailed physical knowledge of the dead—to the local conceptualisation of physiognomy and knowledge of an individual. The features that constituted knowledge of the dead within my field sites diverged in subtle but discernible ways from the utilitarian forensic paradigm, but were also used to mediate the gap between what local people considered uniquely individuating features of a person and the techniques by which the bodies would ultimately be identified. This process of mediation was primarily undertaken by my key informant in Villavieja, Julio, who held the privileged position of being both a local with a deep knowledge of the village and its history and an active member of ARMH who was familiar with the basics of the science underpinning the identification process. Julio's use of the physicality of the dead when communicating with the relatives and locals, particularly those who were reticent or ambivalent about the exhumation process, in order to draw them in and engage them more deeply, was highly revealing. In particular, his use of nicknames and his speculations over the physical resemblance between the living and the photographs of the dead revealed his local understanding of what constituted individuality and relatedness. His method to engage the ambivalent relatives of the dead depended on his capacity to impart his knowledge and imbue them with a sense of their own physical knowledge of the dead. By filling the vacuum of memory with the knowledge of physical characteristics, he triggered a sense of physical relatedness, a legitimate basis upon which to take a proprietary interest over the human remains (Renshaw 2010b).

The way Julio used nicknames was highly significant. He invested time in collecting and confirming the nicknames of the dead. He used those nicknames frequently when speaking about the exhumation in the presence of elderly locals and relatives. The nicknames of most of the dead, although occasionally derived from physical attributes, were of very little relevance to the scientific process of human identification, but I came to understand from observing Julio that a parallel process of village identification was underway, and that nicknames were a key form by which individuals know each another. Some nicknames might be mundane or inherited, but unique nicknames might be highly revealing, a conflation of moral and physical traits that captured the essence of an individual (Gilmore 1980; Kenny 1966). They often related to "fatal" character flaws, or made oblique references to embarrassing anecdotes that typified an individual's style or modus operandi in the world, or commented wryly on their fortune or fate. In this context, nicknames were open to a fatalistic reading strongly dependent on the notion of hubris, in a similar way to the precious objects discussed in chapter 2 such as suits, watches, and rings that draw the envious gaze. An interest in nicknames revealed the idea of an intangible affordance possessed by both people and objects that attracts and contains their fate. In Gilmore's characterisation of the egalitarian ideal in Spanish village life (1980, 1987) there is a type of hubris inherent in standing out from the crowd, and this outstanding trait, an intangible affordance of a thing or person, contains the fate of that object or individual. The nickname may contain a clue, not only to the bearer's physical appearance, but also to how this particular fate came to befall the dead, which is why it is invoked alongside conventionally "forensic" data that will enable the scientific reconstruction of these events and identities.

Julio also referred to the physical resemblance, sometimes tenuous, between the dead and their relatives. He collected and copied photographs of people in the village from the 1930s and tried to identify and corroborate the identity of those depicted. Photographs were a luxury item at this time, particularly amongst this socioeconomic group in a rural village. This meant that on a few occasions Julio might show someone the visual image of a dead relative that the person had never seen before. He also encouraged them to find resemblance between the photograph and other members of the extended family, effectively reinserting the dead into a network of relationships on the basis of physiognomy. In a conflation of scientific and affective or familial identification, I heard Julio point to distinguishing features in a photo and confidently predict to a relative that this could form the basis for a successful identification of the skeleton. He suggested vaguely to the relatives that photo-superimposition or facial reconstruction could be used to identify the bodies, thus locating their identity in readily apprehended facial features rather than in the much more complex skeletal characteristics of the rib, spine, or pelvis that in reality would be analysed in the laboratory, which are too far removed from a vernacular notion of recognition. On occasion he invoked "unique" features such as hair colour, freckles, skin tone, and even the intensity of gaze, which logically the skeleton no longer possessed; nevertheless, this emphasis encouraged the relatives to reflect on the appearance of the dead when they were still alive.

Julio also used photographs to situate the dead within the physical space of the village, asking relatives if they recognised the backgrounds depicted. It was clear that at some point in the 1930s a commercial photographer had set up a stall in the village square, as a small number of photos had the same background, a building that was still standing. The recognition of this recurring backdrop was an exciting discovery for Julio, and elicited an emotional and slightly disquieting response from Pedro who, as noted in chapter 1, found Julio's investigations into his family's past to be threatening. The familiarity of this village setting strongly conveyed the reality of these past events to Pedro, and perhaps hinted at their continuity with the present. The power of photographs of buildings or locales that are still standing in the present to engender disquiet and a sense of collapsed time has been noted by several authors writing on memory and photography (Barthes 2000; Hirsch 1996, 1997). A particular marker in the masonry of this building is still visible today. I overheard Julio predict to a relative that the height of the deceased in the photograph could be calculated in relation to the masonry, and prompt him to stand in this spot to calculate his height in comparison to that of the dead man, effectively encouraging a spatial and physiological point of connection via the photograph.

In his use of nicknames and photographs, and his simplified presentation of the identification process, Julio spoke to local conceptualisations of both individuation and relatedness, and mediated the sense of illegitimacy felt over the unremembered body of the father. Julio's practices helped instil a sense that the dead were known and knowable, and that the past was accessible, if members of the community pooled their memory resources. He explicitly acknowledged the contribution or confirmation of the smallest detail, thus democratising the process and drawing in those who might otherwise have felt they had no valuable knowledge of the past. The assertion that the dead are known and knowable is the first step in making them less remote and fostering new affective bonds between the living and the dead. In chapter 4 I will discuss the more formal and structured attempts to explain the principles of scientific identification to the relatives of the dead undertaken by expert practitioners, and how they helped develop affective bonds between the living and dead using a similar logic to the one employed informally by Julio.

CARDBOARD FATHERS: MUTED PHOTOGRAPHS AND MEMENTOES IN THE HOME

Not all relatives of the dead had access to, or an awareness of, photographic images of the dead. For those who did, it is interesting to consider how the condition of atomisation described in the previous chapters shaped the use of photographs and mementoes within the homes of the Republicans. The absence of detailed knowledge surrounding the biography of the father, the taboo around his political activities or the reason for his death, and the impossibility of mourning openly, all suggested a muted or censored use of photographs in the home. It is therefore important to ask whether the photo was talked about and used as a prop to elicit or structure narratives about the dead. My strong impression is that the portrait photograph of the father was not used in such an active mourning or transmission of memory in the majority of Republican homes in my field sites. I had assumed prior to my fieldwork that the discussion of photographs and mementoes in the family home would be fertile ground for discussion, but my questions on the father's photograph elicited limited, even bewildered responses. There was a high degree of uniformity in the way my elderly informants described their early memories of the practices surrounding those photographs. Relatives would point it out to children from a very young age by simply saying "That is your father," or prompting them to identify him by asking "Do you know who that is?" Several informants recalled the photograph as being in the *salon* or lounge, or above the dining table, which is often in the *salon* in smaller village homes. When I pressed for details over strategies of display or embellishment, the response was that they could recall "nothing special." The photograph was visible but not signalled, and only the inner circle of family or friends would make reference to it in front of the child. The photograph served to refute the "fatherless" state of the family, as material evidence of the fact that he had once existed. Further verbal elaboration was dangerous under Franco, and the materiality of the photograph was safely wordless, allowing it to be visually displayed but never verbally elaborated upon. The significance of these photographs was to assert the family's legitimacy, combating the "sin" of fatherlessness, rather than to elicit narratives or a detailed transmission of memory.

The tangible presence yet limited power of photographs to transmit memory in the absence of verbal elucidation is brilliantly communicated by an open letter written by Manuel Martínez Hinchado, the son of a murdered Republican, as part of the memory campaign in Extremadura. He dedicates it to a "cardboard father" and describes his generation of the bereaved children of Republicans as "those of us with cardboard fathers." In the absence of verbalised memories or narratives of his father's life, his characterisation of a "cardboard" father emphasises the dissatisfying two-dimensionality of the photograph and is sugges- tive of the photograph's function as a place marker or token. Martínez Hinchado describes how bedtime prayers with his siblings, overseen by his mother, always finished with a kiss to the father's photograph, word- lessly, as part of the ritual sequence. This explicitly ritualised use of the father's photograph resonates with the semiritual format of question and answer described by my informants that was used didactically by visi- tors to the house, like catechism, to instill an awareness of the father's photograph but nothing more. This rote form of question-and-answer communicated the fact of paternity but did not permit a wider ranging discussion of the dead. Miller and Parrott have noted the wider tendency for photographs of the dead to be used in "a quasi-ritual of declared intention and a commitment to remember" (2007, 153). The two acts of praying and kissing the photograph were conflated in Martínez Hinchado's childhood cosmology. Commenting further on the inculca- tion of Republican children with the Catholic doctrine, he wryly suggests that a cardboard father was good preparation "to believe in what you could not see [...]. For those of us with invisible fathers, it wasn't so hard to accept the existence of an invisible God."[1]

The insertion of a cardboard father into the ritual of bedtime prayers and the conflation between God and father implied in Martínez Hinchado's last observation recall the murals and portraits in Cyprus that combine the visual styles of photorealism and Orthodox Christian iconography (Sant Cassia 2007) and depict the disappeared in proxim- ity to divine figures, surrounded by halos or radiating beams of light. These images underscore how the Greek Cypriot victims are under- stood through the quasi-religious category of martyr, in reference to the religious divisions in the conflict: this imbues the absent male rela- tives with protective powers over their families and foregrounds their spiritual existence in the absence of their physical remains. Kwon (2008) describes how the war dead in Vietnam are inserted into the family's ritual practices of ancestor worship. Pinney (1997) illustrates how the physical arrangement of photographs of both living and dead relatives—placed in shrines, inserted into framed picture of deities, or set against a backdrop of religious figures—brings the deities closer to those depicted in the photographs. This spatial arrangement is described as proximal empowerment: "Images in Bhatisuda often mobilise an idiom of proximal empowerment through which persons, objects and images can come closer to divine power" (ibid., 173). However, despite points of comparison between these cases and Martínez Hinchado's account, wordlessly kissing a photograph during a private prayer in a bedroom is materially very different from situating the dead in a visible family shrine in a central domestic space, or painting them in the company of saints in a mural on an external wall.

As stated above, my questions on the relationship between memory and photographs of the dead elicited a very limited and homogeneous set of answers, and it is important to situate this response in the historical context of the access to photography in this era. In their ethnography of contemporary South London, Miller and Parrott (2007) describe the multiple ways in which photographs structure grief, as individuals gather photographs to assemble a collection, disseminate them to members of the extended family, or order them sequentially in albums to reconstruct the biography of the dead. Their ethnography also details the decision making behind the selection of a particular photographic representation of the dead for prominent display, including the decoration of the image and its elaboration through the arrangement of associated objects. These strategies of assemblage, dissemination, and selective display are dependent on a temporal and geographical context in which multiple photographic representations are produced throughout an individual's lifetime, which was certainly not the case for the rural working class in 1930s Spain.

The arrangement of photographs in a chronological sequence in order to make a particular biographical representation, as analysed by Langford (2006), is also dependent on multiple images. Pinney, by contrast, works in an ethnographic context in which informants have differential access to the photographs and the resources to pay for them. He has illustrated how this use of photography to structure perceptions of biography, family history, and temporal relationships, which he calls "the development of intimate historicity" (1997, 150), can be structured around a temporal sequence in an album, but may as well be structured around a single materialisation of the past, for example a photograph of a dead parent. Edwards's analysis (1999) of a single photograph of a soldier killed in World War I, displayed in a handmade frame with commemorative phrases embroidered around the central image, refers to a temporal context comparable to that of my informants' childhood; yet, the photograph of this soldier reveals a strategy of display that makes an explicit verbal elaboration around the dead, which is in sharp contrast to the strategies of display recalled by my informants when they spoke of the father's photograph in the family home. My informants recalled the photographs of their dead relatives as both verbally and materially unelaborated.

Edwards's proposal to focus on the materiality of photographs (1999) is highly relevant to my fieldwork. She proposes that any analysis of photographs should pay attention to the "historically and culturally specific material cultures of photographs, whose meaning is too often subsumed in the contemplation of content, which would benefit from a more rigorous form of material analysis" (ibid., 236). This accords with the way my elderly informants refer to these photographs, placing their materiality, as a tangible and irrefutable materialisation of the father, over their content communicating who the father was in life. An informant in Villavieja, Chencho, observed: "I have some photos of him at home, so that people can say 'That is your father'." This blank statement of fact, without elaboration, and the particular use of reported speech are significant, as they suggest that the photograph is oriented toward a social display, perhaps of paternity and legitimacy, rather than a deeper private reflection, which underlines the use of the photograph as a place marker rather than a portal into the past.

The absence of verbal elaboration upon these photographs is redolent of Hirsch's identification of a particularly painful category of photographs in the homes of Holocaust survivors, namely portraits of children born before the war who had not survived (Hirsch 1997). These were often large and ever present but too painful for verbal elaboration. Hirsch identifies the power and fascination these mute photographs exerted over the children born after the war, the siblings or half-siblings of the dead (ibid., 18). Both Hirsch (1997) and Young (1998) focus on the repertoire of photographs referred to or reproduced, alongside letters and diaries, as part of the intertextual layering in Spiegelman's *Maus*. Young conceives of these photographs as "afterimages," as a correlate to postmemory. Afterimages are problematic images associated with the traumatic past that are of great emotional significance to the older generation. However, because their content is too charged for verbal elaboration and their context has been irretrievably lost, the younger generation struggles with these images in an attempt to assimilate them into its own framework of meanings and emotional responses in the present. In contrast, Emiko McAllister (2006) describes how the photographs of wartime internment in the album of her Japanese-Canadian family were made familiar and benign to her as a child by constant verbal elaborations from older relatives on the theme of "adventures" in the camp. These were detailed narratives of resistance and survival during internment that instilled a sense of family pride and unity in the next generation.

In my informants' accounts there is some evidence of the presence in the family home of personal possessions of the dead used as mementoes, but this is very limited, and the majority of my informants stated that they had no physical objects that had been inherited or passed down from their dead parent. This is understandable in terms of the widespread theft and appropriation of objects explored in chapter 2 and the baseline condition of poverty that limited the number of conventional "heirloom" objects that these families might possess, and may have necessitated the sale, pawning, or exchange of valued objects. The focus on valuable and remarkable objects in the extended discussion of *envidia* in chapter 2 could potentially be read as an expression of mourning for these potential mementoes of the father, but this was never articulated explicitly by my informants. One informant described how her mother removed an object from the gravesite in the immediate aftermath of the killings that would perform the function of a "memento":

> Julio: "After your father died, your mother brought you out here, all you children, didn't she?"
> Tina: "Yes, that's right, we came here and my mother made a cross, she made a flat space on the soil and she put a cross with some stones to mark where the bodies were. You could see clothes. And my mother pulled out a beret from the grave, and we always kept that beret at home as a memento. We still have it, I don't know if it's his." (Villavieja)

From this account, in which the informant seems ambivalent about the significance of the beret and whether or not it had in fact belonged to her father, these mementoes seem to have a censored or muted presence in the home, comparable to that identified for the photographs of the dead. This informant, when prompted, was unable to recall any verbal elaboration on the beret or any specific actions, gestures, or placements within the home that called attention to the beret or structured memory around it. The only action was to keep the beret. Its significance as a material reminder of the mother and children's shared visit to the gravesite was perhaps of greater importance than the beret's belonging to the father in particular, and it certainly did not elicit any verbalisations on the subject of their lost relative. This conversation with the informant, which occurred at the graveside, reminded me of the account by the oral historian in Burgos described at the beginning of chapter 2. He described interviewing the elderly daughter of a Republican killed in Burgos whose only memento of the father was his Communist Party membership card; yet, she was emphatic throughout the interview that her father had not been a communist. Here the membership card is equivalent to the portrait photographs discussed insofar, in that it is a tangible place marker, but its specific content is muted.

The clearest example of muted or censored objects that I encountered during fieldwork was in the *salon* of Faustina and Federico. During a wide-ranging conversation, they drew my attention to their bookcase, which was well stocked with classics of Spanish literature and poetry. They told me that they loved poetry, and that their children were great readers. This was part of a longer story on how one of their grandchildren had written them a poem on the occasion of their anniversary that was now framed on the wall. When I asked if they read any history, they became very embarrassed and laughed while gesturing to a series of three books that were aligned with the rest on the shelf but had their spines turned against the walls, so that the pages rather than the titles were visible. These were recent publications on the Spanish Civil War they had acquired once exhumations had started in other villages in the region. One volume was *La memoria de los olvidados* (The memory of the forgotten) by Silva and others (2004), which tackles these very issues of verbalisation and visibility. They said that they were reading them currently and wanted them ready to hand, but they needed to be invisible "because neighbours are always coming and going." I asked them to expand and they said that people would gossip about having seen the books on their shelf and that there was "no sense in upsetting neighbours if you have to live with them." It became apparent that my questions had caused them embarrassment and discomfort, perhaps due to their awareness of the paradoxical tension between the content of these books and their censored form of display on the bookshelf.

THE LAST LESSON: EXEMPLARY BODIES

For some informants in Villavieja the period of limbo and frantic searching triggered by the seizure of their male relative came to an end with their encounter with the dead bodies that were temporarily exposed in the mass grave, or were covered in such a rudimentary way as to still be visible. It is important to clarify that the site of the mass grave in Villavieja was also the execution site. The first grave excavated, containing twelve men, lay in a small grove of coniferous trees that bordered a track and was surrounded by agricultural land. Based on eyewitness accounts, the grave had been dug before the victims were rounded up in lorries and transported to the site. The grave cut was extremely shallow, suggesting that this burial site, although planned in advance, would have been inadequate to fully conceal the bodies. It is worth reflecting that if this material evidence that spoke of a scene of carnage was still detectable after sixty-five years, it must have been horrifying in the aftermath of the killings. The current gravesite was deeply troubling, yet it was sanitised in comparison to the scene that must have appeared back then, which most probably included blood, bodily fluids, clothing, shell cases, disturbed soil, and bullet holes in the trees, partially exposed and decomposing human remains visibly bearing their deadly injuries, necrophagous insects, and odours of decomposition.

It became apparent early in the exhumation at Villavieja that a proportion of the relatives of the dead had indeed visited the scene in the immediate aftermath of the killings and had thus experienced it firsthand as children. These encounters with fatally injured and decomposing bodies were clearly highly frightening and disturbing to my informants. It was not an area of discussion that anyone would voluntarily elaborate upon, and they would mention it only tangentially, especially since a small number of children in Villavieja appeared to have been taken to see the dead not by adult relatives but by other adults in the village who were in some way implicated in the killings, in orchestrated and sadistic "showings" that initially I found hard to comprehend and that my informants found difficult to talk about. I think the anger and bewilderment still detectable in my informants when broaching the subject of showings indicates that this topic is akin to that of the ritualised humiliation of Republican women brought in procession through the village, in that both subvert the normal classification of what is public and private or what should be revealed and what concealed. It was an act that demonstrated power while visually and physically communicating powerlessness in the recipient and engendering shame. The two extracts below drawn from interviews with my informants give an indication first of the difficulty of understanding and articulating the logic underpinning the showings, and second of the trauma of the encounter, as the visual image of human remains is described as physically engraved on the mind:

Q: "Why did they show you the bodies?"
A: "I don't know."
Q: "Were they proud of what they'd done?"
A: "No."
Q: "Was it decency, so you'd know where they were?"
A: "No! Not them. They showed us, to show what had been done."
(Carla, Villavieja)

"My mother knew from the first day that they were here buried in the grave, she saw them with her own eyes. And later, too, came a sister of mine that now is dead. And a man from the village, who had buried him, came and said, "Do you want to see your father? Yes? Then come with me." And he took her walking out of the village to this spot, where they have the very tall pines growing, and he asked, "Do you see this white stuff on the tree? Well, that's the brains of your father." My sister had this engraved upon her mind all her life, the brains of her father where they had tied him to a pine tree and put eight bullets into him." (Luis, Villavieja)

The visual images and sensory impressions of destroyed and decomposing bodies at this site were visceral and violent. I think the ARMH campaigners who so strongly advocate exhumation, and the archaeologists who work for them, envisage the encounter with human remains being mediated by the techniques of archaeological intervention, creating a gravesite that can be sanitised and controlled to a degree. They envisage exhumation as producing an encounter with odourless, clean, white skeletons, far removed from the fleshed body. The elderly relatives whose last encounter with human remains was visceral, traumatic, sensorially overwhelming, and possibly enforced or outside their control, are bringing a very different frame of reference to the rematerialisation of these bodies, one that the activist or archaeologist cannot share, and therefore may not be able to mediate or control.

The showings of bodies, the voluntary visits to the gravesite, and the current exhumations must all be situated in the broader historical and cultural context of the perceived qualities of the dead or suffering body. The exposure or display of human remains in public spaces is a characteristic of the Spanish Civil War remarked upon by a range of authors. Graham (2004) comments on the prevalence of both public executions and the public burning of bodies, performative or ritualised acts redolent of the Inquisition. Ruiz Vilaplana (1938) notes the "findings" of unburied bodies. Both sides in the Civil War produced visual representations and a rhetoric in their propaganda that made reference to the exemplary power of human remains. Several active members of ARMH made repeated reference to a powerful illustration by Republican artist Castelao, whose work during the war combined reportage and propaganda for the Republican cause and has become a significant source of visual imagery for the Republican memory campaign. In this illustration, a group of young boys look at the broken body of a man left exposed on the road. It is entitled "The last lesson of the schoolteacher." The conjunction of image and text is chilling and highly ambiguous: the message intended by its creator was that the body of the dead schoolteacher represented his sacrifice, and the sight of this body was inspiring to his young students, communicating that his ideals were worth dying for and that they should be prepared to emulate him. Yet, the lesson encoded in the schoolteacher's body could also be a warning of the violent retribution that would befall Republicans, a case of exemplary violence. This is clearly the sense in which the showings in Villavieja took place, and from the way my informants referred to these events, they were experienced as exemplary violence. The repeated reference to and circulation of the schoolteacher cartoon via the ARMH website[2] is highly significant in that it indicates that the organisation conceives of a parallel between the contemporary exhumations in Spain and the ideologically inspiring or morally instructive encounter between the small boys and the body of the schoolteacher. It reveals that ARMH explicitly conceive of a lesson transmitted from the dead to the living.

The most sustained enquiry into the significance of visible bodies in the context of the Spanish Civil War has been undertaken by Lincoln (1985), who looks at the spate of mass exhumations and subsequent public displays of the human remains of nuns, monks, and priests by Republican activists in July 1936, in the first weeks of the Spanish Civil War, as a revolutionary statement against Franco's military uprising. The majority of these human remains were buried in crypts or under the flagstones of churches, and the opening of these coffins was part of a broader protest against the Catholic Church that entailed the destruction and desecration of religious buildings and paraphernalia (Maddox 1995). Under these burial conditions, the majority of the bodies were desiccated or naturally mummified, which is significant because this form of postmortem change created an uncanny mix of skeleton and skin, with the appearance of hair, facial feature, and sexual organs in conjunction with bones compounding the obscenity of the exposure. Lincoln has found reports of this phenomenon in at least ten towns and cities such as Madrid and Barcelona; it was also well documented in contemporary photographs and widely reported by both the Spanish and international press at the time: "In Barcelona, where the bodies of nineteen Silesian nuns were exhumed and exhibited flanking the doors of the church and spilling out onto the street [...] more than forty thousand people filed past them, sometimes silent but more often jeering" (Lincoln 1985, 244). This can be interpreted as a binding act of ritualised collective obscenity (ibid., 253), similar to the idea, discussed in chapter 1, of a fellowship of blood between those among Franco's supporters who engaged in acts of extreme violence. The obscenity of these displays created a rupture of normality that marked a point of no return for the participants, unifying them in a shared responsibility.

In the Portuguese context, Pina-Cabral has identified a highly elaborated set of beliefs surrounding human decomposition and sin that equate physical and moral corruption. As secondary burial is common in Pina-Cabral's field sites, as in much of the Iberian Peninsula, where most individuals are disinterred after three to five years to be moved to niches or ossuaries. If the bodies are found to be well preserved or "fresh" and lifelike, this is taken as evidence of great sanctity or purity, and a cult may spring up mythologising events in the lives of the dead or even calling for their beatification. This link between sanctity and postmortem preservation is part of a wider Catholic tradition surrounding the circulation and display of body parts as relics. The anticlerical exhumations have been interpreted as simple iconoclasm, an extension of the desecration of cultic objects and images, but Lincoln stresses the particularity of bodily exposure: "Within the context of exhumation, the category of corruption is an extremely important one, for like its near synonyms, rottenness and decadence, corruption is most concretely and emphatically manifest in the state of bodily decomposition" (ibid., 257). Furthermore, as demonstrated by Verdery (1999), there is a powerful symbolic link between preserved or uncorrupted human remains and claims to eternal or enduring power. The corpses of these clerics communicated their mortality and their progressive withering over time: "Despite its claim to eternity, the Church stood naked in its temporal reality" (Lincoln 1985, 258).

In my informants' responses there was no suggestion that the state of preservation of the exposed bodies would contribute to a reading of the morality of the dead, as it did in 1936. Nevertheless, the current exhumations should be situated in the context of a civil war in which there were multiple incidents of exposure of human remains as a spectacle, demonstration, or "lesson"—as a warning, a model of heroic sacrifice, or evidence of mortality and corruption. All these cases assign powerful agency to the remains of the dead. Arguably, the contemporary Republican exhumations in Spain seek to effect a transformation from bodies exposed as instruments of exemplary violence into bodies exposed as models of exemplary sacrifice, like the schoolteacher's. As seen at the end of chapter 1, this was expressed by forensic expert Gabriel who highlighted the "pedagogic value" of exhumation, a term which has some resonance with the "last lesson of the schoolteacher." The excerpt taken from Pedreño's critique also echoed the idea of the exemplary or pedagogic value of bodies in terms of "the lessons we can take back."

When one reflects on the violence and collective obscenity associated with the "revolutionary" exhumations of the recent past, it becomes clear that archaeological and forensic methodologies play a vital role in distancing this history, by communicating the scientific objectivity, political neutrality, and calm and methodical orderliness of the current exhumations. The clear emphasis among expert practitioners on the scientific analysis of human remains, in which bodies are meticulously recorded and individuated, distances these current practices from a cultural history of exposing bodies for their symbolic properties, in order to generate revolutionary ruptures. An emphasis on materialising *individuals*, rather than simply materialising *human remains*, enables the campaign to distance itself from these disturbing historical precedents. This suggests that a further affordance must be considered for these particular human remains, and that they must be seen not simply as bodies materialised in conjunction with injuries and possessions, but also as bodies materialised in conjunction with trowels, measuring tapes, grids, cameras, laptops, and surveying equipment. All of these provide an archaeological or forensic "dressing" to the scene of the open mass grave.

SCATTERED BODIES AND BODIES AS SEEDS

Despite the encounters with damaged, decomposing bodies at the gravesite discussed above, through the subsequent sixty-five year of enduring absence a dramatic transformation took place in the way the location of the bodies was conceptualised, and my informants established a structural distance between the village and the grave, perhaps to make its proximity and memory bearable. In both villages I found that knowledge of the gravesite or firsthand encounters with it were more widespread than my initial impressions suggested. My first understanding that the bodies had been lost to their families, missing, literal *desaparecidos*, was based on the way the location of the bodies was spoken about in my initial interviews and in more general conversations amongst villagers and relatives (although they rarely used this term). This understanding was also based on the background information furnished by the ARMH coordinators. The discourse within the campaign, particularly during its early phase, consistently referred to the Civil War dead as the *desaparecidos*, drawing on the associations of this term with the truth commissions of Latin America and in particular the forensic investigations in Argentina, as evidenced in Silva's pivotal newspaper article "My Grandfather, too, is a *Desaparecido*" described in the introduction. In the years of my observation of the ARMH campaign, I have noted a shift in usage toward the term *represaliados*, meaning "the ones who were repressed," a collective noun that perhaps reflects a growing awareness of the repression endured by Republican survivors, and particularly the female experience of Francoism.

On numerous occasions, I heard my informants who were active in the ARMH campaign discuss the verbal distinction between *desaparecidos*, "the disappeared," and *desconocidos*, "the unknown." The point here is that in the case of the disappeared, there is a broad awareness of their absence, they are actively missed, and therefore this absence is experienced as a site of active political tension, as exemplified by the ongoing campaigns about the disappeared of Argentina. The tension surrounding the status of the disappeared is also compounded by the mystery surrounding their fate, as some of the haunting power of the term *desaparecido*, like "missing in action," lies in its liminal status between living and dead. In comparison, the *desconocidos* are not just absent, but their absence is unknown or unacknowledged. In the light of the rhetorical use of these terms within the campaign, it is highly significant that the collective noun I most frequently heard from my elderly local informants, the term that could be described as "indigenous" to my field sites, was *los fusilados*, meaning "the ones who were shot." Contrary to the other terms, this one conveys certainty and knowledge on the fate of the dead. It is final and definite to the point of sounding matter-of-fact, and appears at first sight to be devoid of the kind of active tension that surrounds the fate of the disappeared (Renshaw 2010a).

In the context of these semantic distinctions and the blunt realism of *los fusilados*, the transformation that occurred in the imagined location of the dead is even more remarkable. People of all ages in Villavieja and Las Campanas routinely spoke of the bodies as being in *los montes*. This term is rich and evocative in Spanish, meaning literally the mountains, but more broadly "the wild country," and is also a generic way of saying "not here" or "outside the village." The land in which these graves were placed is very close to the village, completely flat, accessible and semicultivated or bordering onto cultivated land. According to some informants, in the 1930s, and to this day, the land was mainly owned by right-wing families believed to be in some way complicit or acquiescent in the positioning of the mass grave on their land, perhaps exacerbating this structural distance. The classification of the bodies as lying in *los montes* communicates their figurative rather than actual distance from the village. They are in a liminal, undomesticated, unquiet space, especially in contrast to the homely village cemetery at the centre of the community. There is also a degree of absolution in maintaining that one's relative is "scattered" in the "mountains," as this implies the practical difficulties of reclaiming the remains. Under Franco, the reclamation of these bodies was indeed impossible, as much as if they had been scattered in the mountains, but this was for political, not practical, reasons that are veiled in my informants' accounts. Another spatial category that is used frequently, which may or may not be a statement of fact, is *las cunetas*, meaning "ditches" or "wayside." This is indeed a common location for clandestine burials in Spain, resulting from roadside executions of prisoners rounded up and driven a few kilometres out of the settlement. In conversation, people elaborate upon it differently from *los montes*, emphasising *cunetas* as an undignified, belittling, liminal "non-place," far away from the communities the dead came from. The word is played with figuratively to imply a group of people "left by the wayside" or "ditched" both by their killers and by the passing of time or the onward trajectory of historical events.

The first book published by the cofounders of ARMH, *Las fosas de Franco* (Silva and Macías 2003), was subtitled *Los republicanos que el dictador dejó en las cunetas* (The Republicans the dictator left by the wayside), and the cover showed a photograph of the exhumation of a ditch. The subtitle seems to suggest a collective category, emphasising the common fate that has befallen these Republicans. However, the way my informants used the notion of scattered bodies arguably had the opposite effect. It was not only a distancing mechanism, but implicit in the scattering was the separation of bodies, even of body parts. It had the opposite structural effect, in terms of the individual and collective identities of both the dead and their surviving families, from the one produced by imagining the relative's remains lying in a shared grave alongside the husbands and fathers of other Republican widows and orphans residing within the same community. The notion of scattered bodies denies the locale of the grave as a potentially unifying locus for shared grief, and reflects the conditions of atomisation described in chapters 1 and 2. The theme of this structural distance and the opposition between village spaces and undomesticated spaces will be returned to in chapter 4, but it useful to reflect on how this structural positioning informs the way that human remains and their rematerialisation are imagined and represented.

The way in which the absent bodies themselves were conceptualised was closely linked to the sentiments surrounding the liminality of the grave locations, as if by being placed in locations associated with animals and rubbish the dead had been transformed into the equivalent of animals and rubbish. The phrases people used to explain why mass graves were objectionable and therefore required exhumation were "thrown out like rubbish," "thrown away like the body of a dog," "shot like dogs," or "they died like rabbits." The spaces outside the village, the semicultivated lands, *los montes*, and the ditches were all associated with waste, pest control, and the disposal of unwanted domestic animals. The images of dogs, rubbish, and, above all, rabbits are extremely passive; the term rabbit in Spanish also has some feminine or effeminate associations, and I was surprised when I heard its frequent use with regard to a group of working men. This characterisation of the dead as rabbits can be understood in the light of the tropes of innocence and unreadiness discussed in the previous chapter. King (1999) also observes that images of passivity and nonviolence are essential to the construction of a memory of sacrifice and martyrdom, as highlighted in the paradoxical norms governing the design of war memorials, which avoid the depiction of the soldier as aggressor.

The comparison with dogs, rubbish, and rabbits serves to convey passivity, innocence, and injustice. It elicits sympathy by implying that the Francoist violence dehumanised its victims, but it is also open to the alternative interpretation that the use of these terms is in itself dehumanising, and that it aims at establishing a structural distance between the living and the bodies described as "scattered in the mountains." The use of animal terms can also be linked to the use of plant metaphors, particularly the recurrence of the verbs "scattered," "sown," and "planted" in relation to the bodies. The potential for organic or plant metaphors to serve a dehumanising, distancing function has been identified by Scarry in her analysis of how injury is imagined:

> A second path by which injuring disappears is the active redescription of the event [...] just as Japanese suicide planes in World War II were called "night blossoms," as prisoners subjected to medical experiments were called "logs," and as the day during World War I on which thirty thousand Russians and thirteen thousand Germans died at Tannenberg came to be called the "Day of Harvesting." The recurrence here of language from the realm of vegetation occurs because vegetable tissue, though alive, is perceived to be immune to pain; thus the inflicting of damage can be registered in language without permitting the reality of suffering into the description. Live vegetable tissue occupies a peculiar category of sentience that is close to, perhaps is, nonsentience. (1985b, 4)

A comparable claim can be made for animals, to which is often ascribed a lesser capacity for pain and suffering than humans. A further association with animals or animal tissue that I noted during my fieldwork occurred in two descriptions of the grave/execution site in the immediate aftermath of the killings, when damaged bodies, blood, fluids, and tissues were present. Visible brain matter was referred to as *sesos* and bloody tissue as *tripas*, which are the terms employed for animal brains and animal intestines respectively. These are the terms used by farmers or butchers to indicate these body parts in the form of edible meat, not the anatomical terms used in relation to humans. This colloquial phrasing graphically emphasises the crude nature of the killings.

The reimagining of these bodies as plant material has a particular significance in the broader context of the use of plant metaphors by both sides in Civil War propaganda and subsequently in ARMH's rhetoric, which differs dramatically from Scarry's formulation. As described in chapter 1, Francoist Civil War propaganda was concerned with the notion of the total erasure of Republicanism, conceptualised as a "pulling up by the roots." Informants in my field site referred to ideologies such as Francoism or Republicanism, and states of mind such as fear, as being "sown" and "planted." A typical formulation of this can be found in Eulalio's words:

> I read on a gravestone "We have only died if you forget us." We haven't forgotten them, we give them dignity, and they haven't died because their ideas have been sown within us. (Eulalio, Las Campanas)

As already observed, the theme uniting these metaphors is a preoccupation with cycles of dormancy and growth, potentiality and resurgence, or continuity and transmission in Eulalio's words. An important variation of these plant metaphors is the conceptualisation of buried bodies as planted seeds articulated by Eduardo, a key founding member of ARMH. Here he describes how the word *semillas* or seeds became an important word and image for the exhumation campaign:

We made a documentary called *Seeds*. The name *Seeds* comes from an event at an excavation in Piedrafita de Babia in the north of León in July 2002, when a miner from that area brought us an old postcard made by a Republican intellectual who died in exile, called Castelao, and it was an illustration from a series he made in 1937 called "Galicia Martyr." In the drawing you can see civilians, villagers who are putting bodies into a mass grave, and you can read the legend below that says, "You are not burying bodies, you are planting seeds." When that card was brought to the excavation it gave us goose pimples because this card represents what we believe we are doing, which is gathering these seeds. We don't know yet what the fruit will be, but I believe it's something better for Spanish society. It thrilled me, this drawing. That he imagined in 1937 that all this was going to happen. It's like a cosmic message. (Eduardo, Madrid)

The equation of buried bodies with planted seeds is highly significant to understand how ARMH conceptualises the materialisation of human remains, and specifically the shifting of material registers between buried bodies and exhumed bodies (Renshaw 2010a). The idea that these bodies possess the inherent potentiality of a seed, and the implicit notion of their coming to fruition, suggest something preordained about the exhumation and the narrative arc surrounding these bodies, which is dramatically reinforced by the invocation of a "cosmic message." Exhumation is the preordained fate of these bodies, and the potentiality for change that they contain is being "gathered" by ARMH. This notion even implies that the bodies wish to be exhumed to fulfil their potential. The message of the "seeds" illustration recalls the "schoolteacher" illustration discussed above. Although the mechanism by which the schoolteacher's dead body transmits a lesson of exemplary sacrifice is much clearer than the way in which these human "seeds" can express their potentiality, both emphasise a cycle of resurgence and both encode a warning to the oppressors that the apparent state of defeat represented by the Republican dead bodies is, in fact, only a temporary state of dormancy. What is clear in this account is that the buried bodies have a power to effect change if they are "gathered" through the act of exhumation. The trope of the planted seeds allows ARMH to transform local notions of scattered and sown bodies, suggesting burial as the condition of being concealed but near at hand, ready to be activated.

CONCLUSION

This chapter has identified the problematic absence of firsthand knowledge and memory amongst the surviving children of the dead, despite their role within the ARMH campaign as the last living link to the Civil War generation. This is problematic for an exhumation process that inherently privileges a bodily connection with the dead. As identified in chapters 1 and 2, this absence is exacerbated by a condition of atomisation that breaks the transmission of the personal or political biographies of the dead and dismantles the Republican memory community in which the children's memories of the dead could be acknowledged and verified. The materialisations of the dead that precede the exhumation—the muted and censored use of photographs and objects in the home, the creation of structural distances between the village and the graves, and the characterisation of the dead as passive "rabbits and dogs"—illustrate that neither strongly personal nor strongly political representations of the dead occurred prior to exhumation. This may explain the potential ambivalence in my field sites toward affective and political representations of the dead, as well as the potential resistance to ARMH's emphasis upon affective bonds between the living and the dead as a rationale for exhumation.

Despite this, the recurring representation of the dead through organic or plant metaphors, both by local informants and within ARMH's campaign discourse, opens up a discursive space for new affective and political representations, as it conceives of these bodies as containing some dormant potentiality, capable of resurgence. The image of the buried seed suggests that aspects of the dead person's identity and agency could be reactivated through the exhumation, thus opening up an opportunity for new representations. ARMH's insistence on the pedagogic value of the bodies shows to what extent that materialisation is fundamental to the formulation of new representations of the dead within the campaign. The emphasis on the "lesson" transmitted from the dead to the living is suggestive of a transmission of Republican ideology, despite ARMH's primarily affective representations of the dead—and this is indeed the central tension within the campaign. The next chapter will look at how the materialisation of the dead through the bodies and objects extracted from the grave allows the emergence of new representations and the transformation of those associated with photographs and mementoes.

Chapter 4

THE OPEN GRAVE: EXPOSED BODIES AND OBJECTS IN NEW REPRESENTATIONS OF THE DEAD

INTRODUCTION

This chapter will focus on the representations of the human remains as they emerge in ever greater detail, as features such as injury patterns and recognisable personal possessions become visible. These possessions include watches, combs, wallets, razors, mirrors, pencils, lighters, rings, shoes, and belts. The affordances of these different possessions will be considered in detail. I will consider the power of skeletal remains in conjunction with personal possessions to humanise and individualise the dead, eliciting particular emotional responses in my informants and fostering new affective bonds. The significance of the progressive emergence of detail through the exhumation process is that different participants may have different encounters with the grave at different times. In particular, the capacity of the expert practitioners to read the injuries on the bodies and make a detailed reconstruction of the violence that occurred at these sites may not be shared by other constituencies who do not discern this evidence during their encounters with the grave. The production of images of bodies and objects by artists and photographers is also considered, in particular to emphasise the wide dissemination of images outside of the immediate community via the news media and internet. These media images also represent the relationships among the different participants in the exhumation, and focus especially on the juxtaposition of youthful investigators, elderly relatives, and the remains of the dead. The dissemination of these images beyond the immediate community is pivotal to the rupture that has occurred in Spanish memory politics since exhumations began in 2000.

I will explore the way ARMH campaigners and expert practitioners represent the process of scientific human identification within these communities to show how this representation of scientific practice can also engender pathos and affective sentiments for the dead. The emphasis here is on the use of antemortem data to achieve human identifications. Antemortem data are the existing materialisations of the dead such as photographs and letters. The unique features of an individual, such as dental traits or the clothing and jewellery visible in a photograph, can then be matched to the remains exhumed from the grave. This confers a new significance to the photographs of the dead and the material possessions found in the grave. The commencement of the exhumation activates new practices—such as bringing photographs to the gravesite, digitally manipulating the images to depict the dead together with their descendants, and taking pictures of the relatives of the dead as they hold images of their lost family members. The encounters with the personal possessions of the dead emerging from the mass grave also activate speculations on the possibility that new mementoes might allow a fuller representation of the dead and structure the intergenerational transmission of memory. The activation of these new practices suggests a rupture with the muted and censored use of photography identified in chapter 3.

THE PROGRESSIVE EXPOSURE OF BODIES AND OBJECTS THROUGH EXHUMATION

The transformation from buried body to revealed body in the Spanish exhumations is not a single moment of revelation, but rather a sequence of discernible shifts in material register. The nature of what precisely is being materialised, and the representations that are made and contested, change as details are progressively revealed and made visible. This is particularly true of the shift from undifferentiated skeletal material to discrete individuals, as bodily postures and signs of injury become apparent and, crucially, personal possessions emerge from the grave. Careful attention to this sequence of material changes through the exhumation produces findings that echo Crossland's analysis of postmortem dissection and autopsy (2009a). Crossland highlights "the categorical instability of the corpse," contrary to its representation in modern scientific discourse and practice as a "fixed and naturalized entity":

> It is an axiom of the anthropological literature that the status of the body as corpse is not fixed at the moment of death, but develops processually, through the interaction of the physical body and those who attend to it. Clearly, this perspective may be extended to encompass practices of postmortem surgery and exhumation, as well as archaeological excavation,

bringing all postmortem interventions within the frame of regularized mortuary practices. (ibid., 104)

During the first preliminary stage of exhumation, an arbitrary selection of skeletal remains emerges before those viewing the grave. The majority of the bodies are still half-buried, but their presence is confirmed, and the possibility of exhumation and identification appears for the first time as a concrete reality to all the participants. The site takes on a sombre atmosphere, with a tangible thrill of anticipation passing between the archaeologists, the ARMH campaigners, and the relatives in attendance (figures 4, 5). There is a respectful and solemn silence at the site in response to this first materialisation of human remains, the new presence of the dead amongst the living. This later fades as work progresses, and the majority of those who attend the grave become rapidly accustomed to the presence of the dead. I recorded the first hours of exhumation at every gravesite as an experience of overwhelming tension, suppressed excitement, expectation, and shock, as a superficially benign location was revealed to contain material traces of horrific events.

It is not possible at this stage to discern the physical relationships between body parts, with some postures appearing perplexing and defying anatomical logic, which contributes to an uncanny feeling. The disjunction of limbs presents images of composite bodies that the mind struggles to process as real or possible (figure 6). The full extent of the grave is still undetermined, and there is a rush of work to extend

Figure 4. Visitors to the mass grave in Villavieja.

the boundaries of the grave outwards and gain a picture of the total number of individuals. The archaeologists constantly assess the emerging evidence in light of the testimonies of the witnesses on the size and positioning of the grave. The archaeologists are noticeably torn between the impulse to expand outward and the desire to dig downward and focus on the visible bodies in order to materialise them further as discrete individuals. There is a tension between the procedural pressure to work systematically or stratigraphically and the human impulse to find an individual by following the bones to their points of articulation.

The archaeologists appear driven and this stage of work progresses rapidly. When the complete grave is exposed and the total number of bodies are visible, the episode of killing is seen in its totality and the

Figure 5.   Archaeologist in the mass grave in Villavieja.

Figure 6.   Human remains uncovered in the mass grave in Villavieja.

bodies are viewed as a collective, forming a tableau that communicates the scope of the event to the observers. This simultaneously materialises both the scale and the particularity of the event, a phenomenon analysed by Laqueur (2002).

This was particularly the case with the multiple bodies found in the long narrow grave at Las Campanas. As word of the number of bodies spread, more visitors attended the exhumation site. The precise spatial relationships between the bodies could be discerned, and the skeletons could be more clearly read as discrete, anatomically viable individuals. Yet the intimate physical contact between them was still difficult to process cognitively, frequently producing the impression of uncannily animated remains. Bodies overlapped; their limbs were splayed and spread-eagled. The angles of the limbs that appeared "unnatural" might indeed have been anatomically "impossible," as they were the result of dislocation and fractures caused by violence or the violent disposal of the bodies (see Nochlin 1994 for a detailed analysis of the visual effect of fragmentary or dislocated bodies). Some bodies lay two deep, with one ribcage interlaced with another and the uppermost body collapsed downward, merging the two skeletons in the eyes of the viewer.

The conventional funerary archaeologists, the family members, and the wider community had few prior visual references for bodies in this condition, as the normative positioning of the dead—face up, straightened limbs, and arms folded upon the torso—is intended to emphasise the integrity of the individual and present the state of burial as one of stillness, peace, and repose. These skeletons instead appeared animated by a violent movement, and their stillness was more suggestive of an action shot or a freeze frame than of repose. The effect was uncanny in that it provoked a sense of confusion between living and dead matter (Freud 2003), a sensation noted in other archaeological encounters (Domanska 2006; Moshenska 2006). The archaeologists had an interpretative framework with which to process these images, and their training or experience provided a lens that allowed them to discern patterns and rationally reconstruct the events that left the skeletons positioned in such an "unquiet" way. Some bodies were "read" as having been thrown from left to right, crumpling upon impact against the far wall of the grave. Others were read as having been dragged into the grave by their wrists, since they had their arms above their heads. It was clear that some bodies had had their hands tied behind their backs and that some individuals had been shot at the grave edge and had fallen forward into the grave. The perpetrators had run out of space at the end and had placed the bodies two deep, thus suggesting the sequence in which the bodies were deposited.

Despite the rational reconstructions or reading of events made by the archaeologists, irrational explanations for the grotesque appearance of the bodies hovered silently nearby. Without the interpretative lens discussed above, certain bodies appeared so animated as to be possessed of some agency or volition after death. This subtext was never explicitly verbalised, either by the relatives of the dead or the community members who visited the grave, but the uncanniness of some postures elicited anxiety. This was discernible in nervous questions such as, "Why do they look like that?" or "Why are they lying like that?" Urgent requests for a rational explanation implicitly contained the possibility of an irrational explanation. Even though the bodies were skeletonised, all observers, archaeologists included, were susceptible to reading body language and gestures exactly as they would have in the living. People stopped and observed skeletons that appeared to be performing particularly lifelike gestures with their hands, or that had their arms interlinked as if in an embrace or a protective gesture (figure 7), or their heads touching as if conferring. Since the bodies in the grave were of neighbours and relatives, these gestures were easily read by the viewers as signs of intimacy, solidarity, and consolation. Pollard and Banks (2008) note the same affective power in the appearance of the skeletons of World War I soldiers lying with their arms entwined.

After a few days of exposure, everyone on site became more familiar with the bodies, and one could overhear archaeologists saying, "These two look like they're talking," "These two are embracing," anthropomorphising the skeletons as part of their growing ease. This affection for the bodies facilitated their work. I noted on occasion archaeologists who permitted themselves to reflect upon the body language of the skeletons but were too self-conscious, or too immersed in their disciplinary

Figure 7. Human remains uncovered in the mass grave in Las Campanas.

prohibitions, to verbalise their thoughts. They would instead gesture to the skeleton and wordlessly mimic the physical position, and others around would nod to confirm that it was indeed emotive, touching, disturbing, without having to utter irrational phrases like "They're talking" or "They're embracing." It was helpful in this phase to have a shared disciplinary background with the excavators, and to endeavour to be reflexive on my own excavation practice. The volunteer archaeologists were making a constant negotiation between emotional detachment and emotional engagement, and were exploring the degree to which we collectively granted ourselves permission to vocalise our emotions or reflections whilst working.

Some of the skeletons' body language was more straightforwardly sinister, particularly that of the bodies that appeared to have their arms raised in self-defence, that appeared to be struggling, or that had their wrists bound. There are unseemly conjunctions of bodies, such as a skeleton lying between the legs of another. Despite the general absence of cosmological or spiritual comments upon the status of the bodies, observers from the village referred to *los bocas abajo*, meaning "mouths down" or "the mouths to the ground," as a collective noun for those in the mass grave, drawing on traditional beliefs around the impiety and indignity of being buried face down or having soil in the mouth. The pattern of injury upon each body became much more readily discernible once the skeletons were cleaned and fully exposed. This is an aspect that would be discerned to differing degrees by ARMH campaigners, relatives of the dead, and expert practitioners, depending on their levels of expertise and experience at reading the physical traces of injury. However, since the large majority of the skeletons had at least one round entry and exit wound visible on each side of the skull, often on the temple, the cause of death was apparent to anyone looking superficially at the body, and did not require any forensic expertise (figure 8).

The responses of locals and relatives to this specific stage in the materialisation of the dead, which revealed the skeletons' unquiet postures and cause of death, were not highly elaborated or articulated verbally in any detail. In keeping with the indignation over "the mouths to the ground," the elderly relatives of the dead expressed some outrage but of a muted quality. The remarks of condemnation I overheard most frequently were "Shameless!" or "Brazen!" which was presumably in reference to the Francoist perpetrators, as well as "Look what a cheek they had!" It is important to emphasise the gravity of these notions of shamelessness and "cheek" in the framework of honourable and shameful conduct within which these constitute severe expressions of opprobrium, particularly amongst the elderly. Nevertheless, these pronouncements of outrage made little reference to the crimes that were being exposed. Apart from

Figure 8. Gunshot wounds to crania of two skeletons in the mass grave in Las Campanas.

seeking explanation and reassurance about the most disturbing postures amongst the skeletons, the dominant response was to reprise the passive characterisation of the dead as rabbits, dogs, and rubbish, along with more general expressions of pity—the pity often centring on the fact that the dead had been left to lie in this way, rather than on their having been murdered. Some of those attending the grave observed for long periods, often in silence and without directly addressing either the archaeologists or the ARMH campaigners, suggesting the necessity of a sustained visual encounter and private processing of what could be seen.

My own experience in Las Campanas was of a progressively dawning realisation of how damaged the bodies had been before or during death. The archaeologists noted more and more weathered but unhealed fractures on the limb bones and fragmentary ribs. I found this evidence of bodily pain and suffering prior to death very disquieting, a response shared by another archaeologist and a forensic anthropologist who had noted the extent of trauma and commented on how deeply it disturbed them. These fractures became linked in my mind with the period of incarceration and with my informants' accounts of those days in limbo while the family waited for the death to be confirmed. I found evidence of this kind of violence impossible to discuss on site in a technical language without feeling overwhelmed, and I was relieved to find that the relatives of the dead and the villagers were not likely to visually detect the fracture injuries by observing the skeletons. I found the material evidence of pain and suffering prior to death to be more emotionally disturbing than the evidence of fatal gunshot wounds, perhaps due to my capacity to empathise with physical pain but inability to assimilate the experience of death. My intermittent realisation of these empathetic sentiments for the physical pain of the dead emphasised the extent to which I had rapidly become inured to the sight of injuries whilst working on the bodies (Canter 2002; Scarry 1985a). *The New Yorker*'s journalist Elizabeth Kolbert attended exhumations close to my field sites, with many of the same archaeologists and activists. She writes on how the progressive emergence of new evidence communicating the cruelty and fear surrounding the deaths changed her emotional response to the grave:

> His skull was shattered indicating he had been shot in the head at close range. Before he had been killed, he had been brutalized, both his arms were broken, one of them probably by a bullet. His position in the grave suggested that he had been the last to be thrown in. The reason for this and the two broken arms [...] was that he had put up resistance. When I thought about this, I felt, for the first time since arriving, that I might be sick. (Kolbert 2003, 72)

The reading of signs of violence and the more detailed reconstruction of the violence surrounding these deaths is primarily limited to a technical discourse amongst the archaeologists and anthropologists, and draws in the representatives of ARMH who are present at the grave edge for sustained periods. For example, there was an extended discussion about whether the sequence of cranial fractures, discernible from how one radiating fracture bisects and interrupts another in relation to the position of the skulls of the surface of the grave floor, was an indication that a *coup de grace* had been administered to a subset of bodies in the Las Campanas grave. Some vigorous and audible discussions occurred amongst the more experienced archaeologists, who later explained their interpretation to the rest of the excavators in a period of the working day during which no relatives were present. The sudden reconstruction of the *coup de grace* whilst immersed in the intimate and delicate process of cleaning the skeletons in the tranquil and secluded gravesite was such a powerful materialisation of a human action in the past, such a detailed rendering of the agency of the perpetrators, that I experienced it as a temporary materialisation of the perpetrators as well as the victims. The perpetrators' sudden presence provoked unexpected emotions of fear and anger amongst us. Small and mundane things, too, can evoke the presence of the perpetrators. Writing on the powerful photographs by Francesc Torres of objects recovered from an exhumation site in Burgos, Monegal observes that "the beer-bottle caps next to the bullet casings tell us what the executioners were doing while finishing off their victims" (2008, 242).

A detailed reconstruction of the perpetrators' violent agency is dependent on the expert gaze and on a sustained engagement with the bodies and the gravesite (also the execution site), and is therefore something primarily experienced by the excavators and activists from which the relatives and locals are largely insulated. The entry and exit wounds in nearly every skull are visible to the untrained eye, but a more detailed reconstruction of the events surrounding these deaths is not accessible to all. The indices of particular acts of violence speak of the power relations inherent in these events and afford a political representation of the dead. Although the archaeologists and expert practitioners maintain a highly objective and neutral discourse at the grave, and rarely make explicitly political representations of the dead, the experience of excavation, the close and sustained exposure to these materialisations, is arguably an experience of politicisation, even radicalisation. This can be seen in the degree to which a single experience of volunteering on an excavation frequently triggers an ongoing and deeper involvement in ARMH campaign activities, and a deeper engagement with Spain's recent past via media, scholarly sources, and one's own family history. The volunteer excavators do not merely facilitate these materialisations through physical labour, or mediate representations of the past through expert readings; they are also profoundly affected by their encounter with the bodies and objects in the grave.

The Possessions of the Dead

In the next stage of the cleaning of the bodies, finer, individuating details emerge, and also the personal possessions of the dead are progressively cleaned and made evident. In my fieldwork I found that the bodies at this stage of work elicited the most reflection from the observers, both from the archaeologists and the relatives of the dead. As personal possessions became clearer, there was a marked shift toward perceiving each skeleton as an individual rather than a mass of homogenous bone. There was extensive verbal elaboration and reflection by both the expert practitioners and the ARMH campaigners upon the objects that were found. The emerging personal possessions of the dead were explicitly brought to the attention of the relatives by excavators and campaigners, mirroring the way Julio had initially fostered a sense of bodily knowledge amongst them, but this time fostering a sense of the individual who had owned those objects and accessories, and emphasising both their ordinariness and bodily intimacy. Prior to a detailed analysis in the laboratory, the skeletons can appear as homogeneous assemblages of the same skeletal elements, but the unique material assemblage on each body emphasises their individuality. Mundane objects underscore the normality of this class of dead, which was so extravagantly demonised and caricatured by Francoist rhetoric. The presence of these objects on the body communicates the indisputable fact of each skeleton's antemortem existence, and the particularity of that existence. The fact that the person was in possession of these mundane objects at the moment of death emphasises the dramatic insertion of extraordinary horror and violence into the ordinary fabric of existence. The capacity for mundane objects at sites of horror that suggest individual narratives of suffering is identified by Shanks and others (2004) in their discussion of the curation of personal objects recovered from the Ground Zero site, following the destruction of the World Trade Center: "Each acts a touchstone; not so much illuminating the topics of political and forensic interest, the exhibits are material correlates for the intimate personal experiences, the individual stories. That is what we mean when we call things iconic" (ibid., 61). Tilley (1990a, 1990b) and Schnapp and others (2004) have identified a modernist sensibility concerning ephemera that applies to encounters with discarded objects and objects emerging from the archaeological excavation. Part of the emotional response elicited by the appearance of quotidian objects in the extraordinary context of a mass grave is due to this sensibility: "A sensitivity to the ephemeral, fleeting and contingent nature of the present [...] a sense of possibility: that the world could be changed, turned upside down" (Tilley 1990b, 128).

Mundane objects such as combs, mirrors, razors, money, and cigarettes are indices of daily routines and habits that may be shared by the living, generating points of connection and a sense of commonality. This was particularly true of the discovery at Las Campanas of a skeleton that still had on it a pocket of fabric. Within the pocket was a heavy old-fashioned cigarette lighter made of metal with a visible wick. Remarkably, the biocidal action of the corroding metal had preserved the man's rolling papers. The cigarette lighter and papers were at first unrecognisable but gradually took shape when cleaned of adhering soil. When the archaeologists who were themselves smokers heard that smoking accessories had been discovered, they automatically and unthinkingly came to examine the skeleton and meet a fellow smoker. Several then laughed in self-conscious recognition of an irrational response. Smoking is a highly visible habit or trait that people use daily to construct an idea of another's persona upon first meeting. The capacity for archaeologists to animate the dead while exhuming their remains has been remarked upon by other authors working on human remains in historical and prehistorical contexts (Boyle 1999; Taylor 2002). The modern accoutrements on the bodies of more recent corpses (Kirk and Start 1999) means that this occurs with greater frequency in the exhumation of contemporary mass graves.

The identities conferred upon the skeletons by the excavators in a large grave like the one in Las Campanas is redolent of the nickname "Sailor" that the forensic anthropologist in Ondaatje's fictionalised account of a human rights investigation in Sri Lanka (2001) gives to the skeleton under analysis. The dead are subject to imaginative reconstructions of their characters on the basis of material clues, and a range of authors including Edgeworth (2003) and Hamilton (2000) have noted the constant interpretative assumptions and narrative reconstructions that occur during excavation. In Villavieja, a skeleton was found with the digits of its hand clutched around a small wallet containing coins and crumbling fragments of paper (see figure 9 for a similar wallet recovered in Las Campanas). The tensed hand bones in the shape of a fist were disturbingly animated in appearance. Once they overcame the initial uncanniness of the tensed hand, the archaeologists were uncomfortable to vocalise the idea that the man had reached for and vigorously held onto his money at the moment of death, as this could have been perceived as a materialistic gesture. One archaeologist suggested that perhaps he was reaching for something else in the wallet, a letter or a photograph, which could be reconstructed as an affective gesture at the moment of death. Another suggested that "perhaps he did not want *them* to have his money," situating the material trace of this bodily gesture in the narratives of theft and envy that were dominant in Republican memory idioms.

Although the great majority of textiles, with the exception of leather, had decomposed, there were various items remaining that gave shape to the garment. Buttons, buckles, and zips, primarily made of metal, could be seen lying in the correct alignment on the body as if held in place by invisible fabric. Thicker concentrations of textiles, or textiles in contact with the biocidal properties of metal artefacts, such as pockets and

Figure 9. Notes and coins recovered in conjunction with human remains from Las Campanas (courtesy of Luis Ríos).

waistbands, survived in fragmentary form, giving some indication of the garment before it decomposed. Some of these fastenings were unfamiliar to the contemporary viewer and evoked the period-specific character of these clothes, particularly braces and waistcoats. The economic status of those in the grave was communicated by the footwear that was prevalent in rural Spain at the time, namely improvised soles made from car tyres or the coiled rope soles of espadrilles. Some of the objects that survived in the grave shared a particular affordance with the lost and stolen objects considered in chapter 2, due to their intimate proximity to the body and their capacity to encircle and contain it—in particular clothing, jewellery, and belts. In several narratives of theft, like those concerning the corduroy suit, the distinctive belt, and the gold ring cut from a finger, the revulsion and abjection surrounding the event were located in the thief's subsequent wearing of the object. Clothes such as suits take on the bodily form of their owners; therefore for killers to return in the suit of their victims equates to assuming their form, or usurping their space. This crosses boundaries of physical intimacy and creates a disturbing elision of the identity of victim and perpetrator. Above all, necklaces and rings are often conceived of as permanent extensions or additions to the body, in that they can be worn perpetually without ever being removed (Miller and Parrott 2007). Rings that become stuck are an example of this connection. The story about the severed finger discussed above in effect underscores that the ring should, in the natural moral order, be inalienable, but is removed by an unnaturally barbaric and immoral act. The power of some possessions to denote whole individuals, rather than simply parts of their body or roles and attributes they possessed, seems related to the objects that are more visibly shaped by use and seem to hold the form of their wearer (Stallybrass and Jones 2001). Enrique, one of the leading members of ARMH, described the first visual encounter with the remains of his grandfather in one of the early ARMH exhumations: "The spade brought up a whole boot, intact. It made a great impression on me because a boot is more human than a bone."

The analysis made by various authors (Barthes 2000; Briggs 2006; Sontag 1979) of the inherent presence of mortality in photography because of the way the image outlives its human subject can also be applied to the effect of encountering these objects in conjunction with human remains, as this is a context in which it is graphically apparent that they have outlived their owners. A category of objects that occur with frequency in the grave and connote a particular intimacy are those associated with personal grooming, such as combs, razors, and pocket mirrors. Of these, combs, razors, and also spectacles, are indices of bodily tissues that have now decomposed. These objects have not only outlived their owners but also survived the decomposition of their tissues. The appearance of this class of objects in conjunction with skeletal tissue highlights not only the fact of death, but also the duration of time that has elapsed since these deaths. This is also true of some of the objects designed to encircle the body, since the vacuum between bones and a surviving boot or belt emphasises the absence, and therefore former presence, of bodily tissues. Objects such as watches and eyeglasses, which have a particular functional nature, seem to have a more readily apparent agency. The moving parts of the watch or a lens that extends the gaze are most readily apprehended as objects that possess their own agency. That the functionality of these objects persists after their function is no longer needed by their owner, in effect outliving human agency, is experienced as uncanny. The emotional responses that these objects can elicit echo with the chilling phrase that recurred in memory idioms of innocence and unreadiness analysed in chapter 2: "*No hace falta,*" or "Where he's going, he won't need it."

Conversely, the conflation of the dead person's agency in life and the functional quality of the object can make eyeglasses (figure 10) and watches (figure 11) seem particularly effective in evoking the antemortem existence of the dead. This inherent redundancy of certain functional objects can elicit emotions of pathos in which the futility of the surviving object becomes conflated with the futility surrounding the violent death. My own strong emotional response to the appearance of glasses in the grave might be helpful to understand the responses to different objects among my fellow excavators. A conscious attempt at reflexivity throughout the exhumation was an important part of my methodology (Hodder 2003) and not only aided in the observation of my fellow excavators' responses to the grave, but also enabled open communication in my interviews with expert practitioners. My emotional response to the glasses was elicited by a combination of the different affordances

Figure 10. Glasses recovered in conjunction with human remains from Las Campanas (courtesy of Luis Ríos).

Figure 11. Pocket watch recovered in conjunction with human remains from Las Campanas (courtesy of Luis Ríos).

identified above. An individual's dependence on his or her glasses evoked for me a sense of vulnerability, and from that I imaginatively reconstructed a narrative of the coercion that surrounded these deaths. This was not a logical reconstruction of events on the basis of material evidence, since the deceased obviously had not lost his glasses or become separated from them. I had conflated the stories of unreadiness told by my informants, concerning relatives taken away without their jacket or half-shaven, with my own association between glasses and dependency, making an imaginary narrative reconstruction.

The uncanny and discomforting association between watches and the dead rests on the presence of moving parts, because of their continuing animation or potential to be reanimated. In my participation in forensic exhumations in Kosovo, I noted that encounters with functioning watches on the wrists of the recently dead exerted a fascination on the expert practitioners, many of them highly experienced and seemingly inured to the psychic effects produced by the material possessions of the dead. A type of discipline-specific mythology or traveller's tale involving the discovery of functioning wrist watches in the morgue or grave has been documented in forensic investigations around the world. Conversely, forensic archaeologists who had worked on the investigation of large-scale massacres in Bosnia reported the eeriness of repeatedly seeing the motion-dependent wrist watches of victims that had all stopped on the same day, thus recording the date of the massacre very precisely (see Edgeworth 2003 on archaeological subcultures and their mythmaking).

These narratives were particularly concerned with the make and appearance of the watch. My interpretation of these discussions was that the preoccupation with the make and technical qualities of these objects was a displacement of the fascination they exerted on a psychic level, which could not readily be acknowledged within the confines of a shared disciplinary discourse that prized objectivity and detachment. The deep association between the measurement of time and human mortality is highlighted by Hallam and Hockey (2001) in their analysis of the kind of material objects that functioned as *memento mori*, or as material reminders of human mortality and temporality designed to focus the mind on the necessity of religious and moral conduct. *Memento mori* often took the form of timepieces, sometimes shaped as a cranium or decorated with depictions of human remains: "Instruments of measurement including hourglasses, watches and clocks were deployed as a means to capture and focus the processes of memory" (Hallam and Hockey 2001, 72).

The propensity of those encountering the bodies in conjunction with objects to make highly elaborate imaginative assemblages can be seen in the two accounts below. Here two volunteer archaeologists draw on objects encountered in the grave, objects from their own memory and biography, and verbal accounts of the past transmitted during the exhumation or within their own family histories. These imaginative assemblages are then used to make narrative reconstructions of the kind that I myself had furnished around a pair of spectacles and that other archaeologists had debated with regard to the wallet in the clenched hand:

> About the bones, when only bones appear, I don't have any feelings because I have spent four years working on excavations, but the objects sometimes move me, and tears come to my eyes because they give life to that particular corpse and I imagine this persons walking around in their corduroy jacket, with their comb and their razor, because these are objects that you might see today, and you suddenly realize that these things didn't happen so long ago, the deaths of these people. It's a thing that never happens in archaeology because the bodies never have names, they have nothing more than a culture, a burial type, but they never have a name so it's not so intimate, it feels much more distant. But the objects are there, so you can identify people. The combs and the watches have been the things that have most affected me, and the ring that we uncovered on a finger today, because that ring is saying "Your wife has been left a widow." My grandmother keeps such objects from her husband, shirts

and a pen [...] For her those are memories that have been able to remain. (Carmela, archaeology student, Villavieja)

The thing that most affects me are the teeth, not just the bones, and yes, the personal objects. There are some with teeth that have all their enamel, that shine: those teeth are just the same, they haven't changed. The pencils are the objects that impress themselves on me. Because they are a symbol of freedom of expression, and under dictatorship they are a form of the power to express yourself. This is the thing that has most impressed me, especially after seeing those letters. Which letters? My grandparents didn't talk much about the war. They had bad experiences; he was a mechanic on the front at Teruel. My grandmother told me of some of the people who were taken away to be killed. In Valencia they saw the processions of people going off to be shot and these people gave them little notes for their families, "Give this to my wife, give this to my daughter," because they knew they would never return. My grandmother, who was very young, was terribly moved by this. She died a long time ago, and you're scared to ask questions when you're little but now I regret it very much. (Concha, archaeology student, Villavieja)

Both these informants were postgraduate archaeology students, and it is interesting that they began their reflections by asserting that bones did not affect them psychologically or emotionally. It is as if they needed to make this assertion of professional distance and objectivity before they could permit themselves to be moved by their encounter with the bodies. This may be an assertion of professional identity or it may rest, in part, on the paradoxical quality of inhumanity or "otherness" of the skeletonised body (Renshaw 2010b; Sofaer 2006). Both accounts imply that certain features "animate" the body: "objects give life to that particular corpse," so that Carmela sees it walking around, and Concha notes teeth that shine as in a living person. Many of the archaeological volunteers referred to the teeth as the aspect of the body that remained unchanged in death and was recognisably human. It is as if the eyes were briefly tricked into seeing a sign of life, causing a jolt of recognition and the fleetingly reclassification of the skeleton as a fellow human. It is this jolt that people need in order to say that they have been moved and impressed. Both informants established a connection between specific objects encountered in the grave at Villavieja and their broader understanding of both the Civil War and the emotional experience of bereavement, which they located with their grandparents, in particular the grandmother.

Carmela's account made a series of connections: from the fact that a wedding ring on a dead man's hand (figure 12) is a signifier of widowhood, to her grandmother's widowhood and her use of small personal objects in mourning, to Carmela's own capacity to be touched by small personal objects in the grave. Concha's account associated the pencil in the breast pocket of one of the dead (figure 13) with the farewell letters described by her grandmother. I was struck by the way Carmela projected into the grave an object that we did not actually encounter, namely the corduroy jacket that had featured in conversations about theft and envy at the gravesite in the first few days. In Carmela's imagination it had now been transposed onto one of the bodies along with the objects that we did indeed find: the comb and the razor. This demonstrates one of the intangible affordances of the personal possessions encountered in the grave, which is their capacity to presence other remembered and imagined objects associated with the dead and with the Civil War.

The period of exhumation in which both the visible injuries and personal possessions of the dead were most apparent was the period in which the maximum number of relatives of the dead, locals, and supporters of the ARMH campaign visited the gravesite. It was also a period of intense media coverage and image production at the gravesite (figure 14). During the exhumation at Villavieja, the schedule of the excavation work was in part shaped by visitors from both national and local news media, particularly the cameramen and professional photographers who came to record visual images of the mass grave and of the exhumation process.

Figure 12. Ring on finger bone of skeleton in mass grave in Las Campanas.

Figure 13. Pencil recovered in conjunction with human remains from Las Campanas (courtesy of Luis Ríos).

Midway through the exhumation of the second grave in Villavieja, there were some extreme fluctuations in the weather: days of intense heat and dramatic thunderstorms accompanied by heavy rain. Several of the volunteer excavators with archaeological backgrounds raised the possibility of recording and then moving the small finds from the bodies, where they had been left. My concern, based on my professional training and experience, was that the complex excavation could disturb or displace the small finds, leading them to be associated with the wrong body in the final recording process. Furthermore, since the sites could not be secured at night, objects might be disturbed or even taken by unauthorised visitors to the grave. The lead archaeologist responded by arguing that the grave must remain exposed and intact until the scheduled visit of a photographer from a national newspaper had taken place. In the words of the lead archaeologist, it was a priority that when the photographer and journalist visited the site, the grave should "have the greatest possible impact." This illustrates the extent to which the exhumation constitutes a site of image production, and that the production and dissemination of these images are a pivotal part of the ARMH campaign.

As we have seen in chapter 1, both Emilio Silva and forensic anthropologist Gabriel identified a "media effect" when trying to assess the significance of exhumations to the rupture in Spanish memory politics generated by the ARMH campaign. Emilio Silva pointed to the role of the media in extending the reach of the campaign, raising awareness and increasing the campaign's momentum by drawing in new participants:

> The media impact that this has had, the media effect, has had a positive effect, because now many people are getting involved, many people set themselves to search, we receive lots of emails now from the grandchildren who begin to search for their grandfathers. (Emilio Silva, Madrid)

The media effect on public engagement with the Republican memory campaign noted here by Silva has been discussed also by Ferrándiz (2006) and González-Ruibal (2008). Forensic expert Gabriel highlighted how a photograph of the material evidence contained within a mass grave allowed campaigners to make a claim to truth, and how the apparent absence of authorship or mediation in a newspaper photograph overcame suspicions around historical representation. He also pointed to the fascination exerted by such images:

> When you read a book, you have to think whether the author is lying or not, but it's irrefutable when we view a photo of a mass grave in a newspaper, and immediately come to the conclusion that it's certain and it's serious [...]. The human race all over the world is impressed by the confrontation with death. (Gabriel, Burgos Province)

The production of images and the rich potential for new representations afforded by the mass grave was a rationale for exhumation that was widely accepted amongst the volunteer excavators, though seldom verbalised explicitly. During an interview with Araceli, a volunteer archaeologist at Las Campanas and coworker of Concha and Carmela, I asked whether the exhumation at Las Campanas was justified, since only half of the forty-six bodies had relatives who were actively involved in the

Figure 14. Cameraman filming excavation volunteer and human remains in mass grave in Villavieja.

exhumation. Araceli's rationale for the exhumation departed from one based on rights, justice, or norms surrounding the proper burial of the dead, and she rejected the necessity of the relatives' participation as a prerequisite to exhumation. However, she did not cite a rationale based on an ideological bond with the dead either. Instead, she formulated a rationale based primarily on the representational and pedagogic potential of the grave, and on the potency of the images that could be produced, saying: "Exhumation is important because there is nothing more self-evident than a mass grave."

The suggestion that the representations of the past made through the production of images of the mass grave are "self-evident" is highly problematic. The potential to manipulate and reframe the powerful photographic record made during exhumation has been illustrated by Paperno (2001) and by the contested investigations into the Katýn Forest Massacre. The lead archaeologist in Villavieja who decided that certain artefacts should remain in the grave until they had been photographed by the news media is not distorting the evidence of the grave. He has not added or changed in any way the bodies, clothing, or bullets uncovered during excavation, which are the material traces of real, and horrific, events. Nevertheless, he is an author actively engaged in image production, and his decision is based on an understanding of the aesthetic and affective affordances of bullets and clothing in conjunction with human remains. This is an illustration of the point made by Buchli and Lucas (2001) that excavation constitutes a production of the past, not simply the exposure of the neutral or natural evidence of a past hitherto concealed.

Analyses of the ethical and political problems inherent in the production and dissemination of images of human death and suffering have been undertaken by a wide range of authors, for a variety of historical and geographical contexts: Hagopian (2006), Kleinman and Kleinman (1997), and Sontag (2004) analyse photography, and in particular its occurrence in news media, while Whitehead's identification of "forensic theatre" (1990) looks at emerging trends in the representation of death and suffering in the moving images of film and television footage, in a discussion that prefigures the televisual representation of the September 11 attacks. Other authors have studied more specifically the representation of mass graves in the news media: Congram and Bruno (2007) and Crossland (2000) argue that the fascination that these images exert over the news media and their public requires a greater reflection from the archaeologists who facilitate the production of these images. Crossland notes in particular the increased occurrence of representations in response to the large-scale forensic investigation into the atrocities committed during the conflicts in former Yugoslavia: "Public interest in forensic techniques may be gauged by the prominence of reports in the popular media, especially during the 1990s, concerning the excavation of mass graves. The potential prurience of these reports has perhaps contributed to mainstream archaeology avoiding the topic" (2000, 115).

A canon of visual images has emerged in the media coverage of the exhumations in Spain, which draws on an iconography that developed during the 1990s and incorporates the media coverage of investigations into human rights abuses in Latin America, the Balkans, and, most recently, Iraq. However, the media coverage of the Spanish exhumations has its own context-specific canon of images, examples of which can be seen in Kolbert (2003) and Webster (2003). The photographs of bodies emerging from the ground are often accompanied by headlines that draw on the ready supply of metaphors for exposure and revelation, in which human remains stand for hidden truths: for example, "Spain disinters its painful past" (Kolbert 2003) or "Spain digs over painful memories" (Sharrock 2004).

In addition to showing the bodies and objects in the grave, the photographs of the exhumation disseminated in the Spanish news media also depict the excavators. This enables a visual conjunction of the youthful volunteers, the great majority of whom are university students, the elderly relatives of the dead, and the skeletonised human remains that are emerging from the grave. These generational juxtapositions communicate the duration of time that elapsed since the deaths, implicitly criticising the long wait endured by the relatives. The recurrent metaphor within ARMH's discourse that describes bodies as seeds and the idea of the lessons of the dead are also significant to an understanding of the production of media images in Spain. The youthful excavators are often depicted in intimate physical proximity or in contemplation of the remains of the dead (Renshaw 2007). These photographs are modern reworkings of the Republican cartoon "The last lesson of the schoolteacher" discussed in chapter 3. This category of photograph suggests some kind of mystical transfer between the living and the dead, and the absorption of the lessons of the dead through the intimate contact with their remains. The dissemination of these images via the news media and internet further reinforces ARMH's rationale for exhumation (for a fuller analysis of image production within the news media coverage of Spanish exhumations see Ferrándiz and Baer 2008 and Renshaw 2007).

Of key significance to this discussion is the fact that the encounters with bodies and objects described above are by no means limited to firsthand encounters by those who come to the gravesite in person. The national and international circulation of images of the bodies and objects, and also of the exhumation process itself, means that the many affordances of both skeletons and personal possessions are experienced by a much wider audience, who is free from some of the representational constraints prevailing in the immediate community in which the grave is situated. These images become divorced from the particularity of a single community and its specific network of relationships to the dead, and thus come to represent the Republican war dead in a more generalised and abstract way. Within the discursive space of the newspaper layout, images can be juxtaposed in a way that real-life encounters would not allow, conflating time, combining material from more than one geographical location, and creating new composite images or new oppositions and tensions for the viewer to decode. The media reproduction of black and white portrait photographs of the dead and close-up images of the bodies and artefacts also furnishes a repertoire, or canon, of Republican Civil War objects, which blends with imagined and remembered objects to create the kind of imaginative assemblages that both Carmen and Concha brought to their encounters with the reality of the grave.

REPRESENTATIONS OF HUMAN IDENTIFICATION

Near the end of the exhumation in Las Campanas, a public meeting was held in the town hall, chaired by Emilio Silva, the head of ARMH, and Gabriel, who has advised on several hundred ARMH exhumations. The purpose of the meeting was ostensibly to familiarise the relatives of the dead with some of the principles of forensic identification and the wider investigative process that underpinned the exhumation, particularly the investigation of archival sources. However, the way in which the past was materialised during the meeting engendered specific representations of the dead and produced particular effects on the attendees.

Gabriel, one of Spain's leading forensic anthropologists and pathologists, is highly authoritative within his discipline, yet possesses a facility for engaging with lay people on the subject of exhumation and identification. He has participated directly in over a hundred Civil War exhumations, and meticulously documents all his work. He records film footage of the exhumations as they progress and photographs all human remains and possessions, both in situ and again in the laboratory as part of his detailed forensic analysis; he uses a range of media, such as digital mapping of the grave and computer graphics, to illustrate his analysis of injury patterns or the trajectory of bullets. His forensic reports are methodically presented and highly visual, which makes them accessible to their intended audience, the relatives of the dead. He is a committed educator who circulates photographs, film footage, and reports amongst the volunteer excavators in order to develop their frame of reference and help them contextualise the material they encounter during exhumation.

He also directs a team of assistant investigators who systematically gather the existing photographs of the dead and search public archives for documents pertaining to the life and death of Republicans in the Civil War—such as military, hospital, and prison records—as well as personal archives for material such as farewell letters or last testaments written by the dead. These are all digitised and stored to aid in the scientific identification of the dead and in the wider project of reconstructing the events surrounding the deaths of Republican civilians. He has amassed thousands of meticulously recorded images, which he proactively disseminates via the internet, academic publications, media interviews and profiles of his work, and via the presentations he gives at public talks and meetings in communities throughout Spain that have solicited his help to investigate their Republican dead.

Gabriel's prolific involvement, his working practices, and his particular affinity for the importance of visual and material indices of the past, fostered perhaps by his years in a forensic role presenting scientific evidence to lay people in a jural setting, make him a pivotal figure in the materialisation of the past in my field sites. His desire for a truth commission can be read, in the light of his intuitive understanding of the existing difference in material registers, as a desire for a forum for the public display of a range of materialisations of the past: verbal, material, and visual. It is the public materialisation of the past that he believes has a "pedagogic value." In the presentations he makes throughout Spain, either in closed meetings designed to train the volunteer excavators or in well-attended public meetings intended to explain the basic principles of human identification to the relatives of the dead and the wider community, Gabriel can be said to be activating some of the "pedagogic value" of a truth commission on a microscale, using the images that he has amassed to achieve a comparable effect. Through this practice, Gabriel has been influential in the formation of an emergent ARMH canon of visual images.

Particular emphasis is placed on the photographs of the dead, as well as on archive material pertaining to their deaths, such as the movements of prisoners or execution orders. Gabriel weaves a series of connections between indices that belong to different registers in a way that is highly significant to an analysis of the effect achieved by these meetings. The forging of connections between indices that refer to the same individual while pertaining to two different material registers is an inherent part of the investigative paradigm used in human identification. The drawing out of points of comparison is inherent to the forensic gaze. A fundamental principle of achieving a positive identification of a set of human remains is the gathering of sufficient antemortem and postmortem data to draw points of comparison until either two features are found to be identical, thus proving the identity, or are found to be incompatible, thus excluding a possible identity for the remains (Byers 2005, 425).

Antemortem data are anything that originated from the dead individuals as they were in life: the fingerprints on a police file, the X-rays held by their dentist, or the buccal cells remaining on their toothbrush that can be used to generate a DNA profile, all of which could be matched to the human remains to achieve a scientific identification. General physical characteristics such as age, sex, or height derived from the detailed measurement and description of human remains can be compiled into a biological profile of the deceased, to match with whatever is known about them in life. This meticulous analysis of the bones constitutes by far the bulk of the identification process in the Spanish Civil War context, at least until genetic testing is applied. Yet the way the investigative process was presented to the relatives of the dead and the wider community at the public meeting in Las Campanas emphasised the achievement of a "match" between antemortem material indices of the dead such as photographs and the human remains and personal possessions recovered from the graves.

Two examples can be briefly described. In the first example, which refers to an identification achieved by Gabriel's investigative team, the portrait photograph of an adolescent male who looked to be between sixteen and eighteen years old was projected larger than life onto a screen in the town hall's central meeting room. This adolescent was wearing a zip-up woollen cardigan, with a prominent zipper below his throat. The portrait photograph was juxtaposed with a photograph of a rusted zipper discovered on a sternum. The zipper was then shown cleaned and in a close-up laboratory photograph to verify that it was identical to the one visible in the portrait. In the second example, a cranium with an apparently normal set of dentition was shown. In the next photograph, a gold and enamel bridge had been removed and was depicted separately. Finally, the cranium was shown without its dental prosthesis, revealing that its top incisors were missing. The individual was identified through testimonies concerning these missing teeth and the prosthesis he had worn. The whole presentation consisted of a series of comparable examples, with positive identifications achieved by triangulating a photograph or a recollection, a personal possession, and a set of human remains. It was a systematic version of the kind of interweaving that Julio attempted more haphazardly as a layman in his own community in Villavieja, as discussed in chapter 3. Both connected memories of the dead, imagined objects, and the photographs that had served as indices of the dead for sixty-five years, with the new materialisation that was happening through the exposure of buried bodies and objects.

It is important to convey the atmosphere of the public meeting in Las Campanas. It was highly charged, and there was a tangible excitement: those attending appeared to be fascinated by the projection of the images onto a large screen behind the stage in the town hall. The faces of the dead dominated the physical space, and the display of antemortem and postmortem matches as a sequence of paired images was redolent of a conjuror displaying a sequence of magical transformations. The audience appeared fascinated to the point of enchantment by the ingenuity of the forensic scientists who wove together these disparate materialisations to reconstruct an individual. Some viewers made murmurs of incredulity or surprise, and some, particularly the elderly, although transfixed, seemed more sombre and subdued, as if they were finding these acts uncanny or that enchantment disturbing.

This was a representation of the dead as discrete individuals, rendering the materiality of their pre-death existence a tangible reality, easier to imagine. The ordinariness of the mundane possessions found in the grave established visible points of similarity between the living and the dead, fostering an empathetic response. Yet it is also important to reflect on the precise affordances of this new form of materialisation, in order to identify how the projection of these images as PowerPoint slides onto the wall differs from an encounter with these same objects as they emerge from the grave. The projections were very large and dominated the meeting room. The objects had been cleaned in the laboratory prior to the close-up, high-quality photographs, and were much more instantly recognisable. In their cleaned state and with their details revealed, objects such as combs, jewellery, and false teeth and other dental prostheses appeared uncannily close to contemporary objects that were still in use amongst the living, by extension situating their owners closer to the living. However, in their cleaned state, objects such as pocket watches and jewellery had a patina from burial that spoke of their unique provenance and history.

The rendering of canonical objects retrieved from other mass graves throughout Spain in this outsized, close-up, and unmistakable form furnished the viewer with a repertoire of images through which to remember and reimagine the soil-encrusted and indistinct objects they had personally encountered as they emerged from the grave in Las Campanas. It also furnished a repertoire of images for those relatives of the dead who never saw a particular object as it emerged, but had heard that such a thing was found. In addition to this, it provided a concrete connection with the many imagined possessions of the dead, particularly the category of stolen and lost objects discussed in chapter 2, which had never been seen but had been imbued with a pivotal role in the narratives surrounding the deaths.

Throughout this presentation, the repeated demonstration of how personal possessions and portrait photographs might hold the key to unlocking the identity of human remains achieved a number of effects. The portrait photograph of the dead which had hitherto materialised the dead in a muted or censored way in the domestic space was suddenly recast as evidence, and through this series of dramatic demonstrations of ante- and postmortem matches, its detailed and specific content was emphatically brought to the foreground. The precedent set by these canonical examples raised the possibility that the photographs that families might have on display in their homes, or in family albums, might contain a uniquely individuating feature, discernible to the expert gaze, which could be matched to a feature of the skeleton or personal possessions emerging from the grave. This activated the power of the photograph to materialise the dead in a new way, as the key to conferring their identity. This possibility necessitated a reexamination of everything that was known, imagined, or remembered about the dead, and all the existing materialisations, such as photographs, letters, diaries, and military or medical records, were reclassified as antemortem data. The gathering in and study of these materialisations of the dead was given a new utilitarian imperative.

This demonstration of the power of a photograph, a personal possession, or even a feature such as a dental prosthesis to confer an identity or unique individuality to the remains of the dead had an electrifying effect on those attending the meeting. The effect must in part be situated in a culturally specific understanding of the power of both personal possessions and physical attributes to exert forms of agency, as discussed in chapters 2 and 3. The objects that were understood to elicit deadly envy, as well as the nicknames that encapsulated unique personal traits, were conceived of as both containing and activating an individual's fate. Antemortem data had the same prescient quality, possessing unique features the full significance of which may not have been discernible at the time, but was laid down for future activation. These unique affordances continue to determine the individuals' fate postmortem, determining whether their body will be identified or not. Some of the enchantment experienced by those attending this meeting might reside in this fatalistic understanding of how objects, photographs, and bodies could aid in identification, as if the minutiae of material objects and bodily traits were fulfilling a preordained purpose. Crossland (2009a) identifies the forensic investigative paradigm as working through metonymy, a part-to-whole relationship between clue and solution. She also notes that the apparent insignificance of the clue is part of its fascination. The seeming insignificance of the part (a zipper or dentures) when compared with the momentous nature of the whole (the reconstituted identity of a missing person) generates the enchantment surrounding the act of detection, as the forensic practitioner performs an alchemic transformation of the insignificant and invisible into the momentous and visible.

The large projections of portrait photographs of murdered Republicans from other locales across Spain that were shown at this meeting had their own aesthetic and affective properties, which require further analysis. Following Edwards's call to pay attention to the materiality of photographs (1999), we can say that the age of these photographs, visible in the tone and quality of the image, had an aesthetic effect that helped overcome the existing prohibitions on representations of the past: "Photographs turn the past into an object of tender regard, scrambling moral distinctions and disarming historical judgements by the generalised pathos of looking at time past" (Sontag 1979, 71). The "disarming of historical judgements" is particularly important in the Spanish context, considering how the dead had been demonised within Francoist rhetoric. The visible historical nature of these photographs, seen not only in the age of the object, but also in the style of clothes, hair, and comportment, conjured an entire epoch, while the particularity of the individual face conjured a single biography. Many of these individuals were depicted on their wedding day or with small infants in their arms, and the optimistic and future-oriented nature of these events added to the pathos of the photographs, while the depiction of these rites of passage underscored these individuals' roles as ancestors.

Domestic images also serve as a counterbalance to the "war photography" that has dominated the iconography of 1930s Spain (Renshaw 2007). Barthes's analysis (2000) of the photograph of a condemned prisoner, youthful and healthy, on the eve of his execution, resonates with the photographs of the younger Republican men. The effect of historical hindsight on the encounters with photographs of World War I soldiers has been analysed by both Fussell (1975) and Briggs (2006) as one of pathos, but also a disquieting and powerless sense of premonition. Both authors identify a type of aura in World War I photographs that depict individuals on the brink of cataclysmic or traumatic historical events, a quality shared by the images of Republicans in the early 1930s.

To conclude his presentation, Gabriel explained how both official and personal archive materials could be investigated to reconstruct the events surrounding the deaths of those in the mass grave. However, rather than selecting official records from the police, military, prisons, or hospitals, all of which his investigative team gathered assiduously, Gabriel projected the scanned images of farewell letters written by incarcerated Republicans prior to their deaths. The text was hard to decipher, but extracts were read out. The letters were addressed to the female relatives of the dead and, as discussed in previous chapters, the surviving relatives of the dead found this category of relationships deeply affecting. The sentiments expressed in the farewell letters elicited pathos in that they were not only expressions of love, but several also showed an urge to reassure and comfort the prisoners' loved ones, revealing selflessness, courage, and a protective instinct toward their families. The farewell letters were produced with the intention that they transmit the agency of the writer beyond his or her death, to achieve a posthumous connection, and this sense of connection was reactivated in the meeting. The letters reminded us that the dead were in a network of affective bonds and drew us into this network.

The inclusion of this class of material in the presentation evoked the agency of the dead more directly than the physical traces, bodies, and objects that happened to remain after death could do, and enabled a more immediate connection with the dead as intentional actors. The projection of these letters, faded and written in an outmoded style of handwriting on improvised scraps of paper, elicited a powerful emotional response from those attending the meeting and constituted a moment of collective catharsis. In the course of this presentation, the dead had been materialised through projections of larger-than-life images of their faces, their possessions, and their bones and teeth. The addition of their handwriting and the vocalisation of their farewell messages brought the meeting to a kind of saturation point in materialisation, similar to that reached at the grave edge when relatives of the dead brought portrait photographs and left messages to the dead.

It is significant that the images shown elicited strong emotions of pathos and empathetic identification also with the unknown dead from other parts of Spain. This cathartic collective and public release of emotion had been structured by a presentation of the evidential value of different materialisations of the dead through the projection of images in a public meeting. The category of "evidence" and the intense scrutiny that this category inherently demands created an intense engagement with those materialisations of the past. By structuring the meeting around the material category of evidence, this engagement had been produced apparently without authorship or mediation. The visual presentation of scientific evidence was perceived to speak for itself through the activation of some hitherto unseen detail by an expert gaze ostensibly free from aesthetic or ideological mediation.

It is certainly true that all of the objects presented had a genuine evidential value, contributing to a reconstruction of the identities of the dead and the sequence of events that befell them. The materials had been gathered meticulously and analysed objectively, and the conclusions drawn from these sources of evidence followed best disciplinary practices. Nevertheless, during this meeting there was also a production of particular representations of the past, which generated pathos and emotional catharsis. The utilitarian investigative framework helped to draw the maximum number of attendees to the meeting and to elicit their fullest engagement with its content, because it was able to circumvent the resistance amongst the relatives of the dead and the wider community to an explicit politicisation of the deaths. A discernible fascination with the technical capabilities displayed in this meeting, and the enchantment of the clue, also put the participants' emotional guard down. This circumvented the more complex resistances to a collective emotional engagement with the dead and the pathos of their deaths, which resided in the ambivalence surrounding affective bonds, uncertain knowledge of the dead, and the condition of postmemory identified in chapter 3.

These canonical images pertaining to other exhumations throughout Spain had the capacity to merge with the objects experienced firsthand in Las Campanas and to become conflated with an existing reservoir of imagined objects. The significance of the emergence of a canon of images of bodies, portrait photographs, and possessions from the unknown dead all over Spain that circulated amongst all the participants in the exhumation process lay, in part, in the capacity of this canon to mediate between the reservoir of imagined objects and bodies identified in chapters 2 and 3 and the firsthand encounters with the bodies and objects that emerged through the exhumation. The canon extended this reservoir, as the images of objects from other places could be assimilated as a repertoire of abstract templates, of pocket watches, letters, rings, zip-up cardigans, or corduroy suits, to give a more concrete material form to an imagined object. The cleaned and restored objects photographed under laboratory conditions also mediated between the pristine objects of the imagination and the soil-encrusted fragmentary objects that emerged from the grave.

The power of canonical objects to mediate between imagined objects and those experienced firsthand in the exhumation, and the significance of Gabriel's presentation, can be illustrated by a reconsideration of the example of the pencil in Concha's account of exhumation discussed in this chapter. Concha's representation of the dead was the result of a conflation of a pencil she had uncovered herself in the jacket pocket of a skeleton, the farewell letters that her grandmother recalled seeing as a young woman in the Civil War, a scene that Concha had imaginatively reconstructed, and the scanned copies of farewell letters that Concha had viewed in Gabriel's PowerPoint presentation. The interpretation of the pencil as an index of a farewell letter, and thus of a moment of parting and loss, had been shaped both by the private transmission of memory within Concha's family and by her exposure to a canon of images associated with other ARMH exhumations. Similarly, Carmela's words, quoted above, wove together the real ring from the grave (which Carmela herself had excavated and cleaned), a reflection on her grandmother's widowhood, and firsthand memories of her grandfather's personal possessions that had been kept by the grandmother as mementoes. In Carmela's words all these references were compressed into almost a single utterance, demonstrating that the materialisations of the dead that occur in the circulation of canonical images, in commemorative acts, and in the exhumation itself effectively become inseparable. The potency of this particular ring as a symbol of marriage or, more broadly, commitment, will be revisited in the next chapter, as it became a key structuring image in the closing ceremony at the end of the exhumation at Las Campanas.

EXHUMATION ACTIVATES NEW PRACTICES AROUND PHOTOGRAPHS AND MEMENTOES

The onset of the exhumation process clearly changed the way in which photographs materialised the dead in my field sites. We have already discussed how Julio's activities at the very beginning had fostered affective bonds by imbuing the relatives with a sense of bodily knowledge of the dead. In the preparatory and early stages of the exhumation, every effort was made to obtain a photograph of the presumed occupants of the mass grave. This means that the onset of the exhumation process triggered a concerted focus on the portrait of the dead. The gathering, copying, and disseminating of photographs was accompanied by speculations on the people and locales depicted and the date the photograph was taken, which constituted a high degree of verbal elaboration on the image, perhaps greater than had hitherto occurred in some households or families. Once this rupture with the old muted photograph had occurred, the use of photographs to materialise the dead took on a momentum of its own, due to the practice of bringing photographs to the gravesite for circulation and display (see also Ferrándiz and Baer 2008). An example can be seen in the photo essay by Francesc Torres (2008, 171), which captures an image of portrait photographs deposited on the soil at a gravesite.

Enlarged portrait photos, sometimes life-size, displayed by relatives of the dead or the missing have become part of an international visual language of protest against human rights abuses: the copresence of the missing with the ones who miss them encodes a narrative of absence and loss that is readily understood by the contemporary viewer, which has been rendered iconic by the format of protest created by the Mothers and Grandmothers of the Plaza de Mayo in Argentina and is frequent in comparable contexts around the world. In the protests of the Mothers of Plaza de Mayo, the photos perform particular functions: presencing the absent and forcing the viewer to engage with the reality of this category of missing people. The individuality of a human face prevents the disappeared from becoming an amorphous or anonymous category that can be rendered emotionally distant. The instinct to engage with a human face and meet its eyes, even those of a two-dimensional representation, can generate a sense of moral responsibility toward the missing individual depicted in the photograph. In this near-universal visual language of loss, a person depicted holding a photograph is immediately understood to be a person experiencing an absence, and suffering because of it.

Yet the visual language of the Mothers of Plaza de Mayo was specifically created to disrupt a public space and confront the passerby, to materialise a marginalised category of people within a central space amongst the living. As the dead are already materialised in the grave by their remains, the bringing of portrait photographs to the gravesite, in close proximity with these remains, generates an additional layer of meaning. There are many ways to interpret this action, the primary one being as a desire to humanise the skeletons in the eyes of observers, reminding them that the dead were once living individuals (as I will discuss later). Moreover, in the context of my informants' preoccupation with mourning as a fulfilment of filial duty, discussed in chapter 1, it must be considered that bringing the portraits of the dead to the grave edge would enable the individuals depicted in the photo to "witness" their own exhumation by "looking" outward from the image. Via the photograph, the dead may be called to witness the belated collective recognition of their death.

It is also possible to argue that in the context of my informants' anxieties over the unremembered body, and the use of the fathers' photographs as a place marker of paternity and legitimacy, the display of photographs in public may be understood as the production of evidence in support of a claim of ownership over a body, and therefore of one's own lineage and descent from an individual in the grave. This desire to demonstrate lineage and to counteract the "fatherless" state is best illustrated by the example of a woman who attended the exhumation of her father at another site in Burgos holding up a large family group photo. The contemporary photo of her children and grandchildren had been digitally modified to place the black and white 1930s portrait of her father in the background, presiding over his descendants. The digital manipulation of the perception of temporal boundaries to conflate or collapse time is another recurring form of postmemory practice explored by (Hirsch 1996; Hirsch and Spitzer 2006). She analyses the effect achieved by artist Shimon Attie, who projects life-size photographs of the former occupants of Berlin's Jewish quarter back onto the sites that form the original background of the photograph, and then photographs the projected figures, effectively allowing the artist and the dead to occupy the same site at the same moment. Both examples, in Berlin and Burgos, exemplify a state of postmemory in that they are attempts to use materialisations of the past to bridge unbridgeable divides. Attie's use of surviving buildings to achieve moments of spatial copresence is also comparable with Julio's suggestion that the height of one of the dead Republicans could be calculated in relation to a building still standing in the village square of Villavieja. There is an element of continuity with the display of photographs in the home prior to exhumation; however, the bringing of portrait photographs to the grave marks a rupture insofar as the marker of paternity or legitimacy that was muted and private within the domestic interior is now writ large in a busy, emotionally charged public space that may be full of strangers and outsiders. The display of photographs at the grave edge is an assertive declaration of kinship that counteracts the ambivalence and stigma that surrounded the descendants of Republicans under Franco.

The digital manipulation of photographs to bring together generations of the same family whose life spans have not in reality overlapped exhibits a similar rationale as the frequent acts of rephotography that occur during exhumation. As stated in the brief analysis of the media coverage of the exhumation, rephotography is a common practice amongst professional photographers who visit the grave. The act of rephotography generates a now iconic image of individuals holding the portrait of their dead relatives, so that both are captured within the same frame. Like digital manipulation, this unites the generations, but without the artifice of image elaboration. The result is not only a photograph that represents familial relationships but also a photograph about loss, memory, and mourning. Professional photographers visiting the gravesites occasionally arrange a more complex composition, with the relative holding a photograph of the dead in front of the exposed human remains in the grave. This photograph contains two materialisations of the dead, before and after the exhumation. On the one hand, it can be seen as a photograph about loss, which reveals more explicitly the precise nature of that loss by depicting the mass grave; on the other hand, it can also be seen as a photograph about mourning and memory that depicts the rupture produced by the exhumation and represents the exhumation as a manifestation of the relative's mourning and remembering. This representation is strongly in keeping with ARMH's rationale for exhumation (Renshaw 2007).

In addition to professional photographers, the act of rephotography is also sought by other visitors to the grave, by campaigners, and by the expert practitioners seeking to make their own records of the exhumation process. The relatives of the dead pose for these photographs and so are coauthors in their composition. The relatives of the dead also use rephotography to create mementoes of the exhumation, situating themselves alongside both portrait photographs of the dead relatives and the relatives' human remains, in the creation of complex compositions. In his ethnography of photographic practices in India, Pinney (1997) found that his interest on the display of portrait photographs in domestic interiors prompted a recurring request amongst informants to be rephotographed holding portraits of family members. The resulting image and the original would then be displayed side by side. The resulting rephotograph could then be held by another member of the family and photographed again, thus visually uniting three relatives. Pinney notes how this request to rephotograph was related to mourning the individual depicted in the original image. Pinney's analysis of this practice is very useful to an understanding of the new photographic practices activated by exhumation: "There is a powerful notion here of the translatability of an affective to a spatial proximity through rephotography, through a sort of recursive binding in of space, a representational involution, as though this photographic recuperation was capable of arresting time itself" (ibid., 168). The notion of arresting time is complex in the Spanish case, as the emerging iconography of exhumation in news media photography seeks to convey the temporality of the situation through the depiction of the elderly relatives of the dead, which highlights the long duration between the deaths and the exhumations and the passing of the last Civil War generation. In contrast, when the relatives of the dead coauthor these photographic compositions by bringing the original photographs to the grave edge and by posing in proximity to the remains, their desires are those identified by Pinney: the achievement of photographic recuperation, the assertion of an affective relation through spatial proximity, and the arresting of time itself.

In her analysis of the material practices of mourning amongst her informants, Gibson (2004) analyses reflexively the final photograph she took of her father in a hospice prior to his death. In the photograph, Gibson poses next to her father but also holds a recent ultrasound image of her unborn child in front of her pregnant abdomen. Realising that her father would not live to see the birth of his grandchild, Gibson uses precisely this kind of recursive binding to photographically configure a relationship among the three generations, arresting the passing of time that will not permit her father and child to know each other. Pinney notes this capacity of photography to reconfigure reality to accord more closely with an ideal, adding that photography is not equated with realism in his field site but rather is "prized for its capacity to make traces of persons endure, and to construct the world in a more perfect form than is possible to achieve in the hectic flow of the everyday" (1997, 149).

Gibson's photograph reconfigures reality to accord more closely with her ideal of a relationship between the three generations, but at the same time its production underscores the gap between reality and the ideal. This is the same duality that can be seen in the Spanish gravesites, in the affective and idealising representations made by relatives, and in the representations of these representational acts made by the professional photographers for dissemination in the news media.

In parallel with the changing use of photographs, after the onset of exhumation there is a discernible shift in the conceptualisation of the personal possessions of the dead as mementoes. The newly created category of objects retrieved from the grave appears to function quite differently from the limited and muted objects found in the home prior to exhumation. In more structured interviews with the relatives of the dead, I asked informants to articulate how they would feel about personal possessions recovered from the grave in conjunction with an identified body; and in particular, whether they would envisage keeping them, or would prefer to rebury the object along with the human remains. It is important to note that these conversations mainly occurred in the initial stage of the exhumation, when the precise material form that these possessions might take was not clear. The idea that personal objects might appear in the grave was clearly an exciting possibility that had not hitherto been considered. Two male informants commented that they liked the idea of having their father's watch, and that they could imagine this object being shown to their own descendants and perhaps passed down in future years. Perhaps the idea of the watch captured their imagination due to its association with both the passing and the continuity of time. Once removed from the grave and the human remains, the potential reactivation of the watch that had seemed uncanny in its capacity to function beyond its owner's death makes it an appropriate symbol of continuity. This is one of the reasons that within the repertoire of male personal possessions, the watch is an archetypal heirloom object, which may be why it came readily to my informants when the new possibility of recovered mementoes was under discussion. In the context of the atomisation and almost total breakdown of the transmission of either personal memory or longer family history between generations in my field sites, even these tentative suggestions that objects from the grave contained the potential to become a new category of heirloom was a radical shift in my informants' willingness to discuss the past with the younger generations of their family.

A more radical and original expression of the desire to possess objects retrieved from the grave was voiced, unprompted, by a female informant, Esther Montoto, during the exhumation of a mass grave in Valdediós, Asturias, in northern Spain, over the course of my initial visit to Spain (see Etxeberria et al. n.d. and Webster 2003 for discussions of this gravesite). Esther made the following comment immediately after a longer reflection on the unsatisfactory or limited capacity of photographs to materialise her father: "I want a button from his coat and the bullets that killed him. I'll frame them and put them on the wall and anyone who comes to my house will get the full story." This remark came after the opening of the grave, when both bullets and buttons were indeed present and visible to the observers.[1] A further referential layer was introduced when Esther, prevented logistically from retaining a bullet from the grave, was instead given a digital image of a retrieved bullet by Ferrándiz (see Ferrándiz 2010). Although, whether it was one from her father's body or not, she did not know.

Esther's intention to frame and display these retrieved objects situates them in relation to the portrait of her father that she already displayed, either in contrast to the photograph or as an extension to it. The conjunction of normality and horror, or the ordinary and extraordinary, is encapsulated in the pairing of button and bullet. The affordances of buttons and bullets require further analysis. Saunders (2000) has conducted an extensive analysis of the multiplicity of possible meanings accruing to matériel once it is assimilated into the domestic setting as a memento. A determining factor is whether the bullet or shell was associated with an individual's death or was a token of survival brought by a returning soldier. The choice of buttons must be analysed in the context of the decomposition of the majority of the textiles. Ash's analysis of the use of clothing as transitional objects in mourning (1996) notes how small or fragmentary items were sometimes a more effective index of the dead than large intact garments that simply emphasised the wearer's absence. Miller and Parrott (2007) report that an informant contrasted the durability of metal with the fragility and transience of textiles used as transitional objects in the process of mourning. Of significance in Esther's story is that visitors to the house will get "the full story," and presumably she envisages that such an unusual display will provoke curiosity in the viewer, thus prompting the "full story" to be told. The button and bullet might encode the beginning and the end of the story, a normal man who died a violent death. This informant envisages how objects may structure or elicit verbal elaboration and a frank account of the past, in stark contrast to the muted and censored way the photographs have materialised the past in Republican homes. The concern amongst the elderly relatives for the representational power of the objects emerging from the grave, for example their potential for display, also prefigures the tension between performative public mourning and scientific identification that will be explored in chapter 5.

CONCLUSION

The emergence of human remains in conjunction with personal possessions and ballistic debris evoked a complex range of responses and a series of different representations of the dead. The contents of the grave emerged over time, progressively revealing greater detail. The physical position of the bodies elicited a sense of uncanniness, but also enabled the expert practitioners to reconstruct the events that occurred at the site. Evidence of injury was discerned at different levels of detail by different visitors to the grave, with the expert practitioners making the most detailed reconstruction of the violence surrounding the deaths. Physical markers of injury as well as ballistic debris were read as indices of the agency and intentionality of the perpetrators. Different categories of personal possession were understood depending on their material, former function, and relation to the body, as well as on a set of imaginative associations that might be specific to this cultural and historical context—such as the pencil acting as an index of freedom of expression, or a wedding ring on a finger bone acting as an index of widowhood. The personal possessions in the grave served to humanise and individualise the dead, communicating the reality and normality of their antemortem existence. The quotidian objects, many recognisable and modern in form, engendered in the living a sense of commonality with the dead. The occurrence of everyday objects in a scene of horror suggested how extraordinary violence interrupted the ordinary biographies of the dead.

Photographs of the bodies and objects in the grave were disseminated via the news media and internet to a far wider audience. The representations of the dead afforded by these bodies and objects and the responses they elicited therefore extended far beyond the community in which the grave was located. The visual juxtaposition in the news media of participants of different ages, particularly youthful excavators, with the skeletonised remains enabled a complex representation of the pedagogic value of the bodies for the future of Spanish society.

The relatives of the dead also encountered photographs of bodies and objects in a presentation held in Las Campanas on the techniques of scientific human identification. This presentation privileged a particular approach to human identification. Rather than explaining how a detailed biological profile of the dead is assembled through observation and measurement of obscure features of the skeleton in the laboratory, the emphasis was placed on identifications achieved through antemortem data, particularly photographs, personal possessions, and letters.

The affordances of this category of evidence echo those of the objects found in the grave, although their material qualities are rendered much more visible, since they have been cleaned and photographed in the laboratory and are enlarged in a PowerPoint projection. Interestingly Torres (2008), reflecting on his own graveside photography, posits an increased risk of "aestheticisation" associated with the artefact in its cleaned state.

The presentation of these examples of human identification elicited strong emotional responses in the audience and showed the capacity of this material to foster affective bonds with the dead and produce sentiments of pathos. These examples were part of a canon of images that circulated amongst the expert practitioners and ARMH campaigners via scientific reports accessible on the internet and via public presentations across Spain. These canonical images became incorporated into imaginary assemblages alongside the objects that emerged from the grave and other remembered and imagined objects.

The exhumation activated new practices around photography and mementoes. Most striking was the practice amongst relatives of bringing photographs of the dead to the graveside. The exhumation also prompted the practice of rephotography, which entails the "recursive binding" of images of the dead, their human remains, and their living descendants. These new images were also part of the news media canon and were thus disseminated across Spain. There was an increased speculation and reflection on the possibility of personal possessions recovered from the grave to act as mementoes, potentially enabling new representations of the dead and structuring the intergenerational transmission of memory.

The materialisation of the dead through their bodies and objects in the open grave elicited powerful emotions and afforded a complex range of representations. The final dismantling of the grave and the removal of the body to achieve scientific identifications in the laboratory would be the next material transformation. After the encounter with the materialisation of the dead, the dismantling of the grave caused anxiety and triggered a new preoccupation with the construction of a more enduring materialisation in the form of a reburial. This transformation from unidentified to identified bodies, and the final transformation from visible bodies to reburied bodies, will be discussed in the following chapter.

Chapter 5

REBURIAL AND ENDURING MATERIALISATIONS OF THE DEAD

INTRODUCTION

The dismantling of the grave and the removal of the human remains and objects from my field sites for laboratory analysis triggered a period of reflection and public debate in preparation for the reburial and the construction of a new and enduring materialisation of the dead. The anxiety discernable around the dismantling of the grave revealed strong preoccupations with the creation of an enduring materialisation and divergent opinions on how the dead should be represented. The collective decision-making process surrounding the preparation for reburial brought to the fore the different rationales for undertaking the exhumation. All the capacities for personal decision-making and agency in the execution of one's personal wishes surrounding reburial and enduring materialisation were entirely contingent on the successful outcome of the scientific identification process. If one's relative was not successfully identified, but instead remained in an undifferentiated group of bodies that had proven impossible to individuate, personal preferences on reburial would have to be subsumed into a compromise with other families. The process by which compromise was achieved will be discussed in full as it had a strong bearing on the degree to which the shared experience of the exhumation process can be said to have engendered the formation of new collective identities and new networks amongst the relatives of the dead. A strong emphasis on compromise and consensus has been identified by several authors as a legacy of the democratic transition and the pact of silence. The theme of compromise and the striving for consensus in the decisions surrounding collective reburial will be explored to see how far this legacy of the "pacted" transition was challenged by the exhumation process.

I will analyse the primary structuring role that the human identification techniques described in the previous chapter ultimately played in the commemorative act in Las Campanas, in order to see to what extent they elicited affective bonds between the living and dead and activated mourning, reprising many of the effects identified in the discussion of the town hall meeting. The representation of scientific techniques in the reburial ceremony, which took the place of either political or biographical representations of the dead, is considered in the light of the critique of ARMH's "privatisation of memory" discussed in chapter 1. The repeated references within the burial ceremony to democracy and democratic values will also be related back to the divisions between the Foro por la Memoria and ARMH, with the Foro understanding the lesson of the dead in terms of the more revolutionary aspects of their leftist ideology, and forensic expert Gabriel presenting the lesson of the dead as a reinforcement of the democratic principles that are now the accepted consensus within mainstream Spanish politics.

The Removal of the Bodies

The following discussion focuses on the period after the exhumation, starting from the final lifting of the bodies that effectively dismantled the composite artefact of bodies and objects that constituted the mass grave. It is important to note that the mass grave was not excavated or recorded in strict accordance with its stratigraphic sequence: the bones and objects that emerged at each layer were cleaned around but remained in situ, pedestalled on islands of soil in order to dig down to the next layer while maintaining the coherence of each individual skeleton. To understand the way the exhumation was experienced by the participants and observers, and the resulting representations of bodies and objects, it important to consider that the grave was exposed in its entirety and kept intact during the process, including layered and commingled remains. The bodies could be said to keep possession of their objects, as even small finds that in a conventional excavation might have been recorded and then removed for safe storage were usually left in situ throughout. The grave existed as a tableau, and then changed through time as it was progressively cleaned to achieve ever greater detail and definition between skeletons. When the maximum level of definition had been achieved, the relative positions and orientation of long bones, skulls, pelvises, vertebral columns, and of artefacts such as ballistic evidence, clothing, and possessions, were recorded using a combination of drawing and digital mapping software.

It is also worth considering the effect of dismantling the grave from the perspective of how both the individual and collective identities of the dead had been perceived up until this point in the exhumation. As described above, the skeletons lay more or less in anatomical position, apart from the overlapping of bodies. In the main, the body parts were articulated correctly as physically bounded, coherent bodies. The great majority were complete and also had some recognisable, though fragmentary, clothing, particularly footwear, and personal possessions such as jewellery. The image of a complete and articulated skeleton in conjunction with clothing strongly conveyed the personhood of the skeleton. It requires little imagination to construct a representation of a living person based on an articulated and dressed skeleton. The attribution of varying degrees of personhood to the dead can be evinced both by the words of the two archaeologists Carmen and Concha, quoted in chapter 4, and by the words of the relatives who visited the gravesites. It was therefore destabilising and disorienting to see the bodies suddenly broken up into their constituent elements—limbs, digits, vertebrae, skulls, and pelvises—to be packed in separate boxes, labelled by body part. This transformation can be conceived of as a transmutation of the rematerialised bodies into rematerialised bones.

In addition to undermining the integrity of the individual body, the dismantling of the mass grave destroyed the physical basis of the collective identity of the dead. They had been removed from the site of their shared death, and from a burial they had shared for sixty-five years in intimate proximity to each other. I did not conduct interviews specifically on the theme of the dismantled grave or the removal of the bodies, but these considerations were explicitly brought up by my informants in their later reflections on the reburial, as I will discuss below. In part, I did not conduct interviews at this time precisely because it was a highly emotionally charged period amongst the excavation team, the campaigners, and the relatives, and I suggest this was due to the way the dismantling of the grave undermined the representations of the dead that had been formed over the preceding weeks. The initial exposure of the remains had felt like a rupture in the community's relationship to the past, and the emptying of the grave felt like a second rupture in the new relationship to the past that was under negotiation through the medium of the bodies. On all the exhumations I attended, I noted that the last phase of exhumation was accompanied by intense emotionality and irritability, exacerbated by exhaustion and by an anticlimactic atmosphere amongst the excavators—the consequence of a period of taxing physical and mental work and of the intense sociality engendered by the team's cohabiting for weeks. Several excavators expressed for the first time at this juncture their strong anger or bitterness at the violence that had occurred in the villages. I think these expressions of anger relate to the conjoining of missing person and human remains that all exhumations are susceptible to. Now that the bones were being packed in boxes, it was finally clear that we had gathered some bones but not brought back the dead. I observed some volunteer archaeologists become tearful, leave the grave to find places to reflect alone, or sit with others in silence.

In both Villavieja and Las Campanas, there were closing ceremonies in the evening of the last day of exhumation, when the final bodies and objects were removed from the grave. The two very different forms these acts took were revealing of the differences in the level and type of collective action and collective identity amongst the relatives of the dead that had coalesced around the exhumations at the two sites.

In Villavieja, after the last skeleton had been removed from the grave of twelve, the archaeologists returned to the site in the evening, after the siesta, and made an improvised form of libation: they took alcohol and cigarettes into the grave, poured the drink on the floor of the emptied grave, and talked to the dead, making also impromptu speeches and toasts to each other. It was unclear if their impulse was to say goodbye to the physical locale where we had worked, to say goodbye to fellow volunteers, or to say goodbye to the dead, who implicitly were felt to still occupy this space, despite the removal of their physical remains. Perhaps due to this confusion, that visit was undertaken in a simultaneously humorous and serious mood, and it was brief and unstructured, with no one taking the lead or organising the act. This was very private amongst the archaeologists, perhaps the final expression of some kind of affective bond that had developed with the gravesite. Significantly, this affective bond was articulated with an imagined presence of the dead, who in the absence of the human remains could finally be addressed and toasted, suggesting that the bones had dictated a professional or technical response, whereas the space left by their absence could finally call forth an affective response. A playful and heady atmosphere suggested a release of the emotional tension that had mounted over weeks of maintaining a professional or technical relationship with the gravesite.

Neither ARMH representatives nor relatives of the dead were present. The absence of the relatives of the dead during the final days of the exhumation was significant. The demographic profile of the community in Villavieja meant that the majority of the relatives were very elderly and insufficiently vigorous to be a strong presence who could steer the exhumation. Several of their younger descendants, the "third" generation, were too young to take responsibility for shaping the course of the exhumation and subsequent commemoration. I think the ARMH coordinators and volunteer excavators expressed an affective bond with the gravesite and the dead in Villavieja in part because their sentiments filled a ritual and affective vacuum. In Las Campanas the campaigners, expert practitioners, and volunteers would observe, while the relatives of the dead and the wider community made the primary expressions of affection and mourning. Overall, my sense was that Villavieja remained subtly more closed and resistant to the very fact of the exhumation, whereas in Las Campanas the fine political balance of the community and the personal dynamism of a few key supporters of the exhumation imbued the entire process with an air of confidence and conviction, which was fully expressed in the closing ceremony. On a practical note, the level of engagement was shaped by the fact that more than double the victims were exhumed at Las Campanas, triggering the participation of a larger network of relatives and neighbours.

Nothing formal or collective was organised at the graveside in Villavieja. That evening it was announced that there would be a dinner in honour of the volunteer archaeologists hosted by Julio and some neighbours in their *merendero*, and contributed to by some of the men in Villavieja with left-wing sympathies. These men had helped behind the scenes with logistical aspects like replacing tools or erecting tarpaulins over the grave, but were not directly related to the dead, nor active members of ARMH. The evening went from more formal speeches and votes of thanks made over dinner, to an alcohol-fuelled and anarchic trawl through the village lasting the whole night. Villavieja is famed locally for its large number of ancient wine cellars or *bodegas* cut into the hillside upon which the village is built. These are cavernous tunnels, built in part with intricate brickwork, and in part hewn out of rock. They are dark and very cold, with reverberating acoustics. The local men took the excavation team on a drinking tour of the caves, some of which connected underground in a bewildering maze. The tunnels were lit by torches and lighters, and finally the drinking continued in total darkness. The local men explained to the volunteers that the *bodega* tunnels had been occupied by the dead Republican men and that they had been a key social space to meet and plan political resistance, and that some of the dead men had even tried to hide or escape capture via the tunnels. Entering these tunnels continued the sense of spatial connection established at the site of the empty grave. The atmosphere of the cellars readily lent itself to the suggestion of a haunted space. The local men were also emphatic that the dead men had been prodigious drinkers, and that we should drink locally made wine in their honour. Republican anthems and chants were sung throughout the night. Toasts were accompanied by revolutionary slogans, curses on the rich and the Francoists of both Spain and Villavieja, albeit made in an exaggerated and self-conscious tone, and crude drinking songs and sexual jokes.

In contrast to this, the closing ceremony at the graveside in Las Campanas was a more formally orchestrated act. It had been planned by ARMH campaigners some time in advance, which placed considerable time pressure on the exhumation team as the last skeleton had to be removed by the prearranged time. All the relatives of the dead who had actively engaged with the exhumation process gathered at the grave edge at sunset, many of them bringing wreaths or bouquets with handwritten messages addressing the dead or longer typewritten texts on their feelings about exhumation. All the volunteer archaeologists and expert practitioners returned to the grave along with the local residents of Las Campanas who had supported the exhumation, making a gathering of around eighty people. It was a highly structured, decorous ceremony that spoke of a certain degree of planning. The lead archaeologist, Ernesto, took a memorial candle into the centre of the grave and lit it, before making a speech to those assembled around the edge. The last body to be excavated in great haste that day had been wearing on the bone of his ring finger what appeared to be a gold wedding band, encrusted with soil. Ernesto produced the ring and announced that in the final hours they had recovered this ring, which had struck him as a symbol of commitment and of promises made. He extrapolated from this central trope saying that the ring symbolised a promise between the living and the dead, which he then explained as the promise we had all made not to forget them, which we had demonstrated by exhuming them. He then said that the ring symbolised the promise to the relatives and wider community on the part of the archaeologists and forensic experts that they would continue working on their behalf to successfully identify the skeletons and bring them back for reburial.

Ernesto then called upon particular relatives of the dead to enter the grave with their flowers and either address the crowd with some impromptu words, or read the message attached to their wreaths. It was highly affecting to see some of my elderly informants take on the role of expressing extreme emotions in this public forum, with the grave functioning as a kind of arena, and to see them be powerfully articulate. I noted in all public gatherings that the elderly relatives of the dead had a striking physical presence, as they combined signs of age and frailty with a slightly old-fashioned physical bearing that communicated endurance and composure. The rest of the attendees who had flowers were then called upon to enter the grave and position bouquets throughout its length in the indentations left by individual skeletons. As the Las Campanas grave was in a clearing in a small stand of pines, the light at dusk was visually striking, creating long shadows over the grave. This, and the distribution of bouquets and wreathes mimicking the positions of the bodies, filled the disquieting absence left by the bodies' removal.

There was a peaceful atmosphere, as some people cried and comforted each other, or embraced and shook hands and thanked each other for their participation in the exhumation. The efficacy of this ceremony could be judged by the fact that it appeared to counter the mounting tension and anxiety I had noted over the previous days as both the skeletons and the grave were dismantled.

These two closing ceremonies were a year apart and in many ways indicate the evolution of the ARMH campaign, particularly the growth of their organisational capacities and the development of newly invented rituals to accompany key stages of exhumation. They also reflect the inherent differences between the two gravesites and the demographic and political profiles of the surrounding communities. Despite the differences in scale and formality, however, some parallels can be drawn between the two.

The first similarity is the use of material objects to structure the expression of affective bonds between the living and the dead. In Villavieja, the consumption of alcohol and cigarettes both at and in the grave, and the act of libation to share the alcohol and cigarettes with the dead, were in keeping with the unofficial and slightly rebellious spirit of the impromptu act, and the use of alcohol eased inhibitions over the expression of affective bonds that went against the disciplinary dictates of archaeology and forensic science. The implicit suggestion here was that the dead could partake in cigarettes and alcohol, clearly ascribing them an agency and intentionality that would have never been explicitly verbalised by those participating in the act of libation.

A year later, the closing ceremony in Las Campanas was much more sober and decorous, yet the lead archaeologist directing the exhumation used the wedding ring in a comparable way to structure his representation of a bilateral relationship, an undertaking of commitment between the living and the dead. This implicitly attributed agency and intentionality to the dead, as one half of the "marriage" between the past and the present. By using an object that had just emerged from the grave, emphasising its appearance just in time to structure the ceremony, Ernesto invoked the same kind of agency that was constantly ascribed to both objects and human remains by ARMH campaigners, which can be characterised as the attribution of a passive intentionality, or a dormant potentiality, awaiting discovery and activation in the future. The idea that the ring had surfaced in time to convey the idea of a promise to the assembled crowd accorded closely with ARMH's metaphor of the buried seeds, its discourse on the lessons of the dead, and the invocation of cosmic messages when describing materialisations of the past. What appeared to be an attribution of some kind of intentionality to the cosmos was in effect an attribution of agency to the past.

The elaboration upon the trope of the wedding ring was in keeping with a discourse that not only attributed intentionality to the dead, but conceived of the exhumation campaign as the activation of that intentionality. The invocation of the ring, displayed during the oration, utilised a material object in a similar way to the memory idioms analysed in chapter 2, reaching for the material as an external verification and validation of the authenticity of one's representation of the past, but also as a catalyst and structuring mechanism to engage with a past so sensitive and traumatic. The second parallel I observed was that both ceremonies employed the occupation of the grave space, filling the disquieting absence and, in the case of Las Campanas, temporarily materialising the absent dead in the form of wreaths and bouquets laid in the spaces they had occupied.

Preparing for Reburial: Individual versus Collective Burial

Among the local community and the relatives of the dead, the removal of the bodies marked the beginning of a period of more intense and focussed speculation on the possible outcomes of the identification process, particularly the likelihood of a confident identification of one's own particular relative. This accompanied a broader speculation on the final outcome of the entire exhumation. The long absence of the bodies during the laboratory phase, over a year in both field sites, elicited reflections and discussions on how the human remains would be handled upon their return from the laboratory. My informants' speculations on the identification and their planning for the eventual reburial and memorialisation of the bodies merits a detailed examination because it reveals some important preoccupations and concerns that are central to both their understanding of the process and their desired outcome of the exhumation. To outline them briefly, the key areas of preoccupation that recurred during discussions on reburial were: the relative merits of individual and collective reburial, and the significance of achieving a scientific identification; the physical location of the bodies, and in particular the significance of burial in the natal village of the dead; the desirability of burying the bodies in proximity to the graves of the relatives (wives, parents, sisters) who had mourned them; and highly conflicting opinions on the inclusion of religious rites within the reburial ceremony, including the problematising of the cemetery itself as an officially sanctioned or sacred locale.

As part of my fieldwork, I read the scientific reports on the graves, interviewed the forensic anthropologists who authored the reports, and conducted limited periods of participant observation in the two anthropology laboratories where the bodies and objects from each gravesite were taken (San Sebastian for the Villavieja bodies and Madrid for the Las Campanas bodies); however, a detailed examination of this element of the investigative process is beyond the immediate focus of this discussion. Although scientific practices within anthropology and osteology are a fertile area for theoretical interpretation (Gere 1999; Sofaer 2006), and the laboratory environment and process of scientific identification are amenable to ethnographic study (Latour and Woolgar 1986; Wagner 2008), I have chosen to focus on the way the identification process is represented, experienced, and understood within my field sites. Some of the disciplinary practices and methodologies of the laboratory phase of analysis will indeed be discussed, but primarily to investigate how the expert practitioners represented the practices of human identification to the relatives of the dead and the wider community in my field sites, both in the occasion of public meetings and as part of the emergent commemorative acts that accompanied the mass reburial of these bodies.

In Las Campanas, the expert practitioners' presentation on human identification discussed in the previous chapter elicited a powerful emotional response at the time of the meeting, but as the identification process took over a year, this unifying experience receded into the past, and I subsequently heard informants make highly divergent representations of both the technical possibility and the necessity or value of achieving scientific identifications. The speculations on human identification practices, both on the form they would take and on their probable efficacy, were strongly dependent on the value placed on the individuation of the dead. The representations of the dead made by ARMH campaigners and by the expert practitioners strongly communicated the value of the individuated dead. This push toward individuation recurred at key points in the process: in the informal conversations on bodily knowledge initiated by Julio, the representations of personal possessions in the grave, the emotionally and aesthetically compelling presentation on human identification, and in the undertaking of a binding commitment between the community and the expert practitioners to continue working upon the bodies, as expressed by Ernesto and the ring in the closing ceremony. The prioritisation of identification was also implicit in the fact that the bodies were held in a remote laboratory for over a year, and that the most enduring materialisations of the dead apart from the monolith took the form of a quasi-forensic laboratory report, the copies of which were finally disseminated. The relatives of the dead, particularly the elderly, and members of the wider community countered the push toward individuation by advancing some limited collective representations, but also by prioritising outcomes or expressing rationales for the exhumation that were not dependent on scientific identification or any kind of individuation of the bodies. These outcomes showed a preoccupation with equality of treatment and normative public mourning of the dead, results that can be successfully achieved without scientific identification. It is important to qualify these observations by asserting that, although the impetus toward individuation was implicit in the campaign and the scientific practice, no explicit direction in this sense was given to the relatives of the dead or the community as a whole. On both exhumations, but particularly in Las Campanas, a highly democratic, consultative, and collaborative approach was adopted to make decisions at all the major turning points of the long investigative process.

As seen in regard to the use of metaphors such as "dogs" and "rabbits," many informants perceived the mass grave as a manifestation of passivity. It was an affront because it was a location of the murderers' choosing, a thing of the murderers' creation and an extension of their agency and control over the dead. As a consequence, the absent bodies were conceived of as suffering an ongoing state of duress. In discussions about the location of the bodies among the relatives of the dead and the broader community, there was a striking absence of religious or cosmological references, despite the high levels of church attendance visible on Sundays, especially amongst the elderly female members of both villages. The denial of a funeral ceremony and burial in the cemetery was framed in terms of the duress or inherent injustice of the mass grave: to lie outside a cemetery was seen as a question of equality, rather than of moral or spiritual danger. In explaining the need for exhumation, relatives made comparisons with the presumed killers, the local Francoists, who had died in their beds and were buried in the village cemetery. The preoccupation with equality between victim and perpetrator and the entitlement to occupy a key symbolic or social space can be seen in the extract below:

> They equally have the right to take their *thirteen feet* and put down a bunch of flowers. If there's no ground for them in the cemetery then build a pantheon in the centre of the village and put all the names on it. (Chenco, Villavieja)

In addition to this concern with equality, informants expressed the importance of the natal village. In both Las Campanas and Villavieja, there was clear evidence that individuals from outlying hamlets and villages had been caught up in the same spate of killings and in all probability were lying in the mass grave. In Las Campanas, over half of the occupants of the grave were from small settlements in the surrounding area. There was also anxiety that there might be some unknown outsiders within the grave, especially likely in a grave the size of the one in Las Campanas, and that bodies might go to the "wrong" village. Initial discussions made it clear that the relatives who maintained any connection, through family or property, to their ancestral village perceived the optimum outcome of the exhumation as a scientific identification of their relative and an individual reburial in their particular village of origin. This, however, was attenuated by an awareness that the scientific process could not guarantee a unique identification, and that if no identification was made, some compromise location would have to be agreed upon with the other families.

My informants stressed the importance of the return of the body to their natal village through a particular idiom, namely referring to the possibility of bringing flowers to their own village cemetery, as seen in the extract from Chencho's interview above. The ability to bring a bunch of flowers to the grave was the uniform response to the question "Why exhume?" that I posed during all interviews. I had envisaged that this question would perhaps elicit thoughtful, open-ended, and varied responses. I was struck and initially disappointed by the absolute constancy with which the leaving of flowers was invoked. When I asked further questions on why flowers could not simply be left at the mass gravesite without exhuming the bodies, I received again a very similar set of responses: "to leave flowers where everyone else does," or "to leave flowers with everyone else." Later on, my field sites and my travels through Spain permitted me to experience All Saints Day, and understand the degree to which taking flowers to the dead on special days and on Sundays was a collective, ritualised, and performative act, which had to be socially visible to have its particular efficacy. The mass visits to the cemetery on All Saints Day are a phenomenon noted by other outsiders living in Spain: "Florists do their best business of the year, selling ten times as many flowers as normal. People flock to the cemeteries to honour dead parents, grandparents, and other relatives" (Tremlett 2006, 11).

My interpretation is that these uniform and formalised responses to the question "Why exhume?" can be related to the prohibition on mourning discussed in chapter 1, and the psychic violence this produces in a society in which visible mourning is linked to family honour. The occupation of the cemetery, the public, socially prescribed space for the dead, is imperative to this. The emphasis on the natal village can be understood, in part, as a focus on the site where the original atomisation and humiliation of one's family occurred, which may be belatedly countered by public mourning in the same community that once prohibited it. The formalised responses to the question "Why exhume?", making reference to collective norms such as the bringing of flowers on prescribed days rather than to personal emotions, can also be connected to the earlier discussion of unremembered fathers. The public yet unelaborated placing of flowers on a grave has an equivalence with the photograph of the father in domestic interiors, which is constantly visible yet never verbally elaborated upon. Both are normative materialisations of the relationship between the dead father and the surviving descendants.

Individual scientific identification becomes less of a pressing imperative in light of this apparent concern with the public mourning and the public reintegration of the dead into the community through their reburial in the cemetery and associated normative acts of mourning. Since this can be achieved through a collective reburial and a single large monolith or monument grouping all the names of the dead, the identification of a particular set of remains may be superfluous to the perceived "success" of the exhumation. In general, I detected amongst the relatives of the dead an apparent generational divide between the younger descendants, primarily grandchildren, who viewed identification as imperative and had particular confidence in genetic testing, and the older relatives, children of the dead, who were much more ambivalent about the necessity of achieving an individual identification. In part, this may be due to a generational divide in the general awareness and understanding of DNA analysis and forensic practices. This generational divide can also be interpreted as a shift over time from the privileging of performative acts of public mourning to a privileging of the private and "authentic" emotion of grief. This trend has been identified by Collier (1997) in her long-term ethnographic study of an Andalucían village. She describes a series of generational contrasts in mourning practices and representations of grief that closely accords with the generational divide in my field sites (ibid., 177–95). It is also worth noting that nearly all the negative representations of human identification I encountered referred to biological identification. This suggests that Gabriel's presentation and recurring elaborations on the power of photographs and possessions (rather than skeletal or genetic analyses) by campaigners and expert practitioners had some discernible impact.

The following extract from an interview with Chencho in Villavieja, who lost a father and an uncle, should be considered in this discussion. It is perhaps revealing of how Chencho conceptualises DNA analysis that at one point he calls it DNI—the acronym for the Documento National de Identidad that all Spaniards must carry—rather than ADN, the correct Spanish acronym. This may be a verbal slip or suggest some imagined conflation between the two as "official" determinants of identity:

> I do want the best for them, but that's exhuming them, burying them in a mass grave in the cemetery, and there you can leave your flowers. I can't say now "That's my uncle, my brother, my father," not now and nor can anyone. Here all that can be done is to take them out of the ground and be grateful for the fact that this has been done after sixty-six years and put them in the cemetery as is proper, and whoever wants to bring flowers can

do so. That's the most that can be done, because for me, when you ask me what feelings I have for my father? I tell you, I don't know him! All I have are some photos of him at home, so that people can say "This is your father." So when this man says "I'll pay a million pesetas to identify my uncle," he's a young man with a family. If you are going to open a grave, you'll have to do the DNI for twenty, and twenty have to be paid for. You can't just say "My uncle was very tall, test him," you can't tell these things from the bones, you have to do all the tests. (Chencho, Villavieja)

This extract unites several of the themes discussed above. Chencho asserts that a collective burial is the most appropriate solution, invoking the amount of time that has passed as part of his reasoning. He expresses the social or public significance of reburial by mentioning the flowers and calling the cemetery "proper." Chencho is quite explicit in acknowledging the lack of a personal in-life relationship with his father and the resulting absence of any visceral or compelling emotions surrounding the father's body. Chencho's lack of personal memory regarding his father appears to inform his ambivalence toward scientific identification. This reluctance or ambivalence surrounding the father's identity helps to make sense of Julio's efforts to elicit a proprietary interest in the human remains by imbuing them with a sense of physical knowledge and reassuring the relatives that an identification could be achieved. Chencho resists the fostering of new affective bonds with his father based on physical knowledge by asserting unequivocally "I don't know him!" He also alludes to the kind of muted or censored use of photography in the home that I have previously identified. He contrasts his sentiments with a "young man" in the village for whom genetic identification is an imperative. I took the allusion to the young man's family as implying that this man should be future-oriented and think of his immediate responsibilities, rather than spend significant sums of money on identifying a long-dead relative. Chencho's pragmatism over the necessity of scientific identification and his privileging of public mourning were fairly representative of the informants of his age and generation—the children rather than grandchildren of the dead—although Chencho stated it more bluntly than most of the other people. Yet, it is interesting that rather than fully asserting this position, he repeatedly emphasises the technical challenges of scientific identification, as if he had weighed up his sentiments in the face of these technical difficulties. His perception of the difficulty and expense of the scientific process of human identification both mediates the degree to which he considers it a necessity and gives him a mode of expressing his preexisting ambivalence around his knowledge of his father as an individual. He qualifies this ambivalence at the beginning of this extract with an assertion of filial duty: "I want the best for them, but…"

As a counterpoint to the ambivalence over the necessity of identification, I noted intense emotions were elicited over the subject of where the mother or wife of the dead man had themselves been buried, and speculations on whether it would now be possible to reunite these male and female relatives by burying their bodies in close proximity. Positive identification of the newly exhumed body is clearly a prerequisite to reuniting male and female relatives, and in relation to this specific goal, a few elderly informants expressed the idea that individual reburial was a more desirable outcome than collective reburial. This can be understood in terms of the constant references by my elderly informants to their own female relatives' experiences of repression and mourning identified in chapters 1 and 2. The degree of emotion elicited by this theme is clear in the extract below and in the episode that followed this conversation:

> My mother never went again to the cemetery either, because her husband was not buried there. When we brought her to live in Barcelona with us when she was getting old, we asked her, "Where do you want us to bury you?" She said, "It doesn't matter. Since I didn't bury my husband myself, I don't care anymore." We cremated her and we have her still at home.
> (Paz, Villavieja)

Shortly after recalling this conversation, during a visit with her siblings to the mass grave Paz became distraught and repeatedly expressed the wish that her mother had lived to see the exhumation. She cried out loudly for her mother in an almost childish voice, exhibiting extreme distress in a way that was highly disturbing for the onlookers and the archaeologists in the grave, several of whom broke down as well and left the gravesite. In a moving account of his fieldwork, also focussing on Civil War memory in Burgos, Fernández de Mata (2010) applies Elaine Scarry's notion of "pre-language" to describe the wracked struggle to find language that can encompass these childhood traumas. While Paz was comforted by her elderly brother and sister and other bystanders at the grave, she tearfully repeated that this process had come too late. In the case of Paz, the memory of her father was shadowy, but the memory of her mother's grief at his murder was vivid and still haunted her. This accorded with other informants who expressed the opinion that the "ideal" place for reburial would be alongside the dead man's mother, wife, or sister. This episode also finds very close parallels in examples cited by Hirsch and other authors working on postmemory (Hirsch 1996; Hirsch and Spitzer 2006).

Once the human remains had been removed to the remote laboratories outside of Burgos, and the scientific identification process was underway, more focussed planning for the eventual reburial and commemoration of the dead was set in motion. In Las Campanas, this prompted a series of meetings with varying degree of formality in which the different forms that the reburial could take were thoroughly discussed. The largest public meeting in Las Campanas was attended by around fifty relatives of the dead. It went on for two hours and I received permission by collective agreement to record it in full, provided that I maintained the anonymity of those attending. Discussion was at times heated and tense, but the meeting was an instructive opportunity to record the public expression of the preoccupations and concerns that my informants had conveyed to me in our one-to-one interviews. The meeting was challenging to follow, sometimes confrontational, sometimes circular and repetitive. Some parts were very dense with references to the local context, particularly family names and places, which have been omitted from these extracts to protect anonymity. At the start of the meeting many individuals appeared to have an entrenched position on the central importance of returning each body to its village or hamlet of origin, but over the course of the meeting, they appeared to become reconciled to the option of a collective reburial in Las Campanas. This process of compromise progressively shifted the focus from the individual to the collective identity of the dead, suggesting that my informants' evaluation of the merits of individual versus collective reburial was fluid in the face of the technical contingencies of identification and the arguments presented by their peers. The dilemma was that if the bodies were separated on the basis on identifications that would later be questioned, a situation of liminality and uncertainty akin to the mass grave would persist.

These discussions convey the kind of collective and democratic processes that are triggered in these small communities by the catalyst of exhumation, and the way individuals are called upon to evaluate competing arguments on the relative importance of individual and collective identity, personal memory, public mourning, religion, and political ideology, all mediated by their newly acquired understanding of scientific practices remote from their daily experience. The meeting in Las Campanas required participants to make public representations of all of the above in a negotiation with their peers. The act of gathering together face to face, seeing their common predicament and family histories, and realising how implicated they were in each other's decision making, may also have contributed to the shift toward a collective burial.

The key issue under discussion in the extract that follows is whether there should be a single collective reburial in Las Campanas or multiple reburials of individuals or groups in their respective villages. It is important to note that the penultimate contribution is made by Arturo, along with Eulalio a key ARMH representative in Las Campanas, who mediated the moments of confrontation but largely refrained from intervening in the debate. The named speakers are informants, while the unnamed speakers attended the meeting but did not wish to be interviewed further:

> – For me, if they don't get all the relatives one hundred per cent, for me they should stay here where they've always been buried. They've always been on the outskirts of Las Campanas, sixty-eight years they've been here, and in my opinion some bones aren't going to worry that much that they stay where they've been their whole life.

> – If they have appeared here, why do we have to separate them? We carry them in our hearts.

> – For me, if my relative is identified then I'm taking him home, if not, they stay here.

> – I heard that in Santa Cruz de la Chapela there were six, and of six, they identified four, they couldn't do the others, and they were all from that village, and they had all the information about heights and so on, and they had their photographs, but two of them were similar and they had doubts...

> – It's very difficult. It has to be through the maternal line. It has to be daughters...

> Claudia – I'm a medical doctor and I know what I'm talking about. We're talking about forty-six people, imagine the best we'll get is twenty or twenty-five identified, of the rest we'll know nothing. We cannot undertake the DNA analysis, through the maternal line, of every single one. It's not viable. What we'll get, like Arturo and Eulalio tell us, is *archaeological* identifications, based on the data we have. My grandfather is from the hamlet of Fuentes but most probably we'll know nothing of him, sixty-eight years have passed...

> – The more we try to separate them, the more problems we're going to have. If they all stay here together, then we all know.

> Arturo – The remains will come placed in boxes, one box each, they're small boxes, each box has a number on it. This is for the simple reason that one day the government may decide to pay for these identifications to be done.

> Laura's daughter – My mother is their niece... She says that if the remains are identified she wants to put them with my mother and my grandmother, who were the mother and sister of the ones who were shot. My mother thinks that for the remains to go there with the others would be better, for him, and for what she told her grandmother.

Some of these speakers appear to accept a collective reburial only if the scientific identifications fail, while others seem to suggest that a collective reburial has its own inherent merit. The first speaker thinks that a kind of relationship among the different bodies and between them and the burial place has built up over time, and with it a certain value has accrued to the location of the mass grave. The question "If they have appeared here, why should we separate them?" also suggests that there is something preordained in the location of the bodies, or that there is some value in maintaining an element of continuity between the physical location of the mass grave and that of the reburial.

It is highly significant that the inherent value of a collective reburial is represented here in terms of a common identity that has developed postmortem, in the grave, rather than in terms of the common identity that these men had shared in life as fellow Republicans, town councillors, and members of the same trade unions and political parties. It is also significant that Las Campanas is represented as the most fitting locale for reburial on the strength of an association that has accrued over time, rather than because of the mass killings that took place there. Returning to the debate between the Foro and ARMH analysed in chapter 1 on whether the exhumation could materialise memory "in its fullest sense," the discourses on the value of a collective reburial in Las Campanas make strikingly little reference to a wider memory of the dead, their biographies, the events of their death, or their ideology and values.

Two speakers in this discussion suggest that the physical positioning of the bodies is not the most significant aspect, by reminding their audience that these are only physical remains, and that "some bones aren't going to care so much." The "so much" is an interesting rhetorical device which implicitly ascribes agency to the dead, only to undermine the idea that the priorities or concerns of the dead might mirror those of the living. The other speaker situates the memories of the dead "in the heart" of the living, rather than in their remains or their burial place.

Over the course of this meeting, some of the representations made in support of a collective reburial came very close to undermining the logic of exhuming the bodies in the first place. If positive identifications were not achieved, and the bodies were not returned to their natal villages but remained in close proximity to the original mass gravesite, exhumation and reburial would have changed little in the material conditions of these bodies. I sensed that the tension surrounding this unstated challenge to the logic of exhumation was present in the meeting but never verbalised explicitly. There was an unstated consensus on the value of exhumation amongst those who had chosen to attend this meeting, based on a shared understanding of the importance of materialising the dead in order to enact formalised public mourning in the normative space of the cemetery. This indicates that the form ultimately taken by the public commemorative acts around these bodies would be central to the perceived outcome of exhumation.

The penultimate statement by Arturo, the local ARMH coordinator, is highly significant to understand the commemorative act that ultimately emerged from this planning meeting. The mention of the "boxes" refers to the standard practice that has emerged over several years of ARMH exhumations, according to which each body is placed in an individually numbered, sealed box, using the same number that has been assigned to it in the forensic report on the skeleton and its possessions. These reports contain a description of the definite and tentative identifications made through skeletal analysis, of the objects found in conjunction with the remains, and also of the bodies that have resisted even a tentative identification. The individual boxes can be placed together in a collective chamber, either a pantheon or a lined subterranean vault, preserving them for the maximum length of time by insulating them from the soil.

This practice has important ramifications for how the exhumation and reburial is experienced. In this way, a collective reburial act may be carried out while maintaining a degree of individuation through the separate boxes. This means that in the future, if a family obtains the money for genetic testing or, as suggested in the meeting in Las Campanas, the Spanish government begins to dispense grants to pay for genetic testing, only the numbered bodies that correspond to known details about the dead, documented in the forensic reports, need be disturbed from the collective burial vault. This effectively constitutes a form of storage as well as a form of burial, and the collective vault may be conceived of as a potentially temporary location. This arrangement must be situated in a local context in which it is a widely accepted funerary practice to have coffin burials followed some years later by the relocation of skeletonised remains to niches or family vaults. Since this ethnography was undertaken, access to the resources and technology for successful DNA identifications has increased significantly (see Cardoso et al. 2008), and requests for genetic testing of human remains has increased exponentially, but at the time of the public meeting, this was a more uncertain prospect.

This particular system of analysing, boxing, and labelling the dead has allowed the emergence of a normative form of reburial throughout Spain that is a synthesis of both an individual and a collective reburial. Arturo was reminding those who attended the meeting of the possibility for compromise contained within this individual-yet-collective form of burial. It meant that the families who had achieved a positive identification of their relative and those who were disappointed could participate in the same reburial ceremony and commemorate the bodies at the same site. It thus resolved potential inequalities and tensions between the families who had achieved a successful identification and those who had not. It also meant that the failure to achieve a scientific identification was no longer final or absolute but could be remedied sometime in the future. Adopting this burial form has had very significant implications for the political influence of ARMH, as it has channelled its campaign efforts and its consultations with government agencies and committees into the question of future funding of genetic testing. Referring back to the semantic discussion in chapter 3 on the collective nouns used for the dead, this particular burial form entailed turning the "disappeared" into the "unidentified," or the "unknown," as ARMH refers to them, thus maintaining the bodies as a site of active political tension or potentiality (Renshaw 2010a), similarly to Argentina's *Desaparecidos*.

This burial practice links the living and the dead in a network of biological relationships, pending confirmation through state intercession and the dispensing of state funds. It endows the relatives of the dead with a new form of biological citizenship (Rose and Novas 2004) that will provide an interesting lens through which to follow the impact of the new Historical Memory Law as it unfolds in practice. The efficacy of this material practice in achieving a particular form of political influence over the Spanish government, which may be interpreted as a biopolitical influence, will be discussed in greater detail in the conclusion.

At the meeting, the option of this burial practice appeared to offer strong grounds for compromise between those who wished to take charge of their own relative's remains and those who preferred a collective reburial. The other arguments on the inherent value of the continuity achieved by a collective burial in Las Campanas also appeared persuasive, as they attracted vocalisations and gestures of support. However, the elderly niece of one of the dead, Laura, who was in attendance at the meeting but preferred to speak through her daughter, resisted the emerging consensus by alluding to the mother and the sister of her dead uncle, reintroducing the theme of Republican female mourning. This final objection was understated, yet compressed within it was a mixture of complex emotions and affective bonds with the dead. Laura challenged the assertion of the first speaker that "some bones aren't going to care so much" by seemingly attributing a form of agency and intentionality to the dead, as reburial with his female kin "would be better for him." It was clear that Laura had made some kind of verbal undertaking in the past to her now dead grandmother, the murdered man's mother ("for what she told her grandmother"), presumably promising that she would endeavour to reunite their remains one day. This is suggestive of the kind of emotionally fraught conversations that Paz described when recalling her mother's cremation. The way this objection was voiced by Laura at the close of a long debate, and remained unchallenged, suggest that her appeal to this promise could not be contested by the other participants to the meeting.

Preparing for Reburial: Religious versus Secular Acts

As noted in the analysis of the planning meeting, very few individuals I encountered in the field questioned the normative value of the cemetery, and by extension the inherent logic underpinning the physical relocation of the bodies through the act of exhumation. The most radical formulation of this sentiment emerged during an encounter with a very elderly man who visited the exhumation of the mass grave in Valdediós, Asturias (reported on by Etxeberria et al. n.d.). He came to challenge and berate the archaeologists and said that he was a Republican who had experienced repression and, most strikingly, urged: "Don't take them to sacred ground, there's no such thing! This ground has been made sacred by the bones of these martyrs!" He was escorted some distance from the grave by the ARMH campaigners whom he continued to berate. I was frustrated in my attempts to find out who he was or establish further contact, as one of the campaigners dismissed my questions by claiming that the man was known locally for having senile dementia. I was not convinced by this characterisation, which I interpreted as a crude strategy to dismiss his critique and divert attention from a deeper consideration of the implications of his words.

This was one of the few occasions in which ARMH campaigners asserted some authority over the otherwise open and highly dynamic environment of the graveside. Their evident irritation and crude attempt to stifle the man's critique may be interpreted as a measure of the extent to which it threatened ARMH's practice as a campaign group. This elderly man's critique accorded with the sentiments expressed in the planning meeting regarding the inherent value of a collective reburial, but was significantly different in that it located this value in the shared political identity of the dead, characterised as "martyrs." This was arguably a logical extension of the rationales for collective reburial that were expressed in the planning meeting, since if both the physical locale of the mass grave and the intimate proximity of the bodies had some inherent value, then why exhume them at all? The invocation of "sacred ground" is also highly significant in this critique. Implicit in this statement is the concern that a normative reburial, particularly a religious one, will traduce the political martyrdom of the dead.

The preoccupation with continuity and the enduring relationship between the dead and a particular locale expressed in statements such as "They should stay where they've always been," and "This ground has been made sacred by the bones," indicate a preoccupation with the form that a materialisation of the dead that will last into the future should take. The critic at the graveside cited above is concerned that the enduring materialisation of the dead achieved at the end of the exhumation process will not represent the dead as fittingly or as accurately as their current materialisation. This is a concern about the multiple representations of the dead that the final result of the exhumation will permit, particularly representations in the future that may slip beyond the control of those making commemorative decisions in the present. The meaning of exhumation, of the rematerialisation of the dead through their bodies, ultimately resides in the form taken by reburial—the shift in material register between visible human remains and some more enduring materialisation that will stand in their place when the remains are once again concealed. As seen in the negative evaluation of "sacred ground" cited above, the place of Catholic imagery and ritual in the enduring materialisations of the dead was the most passionately contested question during fieldwork and in the wider debates on the relationship between exhumation and memory that have arisen since the first exhumation in 2000 (Ferrándiz 2006).

Returning to the central debates and schisms between the different groups within the Republican memory campaign outlined at the end of chapter 1, the chief critic of ARMH, Jose Maria Pedreño, claims that in the way it practices exhumation, "ARMH don't even pretend to resurrect the Historic Memory of the anti-Franco struggle [...] only the bodies." I would argue that his critique is centred not so much on the "resurrection" part of ARMH's practice as on the reburial part, and above all on the absence of explicitly political representations of the dead in the reburial ceremony. Pedreño (2004) characterises ARMH's practice as follows: "They give private treatment to those which were political murders [...] for them the important thing is the 'bones of the grandfather' and to take them to the cemetery without further consideration." As my recordings of numerous public meetings and more private discussions show, it is clearly not the case that the reburials in my field sites occurred "without further consideration," but they did occur in the absence of a political representation of the dead and sometimes with an explicitly religious content, depending on the form devised by the relatives of the dead in that particular community. That ARMH ultimately delegates decisions over reburial to the families is exactly what Pedreño objects to with the words "private" and "grandfather." His conclusion states this objection clearly: "When they died as a result of their struggle [...] they transformed themselves into the dead of us all." In Pedreño's formulation, because the collective political identity of the dead was the reason for their victimisation, this aspect of their identity becomes the defining one, overriding the affective or biological relationships they had established during their lifetime.

The most striking account of the anxieties surrounding reburial and the enduring materialisation of the dead that I heard during my fieldwork was articulated during an interview with a member of the Foro por la Memoria, Mariano, who was highly critical of the type of reburial ceremonies that ARMH organised for the bodies it exhumed:

> If you want to respect his memory, and this man was a socialist, the right thing to do is to use socialist rituals. Later the family can do whatever they want, but the collective ritual has got to be a ritual in keeping with the ideas that he professed, because he died for those ideas… This is historical revisionism. If, in a hundred years, all the dead killed by Franco are lying buried under crosses, they are going to think that they were killed for being Catholics. (Mariano, Foro campaigner, Madrid)

I was struck that Mariano, a person immersed in the immediacy and urgency of the political debates surrounding exhumation, also exhibited a keen archaeological awareness of how this material record would be interpreted in "a hundred years," when those who had created these materialisations would no longer be present to control their meaning. Writing from a museological perspective, Monegal (2008, 242) notes that while the Historical Memory Law makes provision for the compilation of oral and written sources, there is no mention whatsoever of the many material traces of the Spanish Civil War. The idea that the shape of the tombstone chosen to rebury the dead may constitute an act of "historical revisionism" shows an urgent concern for the misrepresentation of the dead. Mariano perceives the dangers created by dismantling the material record without a clear formulation of what will be materialised in its stead, a concern I detected also in some of my informants' comments on collective burial, albeit articulated less forcefully. Mariano equates two forms of materialisation that he considers to be enduring: the collective ritual, which he thinks should be a "socialist ritual," and the funerary monument, which should reflect the Republican ideology of the dead and not leave them "buried under crosses." It is significant that Mariano conceives of the public representation of the dead made during a collective ritual as an enduring one, despite the fact that it is temporally fleeting. The dominant understanding amongst all the participants to the exhumation in my field sites was that the memory of the collective reburial act, and its reprise in subsequent commemorations, constituted an enduring materialisation. Indeed, the form of the ceremony ultimately provoked greater debate than the burial location, its individual or collective form, or the funerary monument. My informants' attitude to the reburial ceremony as the opportunity to produce lasting representations was redolent of Küchler's analysis of the way Malanggan are materially transient but enduring (1999). Unlike conventional funerary architecture and monuments, which aspire to physical permanence, Malanggan endure by being witnessed and remembered by those who attend the funerary ritual. There was a notable absence of discussion over the funerary monument in Las Campanas, with the overall consensus being that the most important feature was that it had all the names and was large enough for the list of names to be legible. The other content considered important was the date and place of the deaths.

The recurring suggestion in both my field sites that clerics were in some way implicated in the deaths, either by inciting the violence or more directly by compiling the blacklists of who should be targeted, has been discussed in chapters 1 and 2, along with the strong, sometimes violent, anticlericalism that constituted a central strand of Republican ideology. In this context, it is easy to predict that strong feelings will arise around the place of religion in the reburial ceremony, and great care will be taken in negotiating related decisions and diffusing this source of tension. The extract below is from the end of the meeting in Las Campanas, when some frustration with the circular form of debate inherent in the process of group decision making became apparent. As before, the speakers known to me as informants are named. The first speaker is ARMH coordinator Arturo, who cites some examples of the ceremonial form chosen in other villages as possible precedents for Las Campanas:

Arturo – Get given the address and telephone number of every family. Once the bodies are here there is more to do than just carry them to the cemetery. In addition, each of you has got to think about what you want. In some places they made a homage in the town hall, in other places they showed a film about how each of the bodies had been identified, others went to the church. There's got to be consultation. Where will you do this?

Eulalio – It's silly but this creates problems and we don't want to have problems. That's why we need to solve this in advance.

– Over here, this lady wants a religious service. [An attendee gestures at a very old lady]

– I'm not religious but it doesn't offend me if they go to the church.

Santi – The Church killed them, their ideas weren't religious. I don't believe they would have wanted a Catholic burial.

Laura's daughter – This could offend other people, perhaps what the dead thought is not what their descendants think today. We've got to be more tolerant.

Santi – The same people always give in, and the same always win. They're going to win everything piece by piece.

Claudia – There are moments when you have to put your foot down. You have to know when you can compromise. I try not to impose anything on anybody.

Santi – They *died* to defend their ideas.

– The day of his death my father had to go along to mass so as not to offend my mother, this I recall clearly. But when they disappeared, she stopped going to mass.

– It seems to me to be a lack of respect for those in the graves.

Laura's daughter – But many of them were religious.

– They were *tolerant* of religion, even though it didn't do them any good.

Claudia – You've got fixed on the idea that we're going to be able to identify all of them.

Santi – People here are very mistaken. Me, when I speak of the dead, I speak of *all* the dead.

This phase of the planning meeting marked the first instance of reflection upon the dead as they were in life in terms of their ideas and beliefs rather than their physical attributes. It was the first time aspects of their biography were publicly considered in terms of the ideology they professed and the link between this ideology and the circumstances of their death. It is striking that even the tentative attribution of a collective identity and a collective ideology contained in the statement "The Church killed them, their ideas weren't religious," was based on a negative, an absence of religiosity, rather than on the positive presence of some other competing ideology. In this sense, the meeting in Las Campanas was very different from Mariano's explicit construction of an opposite and alternative form of commemoration contained in the statement "This man was a socialist; the right thing to do is use socialist rituals." At no point in the Las Campanas planning meeting was there any discussion of the specific political affiliations, biographies of political action, or ideologies espoused by the dead, or the suggestion that any of these traits could form the content for a new commemorative act. It must be remembered that a significant proportion of those awaiting reburial had held or run for public office under the Popular Front government and had held roles in the *casa del pueblo* and the predominant trade unions of the period. The word Republican was not used in this meeting. The characterisation of the collective identity of the dead as primarily irreligious in nature was strikingly similar to the characterisation of Republicans as godless Antichrists in Francoist discourse.

As we have seen, Pedreño stated that the goal of exhumation was to resurrect not only the bodies of the Republicans, but also "their way of thinking, their struggle, and their lives." ARMH as a campaign group devolved the power to make decisions on reburial to a democratic process amongst the families—families that had suffered atomisation and a breakdown in the transmission of memory, which means that no one within this process would make reference to the thinking, struggle, or lives of the dead. The primary opportunities that ARMH had during the exhumation process to represent the dead, at the graveside and at the meeting on identification, were used to represent the individuated dead, to foster affective bonds with them, and to represent the pathos of their deaths. It is important to highlight the three precedents presented as options by Arturo: the conventional funeral mass in the village church; the town hall homage (from the way the Spanish term *homenaje* is used within ARMH and in my field sites, it connotes a subtly more politicised form of commemorative act); and a film showing the scientific techniques and the range of materialisations used as evidence to reattribute individual identities to the dead. Between the two poles of homage or mass, the format of scientific explanation offered a third way of neutrality and compromise, attractive to those struggling with the collective decision-making process. As in the case of the human identification meeting, a film about how the bodies and objects had been analysed offered ARMH an opportunity to represent the individuated dead. It was also another opportunity to show particular materialisations of the dead and personal objects that possessed specific aesthetic and emotive properties, fostering affective bonds and eliciting a cathartic release of emotion.

A very elderly daughter of one of the dead, speaking through the friends or neighbours who had brought her to the meeting, immediately indicated her wish for a church service. The elderly lady spoke quietly to those seated with her, who then voiced her comments to the meeting. Laura, who had spoken through her daughter to express her desire to rebury the body in proximity to female relatives, also gestured her agreement. Neither of these elderly women then participated in the ensuing debate, but their presence was referred to by a younger speaker: "Perhaps what the dead thought is not what their descendants think today." The fact that some of the elderly attendees at the meeting, those perceived generationally and affectively to be "closest" to the dead, seemed to favour the church certainly conditioned the subsequent debate, in the same way that Laura's intervention appeared to be a potential stumbling block in the emerging consensus on collective reburial. This was an illustration of the paradox many immersed in the ARMH campaign struggle with: a proportion of the elderly female relatives, who generationally and affectively are closest to the dead, are the most distant ideologically, particularly as a consequence of having been immersed from an early age in Francoist schools, churches, and welfare institutions. Three representations of the religiosity of the dead emerged during the meeting: "Their ideas weren't religious"; "Many of them were religious"; "They were *tolerant.*" The final point was a reference to the coexistence of different levels of religiosity within Republicanism, and more particularly to the male concessions to female religiosity that occurred within Republican households, also expressed in the memory "My father had to go along to mass so as not to offend my mother." This history of compromise and concession creates some uncertainty about how vigorously a religious reburial should indeed be contested by the living. It is significant that the culpability of local clerics in these deaths was not expanded upon further, despite the fact that many informants spoke about it in one-to-one conversations, indicating the degree to which this was still perceived as a dangerous assertion to make in public.

Notably, the main theme during this phase of the meeting became that of tolerance and its desirability. In public discourse in Spain, both on the macro and micro scale, the themes of tolerance, compromise, and consensus have a specific meaning and significance (Aguilar 2002). The words are used in an implied opposition to the extremism of the Civil War and the dictatorship, and as an inoculation against repeating history (Desfor Edles 1998). That tolerance and compromise were invoked so early in the debate in Las Campanas is a mark of the palpable degree of tension and apprehension about confronting the past so directly and publicly after the kind of atomised silence or idiomatic encoding of memory that had dominated in these communities. The statement "They died to defend their ideas" challenged the ideals of tolerance and compromise by holding up the dead as an example and an inspiration to be courageously uncompromising in one's beliefs. These ideals were also criticised in the final comment "The same people always give in," which situated the demand for compromise in this meeting in a continuum with both the Republican defeat in the Civil War and the heavy concessions extracted from the Left during Spain's transition to democracy. The "ideology" of reconciliation at all cost, privileging compromise and a shared responsibility for the past, has been critiqued by Vinyes (2010) in a recent article for *El País*, as it results in a masking of the asymmetries and injustices of the past that may persist into the present.

This phase of the meeting was the first time I heard relatives of the dead explicitly invoke the deceased and their ideals as an inspiration for action in the present day. However, this was only a brief and limited mention, as the contingencies of human identification were once again invoked to remind those at the meeting that compromise might be a necessity, since the bodies might return as an undifferentiated collective. The meeting arrived at an angry impasse with the accusation of "intransigence" on both sides, and the final decision was to reflect, continue the discussion by telephone, and reconvene. Most people were measured and restrained in their vocalisations within this public forum, but a few left the meeting visibly angry and dissatisfied. One attendee said upon leaving: "I'll bury him in my garden rather than take him to the church."

The Reburial Ceremony in Las Campanas

On a weekend morning in late July, two years after the summer during which the bodies had been exhumed, several hundred people started to gather in Las Campanas from the surrounding villages and further afield, including the major cities of Madrid, Burgos, San Sebastian, Bilbao, and Santander. People arrived in extended family groups, with a large proportion of elderly people. They gathered in the main square outside the town hall building. The external walls of the town hall around the main entrance had been covered with black and white photographs of the dead, all the photos that had been gathered during the two-year process of investigation and exhumation. The majority were enlarged so that the faces could be clearly seen, and the images were interspersed with small pieces of text, some factual or explanatory captions and some memorial messages or notes addressing the dead. These texts were comparatively few in number and less prominent than the photographs.

It took a considerable period of time to organise the crowds into the hall, filled well beyond capacity, since there was concern that the closer relatives of the dead be positioned as close as possible to the front of the hall, and that the large proportion of elderly attendees be seated comfortably and be reassured as to how the ceremony would unfold. A proportion of the relatives, particularly the women, were dressed smartly, not in sombre colours but as if for a public or social occasion. In the preparatory phase there was an atmosphere of mounting tension and an increasing emotionality awaiting some cathartic release. The low stage at the front of the town hall was piled with forty-six boxes, which occupied it almost entirely. These were sealable plastic storage boxes, under a cubic metre in dimensions. The plastic was not visible, as each had been draped in a square of red satin. They were labelled according to the numbering system used in the investigation, but this was invisible to the audience. The sense of dissonance between the familiar municipal space of the village hall and the boxed human remains of forty-six people contributed to an extremely emotional atmosphere.

Two of my informants—supporters of ARMH from Las Campanas who had been heavily involved in the daily logistics of the exhumation, and particularly in hosting the volunteer archaeologists—made brief welcoming speeches. They gave a summary of how the exhumation had been initiated and had gained momentum within the surrounding villages, and acknowledged the funding and support from the local council and other sources. A clip of video footage of the exhumation was projected onto a large screen above the stage, thus evoking the presence of the bodies in situ alongside the boxes. This was a vivid reminder of the shared experience of the exhumation that had occurred two years before. Many of the expert practitioners from Madrid had returned to participate in the reburial ceremony, and the footage of them working on the grave reminded the audience of their participation and of the bond that they had formed and maintained with the community. It also reminded the audience of how far the process had come, of the structural distance from the mass grave to the town hall that had been bridged over the two years.

The stage was then occupied by the lead forensic anthropologist who had authored the report on the identification of the forty-six bodies, Jorge, who projected an extensive PowerPoint presentation onto the screen behind the bodies. Jorge endeavoured to explain the principles of human identification using the analysis of skeletons and objects, but in layman's terms that engaged his audience. He also had to announce which bodies had been successfully identified and which had proved impossible to identify, news that elicited a great deal of excitement and emotion. The majority of the families engaged with the exhumation process and in contact with ARMH had received a scientific report that communicated this information. However, this ceremony took in a much larger constituency, and most people were eager to hear the outcome. Also, to have the report condensed verbally and presented visually brought home its significance to the audience, even those who had been briefed, as was made evident by their emotional responses.

After running rapidly through some scientific principles on age, sex, stature, and skeletal markers of disease and injury, Jorge projected a results table showing the number assigned to each skeleton and the presumed identification, with varying degrees of certainty. Jorge's laboratory analysis represented a considerable technical achievement. Deprived of the resources of a criminal investigation and with so little antemortem data, Jorge had conducted a painstaking and systematic analysis, and by a series of logical deductions had achieved remarkable success. Nine out of forty-six bodies had been confidently identified, a further twelve had been tentatively identified, and the remaining names had been assigned the numbers of the multiple skeletons considered to be biologically "compatible" with what was known of that individual.

The projection of this slide caused a pulse of excitement around the room. I noted an elderly couple who had not participated thus far grasping each other's hands when their relative's name was announced. He appeared to be restraining his urge to go straight to the stage and find his box. The audience craned their necks to look at the boxes and see if they could discern their relative's remains. It was extremely moving to observe people experiencing the emotions raised by this encounter not simply with rematerialised bodies, but finally with a rematerialised individual, yet attempting to contain them within the behavioural confines of a public space and a collective act. Others in the audience were presumably disappointed or resigned to the fact that a tentative identification had not been possible for their relative.

The evidential basis for some of the identifications that had been achieved was then explained in detail through the rest of the slide show. The identifications were based on the matching of ante- and postmortem evidence through a triangulation between bodies, objects, and photographs, as observed during the human identification meeting described in chapter 4. The images included photographs of a pair of spectacles, a pocket watch, and some old-fashioned ceramic brackets used in 1930s electrical wiring that had been found in the pocket of an electrician. Significantly, there was a strong emphasis on images of dentition that resonated with Concha's observation: "Those teeth are just the same, they haven't changed." In the first example of the presentation of dental evidence, images of four different sets of dentition were juxtaposed, photographed from the same angle in the laboratory in order to show the lingual surface of the anterior teeth. Each exhibited the same distinctive traits of an extra cusp and a curvature of the surface known as shovelling. This is known to be an unusual but highly heritable trait in individuals of European descent, and to find three examples in this population strongly suggested that the four individuals were closely related. A father and his three oldest sons were known to be in the mass grave, an example of the wider web of relationships amongst the bodies in that site. The ages of these four bodies were a good match, and the four sets of remains exhibiting these dental traits were identified as the man and his three sons. This was followed with rapt attention. The grouping of these four sets of teeth provided a powerful metaphor for the survival of familial bonds postmortem.

In the second example, a portrait photograph of a young man was projected onto the screen. The set of his jaw and an asymmetrical bulge in his cheek suggested some kind of dental anomaly or infection. The next photograph was from the laboratory: the maxilla and mandible had been separated, cleaned of soil, and were viewed from above, and the anomaly was pointed out to the audience. The bulging cheek in the photograph of a named individual had thus been triangulated with the dental anomaly of a set of remains, and the individual's identity had been restored. Some of the attendees became tearful during this presentation, and when Jorge had finished speaking there was an outbreak of applause and thanks. The participation of Gabriel, the senior forensic anthropologist and pathologist who had made the original presentation on techniques of human identification, was acknowledged and received a thunderous applause. The applause for the identifications released much of the tension and emotion that had mounted during the presentation of the images.

The final speaker, Claudia, was one of the most articulate spokespeople for the relatives of the dead in Las Campanas. Having a medical background, she had engaged confidently with the expert practitioners and with the practicalities of identification, and had tried to act as a conduit to the other relatives. She took the stage to give a brief speech on the theme of injustice, focussing on the illegality of the killings in Las Campanas. She drew an analogy between the injustices of these deaths and the occupation of Iraq in the present day, a parallel framed in terms of the needless death of innocent civilians, and said that this was a contemporary injustice that should be resisted in the same spirit of Republicanism. This received an emphatically positive response from the audience. I did not find the historical parallel anomalous, as the same analogy between Iraqi civilians and Spanish Republicans regularly arose in conversation with my informants, who saw a clear continuum between the exhumation campaign and the contemporary antiwar campaign. (For a comparable reference to the analogies between the repression of Spanish Republicans and the occupation of Iraq see Chacón 2004, 75.)

Claudia then read the names of the identified bodies and handed the boxes to the relative or community member previously designated to carry the box of remains to the cemetery. Boxes containing unidentified remains were apportioned amongst the rest of the relatives. This was done solemnly and the atmosphere remained charged, suspenseful, and serious, seemingly in anticipation of the committal itself. Under Claudia's direction a single red rose was then placed on top of each satin-covered box. The relatives carrying boxes began to line up outside in the square in preparation for the procession through the village to the cemetery. When the rest of the audience came out into the square, the long line of forty-six red boxes, each carried by one or two relatives, made for an impressive sight. They filled the square, communicating the scale of both the killings and the reburial ceremony.

The line of relatives carrying boxes then processed through the village, followed by around one hundred of the attendees at the ceremony. The procession took a winding route that passed through the main quarters of the village. People did not come out of their houses to look at the procession nor watched it from their windows or porches, and it occurred to me that everyone in active support of the reburial ceremony was already there, while those who had chosen not to attend the event did not want to be involved in the ceremony or even acknowledge it, perhaps due to their own political or familial allegiances. The procession was therefore a powerful form of spatial occupation, dominating all the public spaces in the village for the day and filling them with incoming visitors and their vehicles. Furthermore, some of the visitors, such as the forensic experts, were high-status professionals who had travelled some distance to demonstrate their support for the relatives of the dead. Photographers and a representative of the local press were also present, showing that this gathering was sending an image of the village to the wider world. All these factors contributed to turning the reburial ceremony into a physical claim on space.

Upon arrival at the cemetery, the ceremony became temporarily fractured as the collective consensus over the sequence of events broke down. A priest was waiting in the cemetery to receive the bodies, standing by the prepared vault and newly erected monolith. My key informant, Julio, informed me that this was a young priest from a community some distance away who had been invited to officiate at this part of the ceremony due to his reputation as a liberal, "sympathetic" to the exhumation campaign. My understanding was that this same priest had officiated at other ceremonies, and that the local priest had either refused or had been rejected as ideologically unsuitable. The involvement of a priest at this juncture was designed as a compromise with those who held atheist or anticlerical sentiments, since it avoided the necessity that either the relatives of the dead or the human remains enter the church building. Yet the intended compromise was largely ineffectual, as a significant proportion of those attending refused to enter the cemetery while the priest was present, and some relatives of the dead did not wish the bodies to enter either. The result was that a large group gathered by the gates of the cemetery, smoking and making some heated but quiet anticlerical comments. Others commented more neutrally that they felt the prayers were a moment for the family only, particularly as the space around the grave was so crowded, and hung back. The priest's words were brief but conciliatory; he pronounced the standard formula used when committing a body into the ground and led a prayer around the graveside. The rest of the attendees entered once he had stopped speaking and stepped away from the grave. A short speech again on the theme of injustice was made, stating that all the dead had died defending democracy and that their democratic ideals should be upheld in the present. The names of the dead were then read off the monolith and the boxes lowered into the large burial vault.

This last phase was accompanied by a cellist who unpacked his cello and a portable chair by the grave and began to play slow and mournful classical music. When I asked who had arranged for a cellist to play during the interment, Julio said it was his idea because it was "better than songs," and made reference to the "problem with singing." In this context "better than songs" referred to a situation I had observed at several other commemorative acts and reburials, including the closing ceremony on the last day of exhumation at Las Campanas, in which some relatives attempted to lead the assembled crowd in a rendition of the *Internationale*, or the prewar workers' anthem, *La plaza de mi pueblo*, or the chant *Republican Spain, tomorrow!* Such an incident can lead to an ideological disunity amongst the attendees resulting in a sound clash of competitive singing that is far removed from the decorous ideal of a funeral service. Although I found the cellist sitting in the cemetery to be visually incongruous, the music was well played and moving. Later, during the evening's drinking, some of the volunteer archaeologists from Madrid, perhaps aware that the purpose of the cello music was to drown out the political singing and chanting, were cynical about this attempt to generate a mournful atmosphere. One punctured the attempt at pathos by commenting, "It was like *Schindler's List*." This highlighted the extent to which these newly created ceremonies are at the frontline of invented tradition and borrow from the genre markers or aesthetics of memorialisation of other historical contexts. But at the moment of lowering the boxes into the vault, I found the music solemn and dignified, and it succeeded in generating a sense of pathos.

As the last boxes were positioned in the vault, some of the organisers gestured to a young adolescent boy who stepped to the front of those assembled at the grave. He said he did not know his great-uncle but had come to know of him through the exhumation. He was very proud of him and hoped, in turn, to make him proud; he reiterated the victims' innocence and the injustice of the killings. The boy was highly emotional while speaking and struggled to complete his prepared words. This elicited a tearful response from many of those present at the graveside, and in some respects represented the peak of collective emotional catharsis during the cemetery phase of the ceremony. As the attendees started to file out of the cemetery, an elderly couple stayed by the grave haranguing the ARMH representatives who were present. Their father's name had been put on the monolith instead of their uncle's name; indeed, the wrong body was recorded as being buried there. They were extremely agitated, asking who was responsible, how it could be changed, and who would pay for the alterations. The ARMH representatives tried to defuse this so that it would not come to the attention of other attendees or spoil the emotional and reflective atmosphere amongst those who lingered in the cemetery.

The rest of the late afternoon and evening was spent drinking and chatting in the *peña*, and circulating between the two village bars buying rounds of drinks and tapas until nightfall, as the crowd became progressively smaller. Finally, there was a gathering for the inner circle of the key ARMH coordinators and the local supporters of the exhumation organised by Eulalio in his *merendero*, the summer house or cabin used for entertaining in Castilian villages. The female members of this *cuadrilla* suddenly produced an extraordinary quantity of food and alcohol prepared over the previous days. The meal went on until the early hours of the morning, and a large quantity of alcohol was consumed. A volatile atmosphere ensued, moving between triumphant and melancholic. There were heated discussions on both the future of Spain and international politics, interspersed by the impassioned singing of traditional Republican and workers' anthems, and older folk songs.

The main substance of the commemorative act within the village hall was a reprise of the public meeting discussed in the preceding chapter, but with several significant modifications and additions. Multiple materialisations of the dead were woven together producing the same kind of saturation, but with the addition of the montage of portrait photos around the door of the town hall, the physical presence of the dead in forty-six boxes on the stage, and the projection of film footage showing the exhumation's unfolding and the bodies' emerging from the ground. The similarities between the portrait photographs, skeletons, and possessions from other exhumations across Spain shown at the identification meeting and the presentation of the successful identifications from Las Campanas situated these particular bodies and objects within the canon. This fostered an awareness of commonalities with a wider network of comparable communities, pointing to a basis for a wider collective identity that transcended the boundaries of one's immediate community or geographical location. It conformed to an existing model of action and fulfilled expectations, underscoring the successful outcome of the Las Campanas exhumation.

The point at which the reburial ceremony radically departed from the identification meeting was in the presentation of the results that correlated a numbered set of remains to the name of a deceased individual. It is important to convey the emotional charge evoked by the presence of the boxes containing the bones of named and identified individuals. The announcement of the identifications and the explanation of how a subsample of these identifications had been achieved strongly reiterated the emphasis on the individual identity of the dead and the affective familial bonds between the living and dead. The power of the sequence of transformations presented at the identification meeting was greatly intensified in the reburial ceremony. The names being conferred upon the individuals were surnames familiar in the community and the family names of those present; the photographs projected above the bodies and framing the entrance to the town hall were photographs that had been an everyday presence in the domestic interiors of each family; and above all, the human remains were there at the moment in which their identity was revealed, occupying the same space as the living.

A unifying theme in ethnographies that attempt to problematise the experience of exhumation (Crossland 2002; Sant Cassia 2007) is the potential for ambiguity or misidentification. The rematerialisation of the dead may be experienced as the return of an absent person rather than the return of his or her human remains. These studies identify the potential for the relatives of the dead to conflate these two at some point in the exhumation process, perhaps as a precursor to separating them as part of the longer process of mourning. The intensity of emotion palpable in the town hall during this ceremony must be understood in this context. The ceremony created an assemblage, reuniting representations of the dead across the full range of material registers: the portrait photographs of the dead as they were in life; their possessions as indices of their everyday existence; the film and photographs of their human remains; the physical remains themselves; and the living indices of the dead, their biological descendants. Using all these available materials, the dead were rebuilt in front of those attending.

The condition of postmemory consists in trying to materialise an unremembered past so that it can be mourned. In Spain this condition of postmemory consists of the attempt to bridge an unbridgeable gulf in lost knowledge of the dead. The dramatic revelation of the particular kind of biological and material knowledge of the dead that constitutes scientific human identification is experienced, at least temporarily, as a bridging of that postmemory gulf. At the moment of this highly public revelation of the newly assigned identities, the transformation from anonymous to identified remains is experienced as the reintroduction of the unremembered person. In this postmemory context, the ceremony must not only act as the catalyst for a public expression of mourning, but also activate the sentiment of mourning itself through the reiteration of affective bonds with an intensely experienced materialisation of the deceased. In the cemetery, the great-nephew stated that he did not know his relative, and that until recently he did not know *of* his relative, but that he had come to the realisation that he felt an affective bond with his great-uncle. He also affirmed that he had absorbed an example or "lesson" from him by saying that he felt pride in his great-uncle as a defender of democracy. The spontaneous expression of familial bonds in the cemetery by the great-nephew, the intense emotionality that accompanied it, and the degree to which it elicited a cathartic release of emotion amongst many of those present are all markers of the efficacy of this ceremony as a catalyst for mourning.

It is also important to reiterate that the presentation of scientific evidence was the dominant structuring activity of the ceremony that occurred in the town hall, and to consider the representations that were *not* made as a result. The expert practitioner and the evidence he presented occupied the stage longer than the other speakers. This filled the time and space that might conventionally be allotted to a eulogy in an individual funeral service. The background investigations surrounding the exhumation in Las Campanas had gathered through archival and oral sources a significant amount of biographical information on the dead, their professions, family relationships, and political activities. However, there were no verbal "portraits" or narratives of the dead during the ceremony comparable to a eulogy. There was no representation of the words of the elderly relatives expressing affective sentiments for the dead or recalling them firsthand or through transmitted memories. Despite the fact that such a large gathering may have been overwhelming to the oldest participants, their written or recorded words could have been included. The experiences of the mothers, sisters, and partners of the dead so often evoked by my elderly informants in the accounts I recorded during fieldwork were not represented in the ceremony. The investigation had also reconstructed the events surrounding the deaths, the periods of arrest and incarceration, but they were not mentioned in the ceremony. The narrative focussed on the reconstruction of identities rather than on a sequence of events. An alternative emphasis on individual memories and verbal representations of the dead would have revealed the reality of the postmemory state—that very few of those attending had firsthand or even transmitted memories of the dead. This absence is striking and highlights the significance of the materiality of evidence. The bodies and objects uncovered in the grave are accessible to all those who have attended the exhumation or the ceremony: a personal or privileged knowledge of the dead is not a precondition for engaging with these remains or forming a representation of the deceased in response to it. In postmemory terms, these bodies and objects constitute materials to assemble, and they construct a kind of memory of the dead. The ceremony clearly necessitates a public representation of the dead, and this detailed elaboration upon the material remains fills the representational vacuum that results from the absence of memory. Furthermore, by appearing to be unmediated and without authorship, the presentation of material evidence could overcome entrenched resistance and suspicion over the authoring of representations of the past in this context, and the persistent fear that surrounds the making of such representations in public.

An examination how the political biographies of the dead were presented during the reburial ceremony reveals common themes of democracy, justice, legitimacy, and legality. The representation of the dead as dying in the defence of a legitimately elected government was made three times during the ceremony: by Claudia, by the great-nephew, and by the enduring materialisation of the epitaph on the monolith. The characterisation of the political biography of the dead as primarily defined by their defence of a democratically elected government following Franco's instigation of a military uprising in 1936 is a highly selective or abbreviated version of the political activities and broader ideology of the dead. The privileging of democracy and the verbal references to justice and legitimacy echoed the emphasis placed on the key values of tolerance and compromise during the planning meeting, in that they situated these dead firmly in the system of core values and symbols created during the post-Franco transition to democracy (Desfor Edles 1995, 1998). Moreover, the parallels between Iraq and 1930s Spain in Claudia's speech were drawn with very broad strokes around the themes of illegal military action, illegitimate rule, rights to self-determination, and violence against a civilian population. In this context, opposition to the occupation of Iraq stood for a prodemocracy, antimilitarist position.

It cannot be overstated how important the core values of democracy, tolerance, and compromise are in everyday discourse in contemporary Spain. The words recur with remarkable frequency in any kind of debate on the micro or macro scale, be it amongst politicians, media commentators, or at a social gathering. In public meetings, even in informal settings, these values are invoked whenever differences of opinion arise. In this respect, the planning meeting in Las Campanas was highly representative. These core values were reached for whenever discussions turned to a theme that might transgress the pact of silence, particularly discussions about the past. In my interviews in Las Campanas and Villavieja, I noted the tendency of my informants to mention democracy near the end, or after the formal interview had finished. The statement was one of self-reassurance: "In a democracy we can say these things," or "Now we are more tolerant." Democracy, tolerance, and compromise were inserted into the discourse when individuals transgressed the pact of silence or when they disagreed with one another, as if to reiterate their commitment to shared values and make their verbal transgression less destabilising.

As with the planning meeting, also in the case of the reburial ceremony an analysis of the political content that went unrepresented is as significant as an analysis of what was represented. It is true that the Republican Popular Front government was democratically elected, but it was perhaps of greater relevance to the onset of the Spanish

Civil War that this was a democratically elected government pursuing a programme of revolutionary change in social relations and economic redistribution, goals that had also been pursued throughout the 1930s, on the micro scale, by those who were killed. When analysing the significance of representing the dead as "killed for defending a democratically elected government," it is useful to reflect on the significance of the alternative representations that were not made, for example "killed for pursuing a redistribution of power and resources within their communities." This alternative representation, with its implicit critique of Spain, and particularly Las Campanas, in the 1930s, would have been highly discomforting and would have had complex repercussions, potentially engendering a critique of present day Spanish society in comparison to the 1930s. This comparison with the present could have revealed points of continuity in the distribution of power and resources, and points of divergence in the levels of organised political opposition to the status quo. The act of comparison itself would have been highly transgressive within the post-transition hegemony of consensus, designed to maintain a safe structural distance between the 1930s and the present. The only permissible comparisons in public discourse were between the affluence of the present and the *miseria* of the prewar years. The emphasis on a prodemocracy, antimilitarist stance reiterated the core values of the post-transition consensus in a ceremony that marked the culmination of a process ostensibly carried out to produce a rupture in the pact of silence. Invoking the occupation of Iraq appealed to the widest possible base of a shared leftist/liberal sentiment amongst the attendees, evoking a broadly defined leftist heritage without exposing the points of tension and political divergence amongst the living and between the living and the dead. The temporal and geographical distance of Iraq circumvented the anxiety and tension experienced, in particular by the elderly participants, at the potential rematerialisation of the polarising politics of the past.

The other key structuring act of the ceremony was the winding procession of the boxes through the village streets. Within the particular cultural understanding of public and private space discussed in chapter 1, being observed while undertaking a visible action was a form of defiant spatial occupation (Gilmore 1987). Given the history of surveillance and atomisation of these Spanish villages, the collective occupation of public space had a political charge. There was a self-conscious atmosphere of defiance and pride amongst many of the participants during this most public and visible phase of the ceremony, notable in their physical attitude and facial expressions. In his description of the reburial of a Republican woman called Virtudes de la Puente along with a group of other female Republicans exhumed in Poyales del Hoyo in Avila,

Tremlett makes a similar observation, calling the procession a "parade" and thus conveying the element of pride and even display:

> With the church bells ringing, the coffins had been carried around the village's narrow streets. It was a symbolic act—the first time the losers of the war that had ended more than six decades ago had paraded their dead in Poyales del Hoyo [...]. The grandson of Virtudes, now a Socialist village councillor, puffed his chest out and held his head high as a local right-winger walked past. "He knows what I'm thinking. This is our moment," he told me. (2006, 12)

Occupying the town hall, the main square, and every street on the way to the cemetery, the participants to the procession enacted a physical reversal of the spatial marginalisation in a mass grave at the edge of the village, and of the structural distance subsequently imposed. The proud and solemn procession of the human remains also constituted a counteraction to the raucous and humiliating procession of Republican women during the period of "terror and *fiesta*." In my experience the procession represented the truly political content of the ceremony, making reference to the broader power relations underlying these deaths via the microcosm of village spatial politics. This highly visible form of spatial claim equated the right to occupy village space with the right to exist. The simple reiteration of the right of this group of people and their descendants to exist was a fundamental challenge to the logic of "uprooting" that underlay these killings. Self-consciously public, this procession was a challenge to the prevailing power structures in the village and to prevailing norms of conduct that privileged secrecy or clandestinity. In this context, the procession had an immediate and concrete relevance to the behavioural norms firmly situated in the local, as opposed to the somewhat abstract references to democracy and the distancing effect of the Iraq analogy. The rich potential of a spatial analysis of the exhumation process in my field sites will be returned to in the concluding chapter.

CONCLUSION

The powerful and heartfelt representation of both the individual and the familial identity of the dead contrasted with the seemingly self-censored representation of their political identities, which conformed to the constraints that were a legacy of the pact of silence. The continuing presence of these constraints sheds light on the role played by human identification in the ceremony. In the planning meeting described in chapter 4, a "film about how the bodies were identified" was offered as a third way between homage and Mass. The compromise ceremony that was finally enacted in Las Campanas, which avoided the physical locale of the church but included a priest and a Christian committal, shows that this suggestion of a third way early in the planning stage was indeed necessary and prescient. The divisions triggered by the priest's presence at the cemetery threatened to make visible the cracks in the collective identity amongst those participating, despite the highly unifying act of the collective public procession through the village immediately preceding the arrival at the cemetery gates. The deployment of a cellist playing wordless classical music, when compared with the enthusiastic singing of political anthems in the privacy of Eulalio's *merendero*, further underlines the perceived necessity not to jeopardise the consensus that had been achieved between the diverse participants in this public and collective ceremony.

The materialisation of the dead through the presentation of forensic evidence had a close structural equivalent in the wordless classical music played at the graveside. It was ostensibly ideologically neutral and free of transgressive content, and therefore able to fill a representational vacuum; but it also possessed aesthetic affordances that underscored pathos and elicited emotion. The perceived absence of authorship or mediation in the presentation of forensic evidence further defuse the risk of making a transgressive representation. The representations emerging from this particular materialisation of the dead overcame postmemory long enough to activate mourning, the cathartic release of emotions, and enduring sentiments of affective familial bonds. The reburial ceremony presented the paradoxical necessity to break the pact of silence, but only to a certain extent. A representation of the dead was clearly required within the ceremony, but it was a constrained representation that maintained the hegemony of consensus. The materialisation of the dead via the forensic evidence used in human identification filled this representational vacuum. Comparably, the procession through the village was the moment in which the political significance of the exhumation process, its potential impact on power relations in the community, and the collective identity of the dead were rendered highly visible. The public procession to the cemetery was wordless, a purely physical performance combining the bodily actions of the living and the physical remains of the dead. Because any visibly authored or mediated public representation of the dead was still too fraught an undertaking, this form of public, spatial materialisation took its place.

The starting point for this ethnography was the identification of a rupture in Spanish memory politics since the first exhumation in 2000, with a proliferation of representations of the traumatic past that seemed able to break the pact of silence. My ethnographic study of these two field sites suggest that only a partial break with these prohibitions on representation has occurred during the exhumation process, and that significant points of continuity can still be identified, particularly in the enduring materialisation of the past produced during the reburial ceremony in Las Campanas. The conclusion will assess these points of rupture and continuity in the way the dead are represented. It is necessary to reinsert my particular field sites in the nationwide context, in order to understand if, and how, the replication of similar exhumation processes in thousands of communities across Spain since 2000 has achieved a rupture in Spanish memory politics.

Conclusion

The different rationales for undertaking a process of exhumation, identification, and reburial of the dead can be divided into three broad categories: the gathering of evidence under the auspices of some centralised authority, intended for a hearing, tribunal, or report that will construct and disseminate an authorised version of the traumatic past; the expression of an affective, often familial, bond between living and dead individuals; and the expression of a bond based on a shared collective identity, be it nationality, ethnicity, or ideology. These categories are analytical distinctions, and exhumations may involve a combination of the multiple, even conflicting, rationales of the different participants. In the case of Spanish Republicans, the attribution of any of these rationales is complex and potentially problematic in light of the way the dead have been represented during the sixty-five-year period prior to the commencement of the exhumations.

As described in chapter 1, the extreme violence of the Civil War and the repressive measures in place during the dictatorship produced a condition of atomisation, particularly amongst Republican families, which effectively dismantled the Republican memory community and resulted in a breakdown in the transmission of the memories of the dead, including memories of their personal and political biographies. The Francoist rhetoric, positing the biological transmission or heritability of the Republican identity, problematised the representation of enduring familial bonds with the dead. The maintenance of these bonds was further undermined by prohibitions on public mourning, which is essential to the expression of legitimacy and family identity in these communities. These repressive acts, and particularly the examples of gendered violence against the female relatives of the dead, served to inculcate fear and shame.

Chapter 2 looked at the Republican memory idioms to demonstrate the complexities of representing the past in my field. These memory idioms countered the Francoist discourse primarily by challenging its representation of the relative morality of victim and perpetrator, or by making a claim of exceptionality and innocence for one's own particular relative. None of these idioms elaborated on the political identity or biographies of the dead, and none explicitly acknowledged the political motives underlying the majority of the killings that occurred in these communities. They did not identify the logic of Francoist violence nor challenged it explicitly. The use of material objects and material descriptions to structure these narratives shows the importance of materiality in contexts in which the representation of the past is highly fraught.

The emphasis on the aftermath of these killings, particularly on the struggles of the surviving wives and mothers of the dead men, was also highly significant. It indicated a condition of postmemory amongst my elderly informants, whose early lives had been dominated by an awareness of the depth of mourning and loss experienced by these women—something they could not fully share due both to their young age during the war and to the subsequent breakdown in the transmission of memory. This condition is further analysed in chapter 3 in a discussion of the unremembered father, the absence of bodily knowledge, and the muted or censored presence of photographs and mementoes in the home. Overall, this demonstrates the extent to which both affective or familial and ideological or collective bonds between the living and the dead were highly problematic in my field sites.

The transition to democracy after Franco's death in 1975 was based on a process of consensus building that demanded the creation and maintainance of a structural distance between the new democratic state and the traumatic past of war and dictatorship. This distance was perpetuated through the pact of silence or amnesia that permeated all areas of discourse, public and private. In this hegemony of consensus, there were strong prohibitions on making any political representations of the past, on both the micro and macro level. This included representations of the Republican ideology, the political biographies of the Republican dead, and the events surrounding their deaths. In this climate, political representations of the dead were judged to be polarising and backward looking, and were experienced as potentially threatening and destabilising to social cohesion, be it on a community or nationwide scale. The exhumation campaign begun in 2000 sought to counteract the sixty-five years of atomisation and amnesia and create a discursive space in which the prohibitions on the representation of the past could be lifted.

The ARMH campaign group was able to circumvent those prohibitions by situating the rationale for exhumation in the familial bond, affective and biological, between the living and the dead, thus privileging the individual identity of the killed Republicans. The privileging of the private and personal dimension of exhumation, and the insistence on locating and reburying the dead in order to achieve proper mourning and psychological closure, were a very difficult rationale for potential critics to oppose. This also helped to overcome the enduring fears of the relatives of the dead, wary of participating in acts that could be construed as divisive, partisan, or "provocative" to right-wing opinion. The privileging of individual identity and familial bonds shaped the exhumation practice of ARMH, as this required a scientific analysis of the bodies and focussed on the individuating potential of bodies and objects in the grave. This approach was also key to the momentum and success of ARMH's campaign. This investigative paradigm was perceived to be free from authorship or mediation and the scientific practices conferred an aura of objectivity, further deflecting suspicions that exhumation would entail a political representation of the dead. However, the repeated shifts in the material register that occurred throughout the exhumation process created multiple opportunities for different representations of the dead to be made by a wide range of participants. The bodies and objects emerging from the grave, particularly when brought together in assemblages, framed, and selected, allowed powerful representations to be made, though still without apparent authorship or mediation.

The materialisation of bodies in conjunction with their personal possessions has been analysed in chapter 4. The encounters with these materialisations elicited strong reactions in the living. The personal possessions of the dead enabled a representation of their antemortem existence that underscored the humanity and normality of the dead, thus countering the dehumanising characterisation of the Republicans within Francoist rhetoric. These mundane objects, in conjunction with the injured bodies, emphasised the interjection of horror into the everyday lives of the dead. The remarkable preservation of some of the objects and their similarity to objects still used in the present generated a common ground between the living and the dead and underscored the temporal proximity of these deaths, despite the "archaeological" appearance of skeletonised remains. Some objects had a particular physical intimacy and thus a particular power to evoke the body as it was in life, such as shoes that had retained the shape of the wearer's feet, or grooming items and spectacles made for bodily tissues now decayed. Watches were associated with temporality and mortality. Wedding rings served as indices of networks of affective and familial relationships left behind by the dead. One informant identified a pencil as an index of agency and intentionality, specifically the freedom of expression.

These material affordances of bodies and objects could foster affective bonds amongst those who had never known the dead. Amongst the elderly children of the dead, they could break down resistance and ambivalence toward ARMH's affective representation of the dead. The dead were materialised through their bodies and objects at key points in the exhumation process, as identified in chapters 4 and 5: at the grave edge; in the presentation of the scientific process of human identification; and in the final reburial ceremony in Las Campanas. These materialisations activated new practices around photography that seemed to follow the logic of "recursive binding" and "proximal empowerment" identified by Pinney (1997). The exhumation process also activated new reflections on the mementoes and speculations on the possibility of new mementoes coming from the grave. The explanation of the investigative and human identification processes in my field sites achieved a particular effect through its emphasis on the comparison of ante- and postmortem data, which entailed the binding together of the existing materialisations of the dead, above all photographs, and the human remains. It located the power of individuation in photographs and personal possessions, mirroring the culturally specific understandings of material culture in my field sites—particularly the form of agency attributed to objects that are thought to contain and activate an individual's fate.

The reburial ceremony in Las Campanas was primarily structured around the revelation of the identities of the dead and the explanation of the wider process of investigation and scientific analysis. The layering of multiple materialisations of the dead across different material registers achieved an effect of saturation. The dead were effectively rebuilt in order to be mourned, and their presence was experienced with great intensity. The dramatic moment in which the identities of the dead were revealed, and their transformation from undifferentiated bodies to named individuals, dramatically reinserted the dead into a network of relationships amongst the living.

Despite ARMH's focus on the the scientific identification of individual remains, for some of the most elderly descendants of the dead familial bonds were primarily expressed through a normative and formalised public mourning. This did not require the scientific identification of human remains nor the separation of a single body from the collective, but only the assurance that one's relative was amongst the others and therefore could be reburied as part of that group in the cemetery, in the normative locale for public mourning. This ambivalence toward scientific identification and the emphasis on collective public mourning, analysed in chapter 5, can be interpreted in terms of the significance of public mourning to family honour and legitimacy, the history of repressed mourning, and the inculcation of shame amongst Republican families. However, the representations of scientific identification and of the individualised dead in both the explanatory meeting and the reburial ceremony seemed highly effective in overcoming this resistance to the necessity of individualising the body.

Materialisations of the dead such as bodies, objects, and photographs are experienced not only by those who encounter the grave directly but also by a wider audience. They are the focus of unprecedented levels of news media interest and coverage. An intense production of images accompanies the exhumation process, primarily through photographs and the recording of documentaries and news films, but also through a range of visual media. The practice of photography at the grave edge suggests that an iconography of exhumation has emerged in Spain, borrowing heavily from the precedents established in the coverage of disappearances and exhumations around the world. Practices of recursive binding—rephotographing the relatives holding portraits of the dead while standing in proximity to the human remains—are dominant in this emergent iconography. The proximity of youthful investigators and elderly relatives to the human remains also affords a representation of the transmission of memory between generations and the passing of lessons from the past to the future, and implicitly marks the time that has elapsed between the war and the exhumations.

In addition to media and artistic representations, the ARMH campaign has assembled a collection of canonical images of bodies, personal possessions, and photographs of the dead, as the number of exhumations has increased exponentially. This canon circulates amongst expert practitioners, campaign leaders, and the wider network of campaign coordinators and supporters in communities throughout Spain. This occurs primarily through the internet, via blogs and photo sharing sites, the galleries on the ARMH website, and the detailed scientific and historical reports prepared after the exhumations and accessible online. The canonical images are also shown in public meetings that explain aspects of the exhumation and identification process in communities throughout Spain that are undergoing the exhumation process or considering it, and are used to demonstrate how exhumation and identification was successfully achieved in other communities. In addition to serving as a precedent, the presentation of canonical images provides a repertoire that gives material form to imagined and remembered objects. The conflation into imaginative assemblages of the objects encountered firsthand during exhumation and those remembered from the past or featured in transmitted memories demonstrates the importance of canonical objects to construct interpretative frameworks and assimilate what is encountered in the grave. Overall, the extent to which the encounters with these bodies and objects are reproduced countless times via the news media and the internet, far from the particular community in which the mass grave is situated, is pivotal to understand the rupture that occured in Spanish memory politics since 2000.

The exhumation also creates the possibility of genetic testing to achieve a positive identification of a body. This plays a potentially significant role in fostering affective bonds between the living and the dead. The matching of DNA samples effectively locates the basis for the identity of the dead in their familial relationship to the living, emphasising the aspect of biological heritability that was problematised by the Francoist rhetoric on the heritability of the Red identity. In my field sites, DNA analysis was presented by ARMH as the second phase of human identification, postponed until the first phase of the laboratory analysis of bodies and objects had been completed. The future possibility of genetic testing strongly shaped the collective decision process surrounding reburial and the form it would take, which would ultimately be a hybrid between an individual and a collective reburial. The potentiality contained within the body as a site of future scientific work may prove significant in determining the direction and success of the ARMH campaign.

However, as outlined in chapter 1, the capacity of ARMH's practice to engender a rupture in the memory politics of particular communities has been radically questioned by a rival organisation within the Republican memory campaign. Foro por la Memoria believes that exhumation is an opportunity to represent the political identities of the dead, their biographies of political action, and their ideology. They believe that the rationale for exhumation should be located in the collective identity of the dead as participants and adherents to a broad spectrum of left-wing politics. The bond between the living and the dead should be conceived of as a shared ideology, and should be actively fostered amongst the living. The Republican dead represent the Left's shared political heritage rather than particular individuals' ancestors: this is why members of the Foro describe ARMH's privileging of affective and familial bonds as a "privatisation of memory." The lesson of the dead for the living is the model of political action presented by the Left during the 1930s. The aims of the Foro campaign are to galvanise and strengthen the Left through this shared heritage and draw people into leftist politics by fostering a wider awareness of the history of Republican Spain, using the intense media coverage of exhumation as a means to further this goal. They also seek to foster a wider awareness of the violence and brutality of the Francoist regime, thus provoking a more critical assessment of the dictatorship and, by extension, a more critical perspective on the Right in contemporary Spanish politics. For the Foro, the explicit goal of a Republican memory campaign should be to achieve a hegemonic shift to the Left.

An analysis of the way in which the ideology of the dead was represented during the reburial ceremony and the planning phase that preceded it allows us to assess the relevance of the Foro por la Memoria's critique. At the heart of this critique is the claim that ARMH makes no representation of the political identity of the dead. The charge is that despite the often extensive archival investigations conducted around the exhumation, ARMH does not go on to disseminate the information they have gathered about the political biographies of the dead—including features such as trade union membership, political party membership, strike participation, the running of organisations and institutions such as the *casa del pueblo*, and the holding of public office. In both Villavieja and Las Campanas, a significant proportion of the dead held public office as mayors or town councillors at the time of their death. These aspects of their biographies were not explicitly represented or verbalised in any public forum over the course of the exhumation process.

In the planning meeting in preparation for the reburial ceremony in Las Campanas, there was a debate on the inclusion of religious content. This discussion included the public acknowledgement of the atheism and even anticlericalism of the dead, and more dramatically, a public reiteration of the charge that local clergy were implicated in the killings, a belief widely held in my field sites. At first sight this discussion would appear to be the opening of a discursive space in which to discuss the motivation behind these killings and the ideology and political biographies of the dead, thus creating a rupture in the pact of silence in the village. However, the existing prohibitions on the political representation of the dead were maintained, and the ideology of the dead was presented in terms of a negative, as "non religious." No representations of positive alternative ideologies were made and none of those present in the meeting, including the ARMH campaign coordinators, suggested an alternative symbolic content for the ceremony, not even the Republican tricolour flag to represent the government in which many of these men held public office. In contrast to this, Foro por la Memoria included Republican flags and anthems as part of the reburial ceremonies that it coordinated. As part of his critique of ARMH Mariano, from the Foro por la Memoria, emphasised the necessity for "socialist rituals": it is important to note that in my experience of ARMH commemorative acts throughout Spain, elements of socialist ritual, particularly flags, anthems, and slogans were clearly present, but they were absent in Las Campanas. ARMH does not have a coherent approach to the political content of commemoration, as decision making is devolved to the communities and families concerned, which is arguably a marker of the democratic, grassroots, family-led nature of the organisation.

As I discussed in chapter 5, when the discussion of religious content in the planning meeting verged on open confrontation, the tension was defused by invoking compromise and tolerance and, most significantly, by discussing whether the dead themselves had been tolerant. During the reburial ceremony, the representation of the political biography and ideology of the dead was selective, focussing solely on their role as defenders of democratic principles. The redistribution of economic and social power achieved by the Popular Front government, the aspects of their agenda that for that period constituted radically progressive, even revolutionary change, and the backdrop of class antagonism were not represented. The narrative constructed around these individuals was that they died to defend a democratically elected government. Democracy, tolerance, and compromise are the core values of the hegemony of consensus, a unifying force in Spanish society since the transition to democracy. They are frequently invoked during discussions experienced as destabilising or potentially divisive. They are accorded primary importance as antidotes to political polarisation and are seen as a safeguard against a return to Spain's traumatic political past. In this way, the representation of the dead in terms of the core values of the transition rather than of the revolutionary politics of the 1930s appears to uphold, rather than rupture, the prohibition on political representations of the past that constitutes part of the pact of silence. By materialising the dead with such detailed particularity in the reburial ceremony, a representational vacuum is temporarily filled, while the structural violence underpinning those deaths remains unrepresented. This use of intense materialisation to fill a representational vacuum is also consistent with the memory idioms that predate exhumation and that invoke materiality (stolen objects and unused talismans) in the accounts of the traumatic past.

The Foro por la Memoria critique of ARMH's depoliticisation of these inherently political killings might appear to be upheld by the analysis of the reburial ceremony in Las Campanas, but this would be an overly simplistic interpretation. In my participant observation of ARMH campaigners and their supporters, it was readily apparent that many of them held a strong personal identification with the leftist ideology of the dead. In private, the majority expressed views on a wide range of social and economic policies that could be characterised as left of centre. They were virulently anti-Franco, but also vituperative in their criticisms to the Right in contemporary Spanish politics. The ostensibly "depoliticised" campaign practice of ARMH has to be reconciled with the highly politicised disposition of the campaign's organisers. A further clue to their politicised understanding of exhumation can be found in their discourse surrounding the lessons of the dead. There was a widely held conviction within the campaign that the exhumations had a "pedagogic value" for Spanish society, as expressed by the recurring trope of bodies as seeds, which suggested that the dead Republicans embodied some dormant potentiality that could be activated through exhumation.

Within ARMH's campaign this was conceived of as the potential to effect some transformation in Spanish society; but unlike Foro por la Memoria, ARMH did not articulate explicitly the precise nature of this transformation. Looking at the ARMH campaign and its members from the perspective of both their individually held political views and their shared discourse on the pedagogic and transformative power of the dead, it is clear that ARMH also sought to effect a hegemonic shift to the Left, but of a different order than the one sought by Foro por la Memoria.

The rupture in Spanish memory politics that is currently underway is a result of the kind of long-term and progressive hegemonic shift that ARMH seeks to produce. This hegemonic shift is based on a more gradual process that repositions the Republican dead within family histories as a precursor to repositioning them in the national narrative. There is an apparent paradox in the way ARMH's exhumation and reburial practices can simultaneously produce a rupture in national memory politics and yet leave the existing prohibitions on the political representation of the dead (at least in the communities studied here) largely unchallenged. This contradiction can be reconciled by considering that every exhumation is viewed by two distinct audiences: the communities involved and those who encounter the canonical images of exhumations, bodies, objects, and portrait photographs one step removed, through their dissemination via the news media and the internet. These images elicit affective bonds and sentiments of pathos and mourning in the viewer; as discussed in chapter 4, they also elicit an awareness of the violence and injustice inherent in these deaths. Taken together, these are the "lessons" of the dead as conceived of by ARMH. Encounters with these images via the news media and internet, particularly by the young or by urban dwellers, will be free from the kind of enduring prohibitions that are so strong amongst the elderly in small rural communities in which contested representations are experienced as intimate face-to-face confrontations. The exhumations in these small rural communities may not produce a rupture in the memory politics of the village, but they produce a stock of canonical images for dissemination amongst a wider national audience that is free to make a more political representation of the dead.

A further rupture in Spanish memory politics is produced through the creation of an enduring representation of the Republican dead as defenders of democracy, conflating the Republican ideals of the 1930s with the core values of contemporary Spanish society. The symbolic capital accruing to these core values of democracy, tolerance, and compromise cannot be overstated. A popular founding myth of contemporary Spanish politics is that democracy was "gifted" to Spain at the end of Francoism by a kindly and paternalistic right-wing establishment. The reappropriation of the core values of democracy, tolerance, and compromise by the Republicans, and by extension the contemporary Left, is thus in itself a significant shift. It situates the Republicans within the founding narrative of contemporary Spanish democracy, presenting the peace and prosperity of contemporary Spain as a Republican legacy. Here the lesson of the dead is that Spanish democracy is the preserve of the Left and that a brutal dictatorship is the preserve of the Right.

Despite the failure to overcome the existing prohibitions on the political representation of the dead in my field sites, multiple transformations occurred as a result of the exhumation, which constituted partial ruptures in the prevailing memory politics and are important to enumerate here. The expression of affective bonds and sentiments of public mourning during the reburial ceremony in Las Campanas marked a radical rupture with the assertion amongst some elderly informants that their fathers were unknown to them or unremembered. The presence at the reburial ceremony of so many younger relatives accompanying the elderly suggests that the dead had been successfully reinserted into a network of familial relationships. Multiple generations of the same family attended the public ceremony together, perhaps providing a catalyst for the subsequent transmission of memory and breaking the pact of silence in the home. The transformation in the use of photography and the speculation amongst some informants that possessions from the grave could become mementoes in the home strongly suggest a new concern for the transmission of memory within families.

For the elderly relatives who expressed a preoccupation with the formal rituals of public mourning, the opportunity to fulfil this crucial filial duty represented a momentous rupture, effectively transforming the narrative arc of their own lives and their family history. The sense of catharsis in finally fulfilling a long-postponed duty was palpable in the reburial ceremony. In terms of the self-perceived status of these individuals and their families within their immediate community, the formal reburial in the cemetery and the inscription of the name of the dead person on a monolith was a profoundly transformative act. Regardless of the Foro's critique of "privatised memory," the incorporation of the Republican dead into their community's cemetery, the proper and dignified repository of the dead, and the public recognition of their family name represented a huge collective achievement. To appreciate its magnitude, it must be remembered that these reburials had seemed an absolute impossibility for almost seventy years. Even if a representational vacuum surrounded their biographies, the physical relocation of the bodies to their "proper" place represented a symbolic vindication of the dead and a final refutation of their killers.

The scale and visibility of the public gathering for the reburial ceremony in Las Campanas marked a dramatic break with the kind of enduring atomisation described in chapter 1, particularly as those attending filled the main square and brought the boxes of human remains through the village streets to the cemetery. Many of the elderly informants had exhibited a fearful awareness of the surveillance and critical gaze of their neighbours. From the old man who walked all the way to the mass grave rather than being seen on a bus headed in the direction of the exhumation, and the elderly informants in Villavieja who encouraged me to visit their homes during the siesta, the consciousness of surveillance permeated village life. The dramatic occupation of public space during the reburial ceremony in Las Campanas laid claim to the public realm for a hitherto marginalised and atomised group of people. The forging of links between different Republican families amongst neighbouring villages, or further afield in urban centres, also reversed the existing state of atomisation. Repeated attendance at the graveside and at public meetings, and the exchange of contact details for the planning process prior to reburial, effectively forged a new network of Republican families. The unfolding exhumation process gradually pulled in greater numbers of relatives. The mass gathering at the reburial ceremony graphically demonstrated that a large number of individuals had a shared family history, and the consciousness of being part of this number was inherently empowering.

The events observed in my fieldwork unfolded over the course of three years, but the ruptures and transformations described thus far should be situated in longer trajectories of change. The new legislation, the so-called Law of Memory, was passed in 2007, after the two communities under discussion here had undertaken the exhumation process. This wide-ranging legislation addresses education, public monuments, and place names of the Franco era, and defines the new uses of Franco's monumental complex, Valle de los Caídos. The strengths and weaknesses of this legislation have been analysed by a range of authors (Blakely 2008; Golob 2008; Tremlett 2007). The legislative build-up and political climate prior to the ratification of the law is described by Davis (2005). The potential for the political Right to see the law as a provocation and for the Left to experience disillusionment in a wasted opportunity (Moreno 2006) indicates the tightrope to be walked by any "law of memory."

Taken together, these commentaries suggest that the very existence of the legislation may constitute a groundbreaking rupture, although its actual substance is limited, particularly on a proscriptive level or in establishing enforceable powers and sanctions. The law acknowledges the responsibility of the state to ascertain and record the whereabouts of clandestine or unmarked graves from the Civil War and the subsequent repression. It establishes the formal bureaucratic framework through which a mass grave exhumation can be solicited from the local authority, and dictates that all such requests have to be submitted to the centralised body, which undertakes the mapping of the graves. The competent public authorities in each region are charged with creating the conditions by which the direct descendants of the dead or their representatives will be able to recover human remains from clandestine graves and subject them to analysis with the aim of identification, and eventually move them to a place of permanent interment. The new legislation also provides a legal mechanism to gain access to privately owned land, if there is good reason to believe that a clandestine burial is located there.

The physical form of reburial finally adopted in Las Campanas, and replicated at other sites, opens the possibility for the relatives of the dead to petition central government for assistance in providing the economic and scientific resources to undertake a genetic identification of exhumed human remains. The hybrid burial form adopted in Las Campanas entailed the placing of separate numbered boxes in a collective vault. The detailed human identification report prepared by forensic anthropologist Jorge included a table of results that showed the sets of remains that could be tentatively identified, and in the most difficult cases, the sets of remains that were physically compatible with the known descriptions of dead individuals. This means that in the Las Campanas case, a relative of the dead might only need to subject three of four sets of remains, out of the total forty-six, to genetic analysis in order to isolate his or her own relative. This new possibility opens up the potential for new kinds of collective action and negotiation amongst the relatives of the dead (Cardoso et al. 2008; Ríos et al. 2010). This would throw into sharp relief the potential of scientific techniques to mediate actions and notions of relatedness, ancestry, and identity. It would constitute a new way to materialise the dead, on the molecular level.

A new metonymy between part and whole is created between the genetic reference material of the living relative and the identity of the dead. This places the living relatives, their status as descendants, and their biological inheritance at the centre of the exhumation and identification process. Instead of viewing as an audience the transformations and triangulations between the evidence of bodies and objects and the identities of the dead achieved by expert practitioners, the relatives of the dead will themselves be constituted as evidence. The physical traces contained within their own bodies will become a vital "clue." Structuring the investigation around this familial bond will have deep ramifications for the meaning of future exhumations in terms of the familial-ideological analytical axis employed here. Just as the discourse of norms and rights has been employed effectively by the Republican memory campaign, and proved hard to counter, a discourse of genetics and biology may prove hard (possibly, even harder) to oppose. The metadiscourse surrounding the primacy of our biological existence and identity, characterised in Foucauldian terms as an era of biopolitics, may be harnessed as a source of power and symbolic capital by the Republican memory campaign.

As more relatives of the dead opt for genetic testing, the next phase of the Republican memory campaign could present an interesting case of biopolitics. This could be examined through the analytical framework of biological citizenship (Rose and Novas 2004) currently used to analyse biological aspects of identity, particularly chronic and inherited diseases, and the way these biological identities can mobilise individuals and mediate their relationship with the state. The bureaucratic framework for genetic testing opens up a new type of claim for recognition and resources that the citizen can make upon the state. It is an area of scientific practice that has been burdened with a particularly complex significance in Spain due to the history of the Francoist rhetoric on the biological transmission of Republicanism through contagion and inheritance. In this context, the claim to state assistance in the scientific identification of one's ancestors is effectively a biopolitical claim to the state's acknowledgement of one's identity and family history. It also represents a reversal in the long history of state neglect and marginalisation of Republican families. This new process could provide a rich ethnographic context in which to examine notions of identity, ancestry, and the connections between biological and political heritage. This book has examined a series of shifts in the way the Republican Civil War dead are materialised, and the way in which these material transformations create discursive spaces in which new representations of the dead can be made and contested by the multiple participants in the process. The new possibilities opened up by large-scale genetic identifications demonstrate that the transformations in the materialisation and representation of the dead are continuous and extend beyond the sequence of exhumation, analysis, and reburial examined here.

NOTES

INTRODUCTION

1. "Conclusiones y Recomendaciones de Amnistía Internacional al Gobierno Español para que haga justicia a las víctimas de la guerra civil y del Franquismo," http://www.es.amnesty.org/.

2. The official title of this legislation is "Ley 52/2007, de 26 de diciembre, por la que se reconocen y amplían derechos y se establecen medidas en favor de quienes padecieron persecución o violencia durante la guerra civil y la dictadura." The full text of this legislation is reproduced in the Official State Bulletin number 310 (BOE n° 310, December 27, 2007), http://noticias.juridicas.com/base_datos/Admin/l52-2007.html.

CHAPTER 3

1. Manuel Martínez Hinchado, newsletter distributed via the Association for the Recuperation of Historical Memory in Badajoz, August 2003, page 9. For a full account of repression in Badajoz, including Martínez Hinchado's contribution, see Chaves Palacios (2006).

2. http://www.memoriahistorica.org.

CHAPTER 4

1. A much fuller discussion of Esther and her family's experience, reflecting further on the memorial decisions regarding her father's remains and the objects in the grave, can be found in Ferrándiz (2010).

References

Aguilar, P. 2001. Justice, Politics and Memory in the Spanish Transition. In *The Politics of Memory: Transitional Justice in Democratizing Societies*, eds. A. Barahona de Brito, C. Gonzaléz-Enríquez, and P. Aguilar. Oxford: Oxford University Press.

Aguilar, P. 2002. *Memory and Amnesia: The Role of the Spanish Civil War in the Transition to Democracy*. New York: Berghahn Books.

Aguilar, P. and C. Humlebaek. 2002. Collective memory and national identity in the Spanish Civil War. *History and Memory* 14 (1–2): 121–164.

Arendt, H. 1985. *Totalitarianism: Part Three of the Origins of Totalitarianism*. San Diego: Harvest.

Arendt, H. 1994. *Eichmann in Jerusalem: A Report on the Banality of Evil*. London: Penguin.

Ash, J. 1996. Memory and Objects. In *The Gendered Object*, ed. P. Kirkham. Manchester: Manchester University Press.

Bandrés, J. and R. Llavona. 1996. La psicología en los campos de concentración de Franco. *Psicothema* 8 (1): 1–11.

Barciela, C. 2002. Guerra Civil y primer Franquismo. In *Historia económica de España, siglos X–XX*, ed. F. Comín. Barcelona: Crítica.

Barrett, R.A. 1974. *Benabarre: The Modernization of a Spanish Village*. New York: Holt, Rinehart and Winston.

Barthes, R. 2000. *Camera Lucida*. London: Vintage.

Behar, R. 1986. *Santa María del Monte: The Presence of the Past in a Spanish Village*. Princeton: Princeton University Press.

Bickford, L. 2000. Human rights archives and research on historical memory: Argentina, Chile, and Uruguay. *Latin American Research Review* 35 (2):160–182.

Blakeley, G. 2008. Politics as usual? The trials and tribulations of the Law of Historical Memory in Spain. *Entelequia: Revista Interdisciplinar* 7: 315–330.

Boyle, A. 1999. A Grave Disturbance: Archaeological Perceptions of the Recently Dead. In *The Loved Body's Corruption: Archaeological Contributions to the Study of Human Mortality*, eds. J. Downes and T. Pollard. Glasgow: Cruithne Press.

Braun, R. 1994. The Holocaust and problems of historical representation. *History and Theory* 33 (2): 172–197.

Briggs, M.A. 2006. The Return of Aura: Contemporary Writers Look Back at the First World War Photograph. In *Locating Memory: Photographic Acts*, eds. A. Kuhn and K. Emiko McAllister. Oxford: Berghahn.

Brysk, A. 1994. The politics of measurement: The contested count of the disappeared in Argentina. *Human Rights Quarterly* 16 (4): 676–692.

Buchli, V. 2000. *An Archaeology of Socialism*. Oxford: Berg.

Buchli, V. and G. Lucas, eds. 2001. *Archaeologies of the Contemporary Past*. London: Routledge.

Bunk, B.D. 2002. "Your comrades will not forget": Revolutionary memory and the breakdown of the Spanish Second Republic 1934–1936. *History and Memory* 14 (1–2): 65–92.

Byers, S.N. 2005. *Introduction to Forensic Anthropology: A Textbook*. Boston: Pearson.

Cabana Iglesia, A. 2010. Passive resistance: Notes for a more complete understanding of the resistance practices of the rural population during the Franco dictatorship. *Amnis: Revue de Civilization Contemporaine* 9 (online). http://amnis.revues.org/265.

Canter, D. 2002. The Violated Body. In *The Body*, eds. I. Hodder and S. Sweeney. Cambridge: Cambridge University Press.

Capdevila, L. and D. Voldman. 2006. *War Dead: Western Societies and the Casualties of War*. Edinburgh: Edinburgh University Press.

Cardoso, S., F. Etxeberria, M.A. Alfonso-Sánchez, A.M. Pérez-Miranda, A. Odrozola, L. Valverde, E. Sarasola, J.A. Peña, and M.M. de Pancorbo. 2008. Contribution of forensic genetics to the recovery of historic memory of the Spanish Civil War. *Forensic Science International Genetics Supplement Series* 1: 454–456.

Caruth, C. 2002. The claims of the dead: History, haunted property, and the law. *Critical Inquiry* 28 (2): 419–441.

Casanova, J. 2002. Una dictadura de cuarenta años. In *Matar, morir, sobrevivir. La violencia en la dictadura de Franco*, ed. J. Casanova. Barcelona: Crítica.

Cenarro, A. 2002. Memory beyond the public sphere. *History and Memory* 14 (1–2): 165–188.

Cenarro, A. 2008. Memories of repression and resistance: Narratives of children institionalized by Auxillio Social in Postwar Spain. *History and Memory* 20 (2): 39–60.

Cercas, J. 2003. *Soldiers of Salamis*. London: Bloomsbury.

Chacón, D. 2004. *La mujer y la construcción del olvido*. In Silva et al. 2004.

Chacón, D. 2006. *The Sleeping Voice*. London: Harvill Secker.

Chaves Palacios, J., ed. 2006. *Badajoz agosto de 1936: Historia y memoria de la Guerra Civil en Extremadura*. Badajoz: Diputación de Badajoz.

Claret Miranda, J. 2006. Cuando las cátedras eran trincheras: La depuración política e ideológica de la Universidad española durante el primer franquismo. *Hispania Nova Revista de Historia Contemporánea* 6.

Collier, J.F. 1986. From Mary to modern woman: The material basis of marianismo and its transformation in a Spanish village. *American Ethnologist* 13 (1): 100–107.

Collier, J.F. 1997. *From Duty to Desire: Remaking Families in a Spanish Village*. Princeton: Princeton University Press.

Congram, D. and D. Austin Bruno. 2007. (Don't) smile for the camera: Addressing perception gaps in forensic archaeology. *Archaeological Review from Cambridge* 22 (2): 37–52.

Congram, D. and D.W. Steadman. 2008. Distinguished guests or agents of ingérence: Foreign participation in Spanish Civil War grave excavations. *Complutum* 19 (2): 161–173.

Connerton, P. 1989. *How Societies Remember*. Cambridge: Cambridge University Press.

Corbin, J. 1995. Truth and myth in history: An example from the Spanish Civil War. *Journal of Interdisciplinary History* 25 (4): 609–625.

Corillon, C. 1989. The role of science and scientists in human rights. *Annals of the American Academy of Political and Social Science* 506: 129–140.

Cox, M. 2001. Forensic Archaeology in the UK: Questions of Socio-Intellectual Context and Socio-Political Responsibility. In Buchli and Lucas 2001.

Crossland, Z. 2000. Buried lives: Forensic archaeology and the disappeared in Argentina. *Archeological Dialogues* 72: 146–158.

Crossland, Z. 2002. Violent Spaces: Conflict over the Reappearance of Argentina's Disappeared. In *Matériel Culture: The Archaeology of Twentieth Century Conflict*, eds. J. Schofield, W.G. Johnson, and C.M. Beck. London: Routledge.

Crossland, Z. 2009a. Acts of estrangement: The post-mortem making of self and other. *Archaeological Dialogues* 16 (1): 102–125.

Crossland, Z. 2009b. Of clues and signs: The dead body and its evidential traces. *American Anthropologist* 111 (1): 69–80.

Cue, C.E. 2007. La Ley Memoria se aprueba entre aplausos de invitados antifranquistas. *El País*, November 1.

Das, V. 1997. Language and Body: Transactions in the Construction of Pain. In *Social Suffering*, eds. A. Kleinman, V. Das, and M. Lock. Berkeley: University of California Press.

Das, V. 2000. The Act of Witnessing: Violence, Poisonous Knowledge, and Subjectivity. In *Violence and Subjectivity*, eds. V. Das, A. Kleinman, M. Ramphele, and P. Reynolds. Berkeley: University of California Press.

Davis, M. 2005. Is Spain recovering its memory? Breaking the pacto del olvido. *Human Rights Quarterly* 27 (3): 858–880.

Desfor Edles, L. 1995. Rethinking democratic transition: A culturalist critique and the Spanish case. *Theory and Society* 24 (3): 355–384.

Desfor Edles, L. 1998. *Symbol and Ritual in the New Spain: The Transition to Democracy after Franco*. Cambridge: Cambridge University Press.

Díaz, E. 1995. The Left and the Legacy of Francoism: Political Culture in Opposition and Transition. In *Spanish Cultural Studies: An Introduction*, eds. H. Graham and J. Labanyi. Oxford: Oxford University Press.

Domanska, E. 2005. Toward the archaeontology of the dead body. *Rethinking History* 9 (4): 389–413.

Domanska, E. 2006. The material presence of the past. *History and Theory* 45 (3): 337–348.

Doretti, M. and L. Fondebrider. 2001. Science and Human Rights: Truth, Justice, Reparation and Reconciliation, a Long Way in Third World Countries. In Buchli and Lucas 2001.

Douglas, L. 1998. The shrunken head of Buchenwald: Icons of atrocity at Nuremberg. *Representations* 63: 39–64.

Edgeworth, M. 2003. *Acts of Discovery: An Ethnography of Archaeological Practice*. BAR International Series 1131. Oxford: Archaeopress.

Edwards, E. 1999. Photographs as Objects of Memory. In *Material Memories: Design and Evocation*, eds. M. Kwint, C. Breward, and J. Aynsley. Oxford: Berg.

Emiko McAllister, K. 2006. A Story of Escape: Family Photographs from Japanese Canadian Internment Camps. In *Locating Memory: Photographic Acts*, eds. A. Kuhn and K. Emiko McAllister. Oxford: Berghahn.

Espinosa, F. 2002. Julio de 1936. Golpe militar y plan de exterminio. In *Matar, morir, sobrevivir. La violencia en la dictadura de Franco*, ed. J. Casanova. Barcelona: Crítica.

Espinosa, F. 2006. La memoria de la represión y la lucha por su reconocimiento (En torno a la creación de la Comisión Interministerial). *Hispania Nova Revista de Historia Contemporánea* 6.

Etxeberria Gabilondo, F. and L. Herrasti Erlogorri. n.d. Informe relativo a la exhumación llevada a cabo en Vadoncondes (Burgos) con el fin de recuperar los restos humanos pertenecientes a seis personas ejecutadas en la Guerra Civil. http://www.sc.ehu.es/scrwwwsr/Medicina-Legal/vadocondes/vadocondes.htm (accessed July 2008).

Etxeberria Gabilondo, F. and L. Herrasti Erlogorri. n.d. Informe relativo a la exhumación llevada a cabo en Olmedillo de Roa (Burgos) con el fin de recuperar los restos humanos pertenecientes a ocho personas ejecutadas en la Guerra Civil. http://www.sc.ehu.es/scrwwwsr/Medicina-Legal/olmedillo/olmedillo.htm (accessed July 2008).

Etxeberria Gabilondo, F., L. Herrasti Erlogorri, and J. Ortiz Lejarza. n.d. Valdediós: la memoria recuperada. Informe relativo a los restos humanos hallados en la fosa de Valdediós (Asturias). http://www.sc.ehu.es/scrwwwsr/Medicina-Legal/valdedios/Intro.htm (accessed July 2008).

Etxeberria Gabilondo, F., L. Herrasti Erlogorri, J. Ortiz Lejarza, and J. Jiménez. n.d. Informe relativo a la exhumación llevada a cabo en Benegiles (Zamora) con el fin de recuperar los restos humanos pertenecientes a tres personas ejecutadas en la Guerra Civil. http://www.sc.ehu.es/scrwwwsr/Medicina-Legal/benegiles/benegiles.htm (accessed July 2008).

Felman, S. 2001. Theaters of justice: Arendt in Jerusalem, the Eichmann trial, and redefinition of legal meaning in the wake of the Holocaust. *Critical Inquiry* 27 (2): 201–238.

Fernández de Mata, I. 2004. The "logics" of violence and Franco's mass graves: An ethnohistorical approach. *International Journal of the Humanities* 2 (3): 2527–2535.

Fernández de Mata, I. 2010. The Rupture of the World and the Conflicts of Memory. In *Unearthing Franco's Legacy: Mass Graves and the Recovery of Historical Memory in Spain*, eds. C. Jerez-Farrán and S. Amago. Notre Dame: University of Notre Dame Press.

Ferrán, O. 2007. *Working through Memory: Writing and Remembrance in Contemporary Spanish Narrative*. New Jersey: Associated University Press.

Ferrán Gallego, M. 2008. *El mito de la transición. La crisis del franquismo y los orígenes de la democracia (1973–1977)*. Barcelona: Crítica.

Ferrándiz, F. 2006. The return of Civil War ghosts: The ethnography of exhumations in contemporary Spain. *Anthropology Today* 22 (3): 7–12.

Ferrándiz, F. 2010. The Intimacy of Defeat: Exhumations in Contemporary Spain. In *Unearthing Franco's Legacy: Mass Graves and the Recovery of Historical Memory in Spain*, eds. C. Jerez-Farrán and S. Amago. Notre Dame: University of Notre Dame Press.

Ferrándiz, F. and A. Baer. 2008. Digital memory: The visual recording of mass grave exhumations in contemporary Spain. *Forum: Qualitative Social Research* 9 (3): Article 35.

Fidalgo, P. 1939. *A Young Mother in Franco's Prisons*. London: United Editorial.

Foro por la Memoria and J. Conde. 2008. Huecos en la memoria. Exhumación de una fosa en Cincovillas (Guadalajara). *Complutum* 19 (2): 131–138.

Foucault, M. 2003. *The Birth of the Clinic*. London: Routledge.

Fraser, R. 1979. *Blood of Spain: The Experience of Civil War 1936–1939*. Harmondsworth: Penguin.

Freud, S. 2003. *The Uncanny*. London: Penguin.

Friedlander, S., ed. 1992. *Probing the Limits of Representation: Nazism and the "Final Solution."* Cambridge: Harvard University Press.

Fuchs, D. 2007. Hundreds of Spanish Civil War "martyrs" beatified. *The Guardian*, October 29.

Fussell, P. 1975. *The Great War and Modern Memory*. New York: Oxford University Press.

Garcia, M. 1972. *Franco's Prisoner*. London: Hart Davis.

Gere, C. 1999. Bones that matter: Sex determination in paleodemography 1948–1995. *Studies in History and Philosophy of Biological and Biomedical Sciences* 30 (4): 455–471.

Gibson, M. 2004. Melancholy objects. *Mortality* 9 (4): 285–299.

Gilmore, D.D. 1980. *The People of the Plain: Class and Community in Lower Andalusia*. New York: Columbia University Press.

Gilmore, D.D. 1987. *Aggression and Community: Paradoxes of Andalusian Culture*. New Haven: Yale University Press.

Golob, S. 2008. Volver: The return of/to transitional justice politics in Spain. *Journal of Spanish Cultural Studies* 9 (2):127–141.

Gómez Bravo, G. 2009. *El exilio interior: Cárcel y represión en la España franquista 1939–1950*. Madrid: Taurus.

González, M. 2006. Apuntes para un método de análisis mnemónico intergeneracional sobre la Guerra Civil. *Hispania Nova Revista de Historia Contemporánea* 6. http://hispanianova.rediris.es/.

González-Ruibal, A. 2007. Making things public: Archaeologies of the Spanish Civil War. *Public Archaeology* 6 (4): 203–226.

González-Ruibal, A. 2008. Time to destroy: An archaeology of supermodernity. *Current Anthropology* 49 (2): 247–279.

Govan, F. 2006. 70 years on, Spain hopes to heal Civil War wounds. *The Telegraph*, July 18.

Graham, H. 1995a. Gender and the State: Women in the 1940s. In *Spanish Cultural Studies: An Introduction*, eds. H. Graham and J. Labanyi. Oxford: Oxford University Press.

Graham, H. 1995b. Popular Culture in the "Years of Hunger." In *Spanish Cultural Studies: An Introduction*, eds. H. Graham and J. Labanyi. Oxford: Oxford University Press.

Graham, H. 2004. The Spanish Civil War, 1936–2003: The return of Republican memory. *Science and Society* 68 (3): 313–328.

Hagopian, P. 2006. Vietnam War Photography as a Locus of Memory. In *Locating Memory: Photographic Acts*, eds. A. Kuhn and K. Emiko McAllister. Oxford: Berghahn.

Hallam, E. and J. Hockey. 2001. *Death, Memory and Material Culture*. Oxford: Berg.

Hallam, E., J. Hockey, and G. Howarth. 1999. *Beyond the Body: Death and Social Identity*. London: Routledge.

Hamilton, C. 2000. Faultlines: The Construction of Archaeological Knowledge at Çatalhöyük. In *Towards Reflexive a Method in Archaeology: The Example at Çatalhöyük*, ed. I. Hodder. Cambridge: McDonald Institute for Archaeological Research.

Hanson, I. 2007. Psycho-social issues and approaches in forensic archaeology. *Archaeological Review from Cambridge* 22 (2): 69–76.

Herrmann, G. 2003. Voices of the vanquished: Leftist women and the Spanish Civil War. *Journal of Spanish Cultural Studies* 4 (1): 11–29.

Herrmann, G. 2010. Mass Graves on Spanish TV: A Tale of Two Documentaries. In *Unearthing Franco's Legacy: Mass Graves and the Recovery of Historical Memory in Spain*, eds. C. Jerez-Farrán and S. Amago. Notre Dame: University of Notre Dame Press.

Herzfeld, M. 1980. Honour and shame: Problems in the comparative analysis of moral systems. *Man* (new series) 15 (2): 339–351.

Hirsch, M. 1996. Past lives: Postmemories in exile. *Poetics Today* 17: 659–686.

Hirsch, M. 1997. *Family Frames: Photography, Narrative and Postmemory*. Cambridge: Harvard University Press.

Hirsch, M. and L. Spitzer. 2006. There Was Never a Camp Here: Searching for Vapniarka. In *Locating Memory: Photographic Acts*, eds. A. Kuhn and K. Emiko McAllister. Oxford: Berghahn.

Hodder, I. 2003. Archaeological reflexivity and the "local" voice. *Anthropological Quarterly* 76 (1): 55–69.

Holguín, S. 2002. *Creating Spaniards: Culture and National Identity in Republican Spain*. Madison: The University of Wisconsin Press.

Holguín, S. 2007. Navigating the Historical Labyrinth of the Spanish Civil War. In *Teaching Representations of the Spanish Civil War*, ed. N. Valis. New York: The Modern Language Association of America.

Hoshower-Leppo, L. 2002. Missing in Action: Searching for America's War Dead. In *Matériel Culture: The Archaeology of Twentieth Century Conflict*, eds. J. Schofield, W.G. Johnson, and C.M. Beck. London: Routledge.

Hoskins, J. 1998. *Biographical Objects: How Things Tell the Stories of People's Lives*. London: Routledge.

Hunter, J. 1999. The Excavation of Modern Murder. In *The Loved Body's Corruption: Archaeological Contributions to the Study of Human Mortality*, eds. J. Downes and T. Pollard. Glasgow: Cruithne Press.

Juliá, S. 2010. *Hoy no es ayer. Ensayos sobre la España del siglo XX*. Barcelona: RBA.

Kadare, I. 2000. *General of the Dead Army*. London: Harvill Press.

Kenny, M. 1966. *A Spanish Tapestry: Town and Country in Castile*. Bloomington: University of Indiana Press.

King, A. 1999. Remembering and Forgetting in the Public Memorials of the Great War. In *The Art of Forgetting*, eds. A. Forty and S. Küchler. Oxford: Berg.

Kirk, L. and H. Start. 1999. Death at the Undertakers. In *The Loved Body's Corruption: Archaeological Contributions to the Study of Human Mortality*, eds. J. Downes and T. Pollard. Glasgow: Cruithne Press.

Kleinman, A. and J. Kleinman. 1997. The Appeal of Experience, the Dismay of Images: Cultural Appropriations of Suffering in Our Times. In *Social Suffering*, eds. A. Kleinman, V. Das, and M. Lock. Berkeley: University of California Press.

Klinenberg, E. 2001. Bodies that don't matter: Death and dereliction in Chicago. *Body and Society* 7 (2–3): 121–136.

Koff, C. 2004. *Bone Woman: Among the Dead in Rwanda, Bosnia, and Croatia.* London: Atlantic Books.

Kolbert, E. 2003. Looking for Lorca. *The New Yorker*, December 22.

Kovács, K. 1991. The plain in Spain: Geography and national identity in Spanish cinema. In "Remapping the post-Franco cinema," special issue, *Quarterly Review of Film and Video* 13 (4): 112–134.

Küchler, S. 1999. The Place of Memory. In *The Art of Forgetting*, eds. A. Forty and S. Küchler. Oxford: Berg.

Kwon, H. 2008. *Ghosts of War in Vietnam.* Cambridge: Cambridge University Press.

Labanyi, J. 1995. Postmodernism and the Problem of Cultural Identity. In *Spanish Cultural Studies: An Introduction*, eds. H. Graham and J. Labanyi. Oxford: Oxford University Press.

LaCapra, D. 1999. Trauma, absence, loss. *Critical Inquiry* 25 (4): 696–727.

Langford, M. 2006. Speaking the Album: An Application of the Oral-Photographic Framework. In *Locating Memory: Photographic Acts*, eds. A. Kuhn and K. Emiko McAllister. Oxford: Berghahn.

Laqueur, T.W. 1989. Bodies, Details, and the Humanitarian Narrative. In *The New Cultural History*, ed. L. Hunt. Berkeley: University of California Press.

Laqueur, T.W. 1994. Memory and Naming in the Great War. In *Commemorations: The Politics of National Identity*, ed. J.R. Gillis. Princeton: Princeton University Press.

Laqueur, T.W. 1996. Names, Bodies, and the Anxiety of Erasure. In *The Social and Political Body*, eds. T.R. Schatzki and W. Natter. New York: The Guilford Press.

Laqueur, T.W. 2002. The Dead Body and Human Rights. In *The Body*, eds. I. Hodder and S. Sweeney. Cambridge: Cambridge University Press.

Larubia-Prado, F. 2000. Franco as cyborg: The body re-formed by politics: Part flesh, part machine. *Journal of Spanish Cultural Studies* 1 (2):135–152.

Latour, B. 2002. From Realpolitik to Dingpolitik, or How to Make Things Public. In *Making Things Public: Atmospheres of Democracy*, eds. B. Latour and P.Weibel. Cambridge: The MIT Press.

Latour, B. and S. Woolgar. 1986. *Laboratory Life: The Construction of Scientific Facts*. Princeton: Princeton University Press.

Layne, L. 2000. He was a real baby with baby things. *Journal of Material Culture* 5: 321–345.

Lever, A. 1986. Honour as a red herring. *Critique of Anthropology* 6: 83–106.

Lincoln, B. 1985. Revolutionary exhumations in Spain, July 1936. *Comparative Studies in Society and History* 27 (2): 241–260.

Lutz Bauer, R. 1992. Changing representations of place, community, and character in the Spanish Sierra del Caurel. *American Ethnologist* 19 (3): 571–588.

Maddox, R. 1995. Revolutionary anticlericalism and hegemonic process in an Andalusian town, August 1936. *American Ethnologist* 22 (1): 125–143.

Marres, N. 2002. Issues Spark a Public into Being. In *Making Things Public: Atmospheres of Democracy*, eds. B. Latour and P. Weibel. Cambridge: The MIT Press.

McEvoy, K. and H. Conway. 2004. The dead, the law, and the politics of the past. *Journal of Law and Society* 31 (4): 539–562.

Miller, D. and F. Parrott. 2007. Death Ritual and Material Culture in South London. In *Death Rites and Rights*, eds. B. Brooks-Gordon, F. Ebtehaj, and J. Herring. Oxford: Hart.

Mintz, J.R. 1982. *The Anarchists of Casas Viejas*. Bloomington: Indiana University Press.

Mir, C. 2002. La represión Franquista en la Cataluña rural. In *Matar, morir, sobrevivir: La violencia en la dictadura de Franco*, ed. J. Casanova. Barcelona: Crítica.

Mitchell, T.J. 1988. *Violence and Piety in Spanish Folklore*. Philadelphia: University of Pennsylvania Press.

Monegal, A. 2008. Exhibiting objects of memory. *Journal of Spanish Cultural Studies* 9 (2): 239–251.

Moreno, J.A. 2006. La memoria defraudada. Notas sobre el denominado proyecto Ley de Memoria. *Hispania Nova Revista de Historia Contemporánea* 6. http:// hispanianova.rediris.es/.

Moreno Gómez, F. 2002. La oposición armada a la dictadura. In *Matar, morir, sobrevivir. La violencia en la dictadura de Franco*, ed. J. Casanova. Barcelona: Crítica.

Moshenska, G. 2006. The archaeology of the uncanny. *Public Archaeology* 5: 91–99.

Muro, D. 2009. The politics of war memory in radical Basque nationalism. *Ethnic and Racial Studies* 32 (4): 659–678.

Narotzky, S. and G. Smith. 2002. "Being politico" in Spain. *History and Memory* 14 (1–2):189–228.

Narotzky, S. and G. Smith. 2006. *Immediate Struggles: People, Power and Place in Rural Spain*. Berkeley: University of California Press.

Navarro, V. 2004. *La transición y los desparecidos republicanos*. In Silva et al. 2004.

Nochlin, L. 1994. *The Body in Pieces: The Fragment as a Metaphor for Modernity*. London: Thames and Hudson.

Ondaatje, M. 2001. *Anil's Ghost*. London: Picador.

Orwell, G. 2003. *Homage to Catalonia*. London: Penguin.

Paperno, I. 2001. Exhuming the bodies of Soviet Terror. *Representations* 75: 89–118.

Parker Pearson, M. 1982. Mortuary Practices, Society, and Ideology: An Ethnoarchaeological Study. In *Symbolic and Structural Archaeology*, ed. I. Hodder. Cambridge: Cambridge University Press.

Pedreño, J. 2004. "Apoyar a la ARMH es enterrar la memoria," message to online forum. http://www.alasbarricadas.org/forums (accessed June 2005).

Perez Diaz, V.M. 1976. Process of Change in Rural Castilian Communities. In *The Changing Face of Rural Spain*, eds. J. Aceves and W. Douglass. New York: Wiley.

Pina-Cabral, J. de. 1986. *Sons of Adam, Daughters of Eve: The Peasant World View of the Alto Minho*. Oxford: Oxford University Press.

Pinney, C. 1997. *Camera Indica: The Social Life of Indian Photographs*. London: Reaktion Books.

Pinto, D. 2004. Indoctrinating the youth of post-war Spain: A discourse analysis of a Fascist civics textbook. *Discourse and Society* 15 (5): 649–667.

Pollard, T. and I. Banks. 2008. *Scorched Earth: Studies in the Archaeology of Conflict*. Leiden: Brill.

Prada, M.E., F. Etxeberría, L. Herrasti, J. Vidal, S. Macias, and F. Pastor. 2002. Antropología del pasado reciente: Una fosa común de la guerra civil española en Priazanza del Bierzo (León). *Antropología y Biodiversidad* 1: 431–446.

Preston, P. 1989. Revenge and reconciliation. *History Today* 39: 28–33.

Preston, P. 1996. *A Concise History of the Spanish Civil War*. London: Fontana.

Preston, P. 2004a. *Las víctimas del francoismo y los historiadores*. In Silva et al. 2004.

Preston, P. 2004b. The answer lies in the sewers: Captain Aguilera and the mentality of the Francoist officer corps. *Science and Society* 68 (3): 277–312.

Preston, P. 2010. Theorists of Extermination: The Origins of Violence in the Spanish Civil War. In *Unearthing Franco's Legacy: Mass Graves and the Recovery of*

Historical Memory in Spain, eds. C. Jerez-Farrán and S. Amago. Notre Dame: University of Notre Dame Press.

Raszeja, S. and E. Chroscielewski. 1994. Medicolegal reconstruction of the Katy Forest massacre. *Forensic Science International* 68 (1): 1–6.

Renshaw, L. 2007. The Iconography of Exhumation: Representations of Mass Graves from the Spanish Civil War. In *Archaeology and the Media*, eds. T. Clack and M. Brittain. Oxford: Berg.

Renshaw, L. 2010a. Missing Bodies Near-at-Hand. In *An Anthropology of Absence: Materializations of Transcendence and Loss*, eds. M. Bille, F. Hastrup, and T. Flohr Soerensen. New York: Springer.

Renshaw, L. 2010b. The scientific and affective identification of Republican civilian victims from the Spanish Civil War. *Journal of Material Culture* 15 (4): 449–463.

Resina, R. 2000. *Disremembering the Dictatorship: The Politics of Memory in the Spanish Transition to Democracy*. Amsterdam: Editions Rodopi.

Rey, D. 2001. La transición: Un análisis marxista. *Marxismo Hoy* 9: 3–26.

Richards, M. 1995. "Terror and Progress": Industrialization, Modernity, and the Making of Francoism. In *Spanish Cultural Studies: An Introduction*, eds. H. Graham and J. Labanyi. Oxford: Oxford University Press.

Richards, M. 1998. *A Time of Silence: Civil War and the Culture of Repression in Franco's Spain: 1936–1945*. Cambridge: Cambridge University Press.

Richards, M. 2001. Morality and biology in the Spanish Civil War: Psychiatrists, revolution and women prisoners in Málaga. *Contemporary European History* 10 (3): 395–421.

Richards, M. 2002. From war culture to civil society. *History and Memory* 14 (1–2): 93–120.

Ríos, L., J.I. Casado Ovejero, and J. Puente Prieto. 2010. Case Report: Identification process in mass graves from the Spanish Civil War I. *Forensic Science International* 199: e27–36.

Robben, A.C.G.M. 2005. *Political Violence and Trauma in Argentina*. Philadelphia: University of Pennsylvania Press.

Rodrigo, J. 2008. *Hasta la raíz. Violencia durante la Guerra Civil y la dictadura Franquista*. Madrid: Alianza.

Rodrigo, R. 2006. La Guerra Civil: "memoria," "olvido," "recuperación" e instrumentación. *Hispania Nova Revista de Historia Contemporánea* 6. http://hispanianova.rediris.es/.

Romero-Maura, J. 1967. Spain: The Civil War and after. *Journal of Contemporary History* 2 (1): 157–168.

Rose, N. and C. Novas. 2004. Biological Citizenship. In *Global Assemblages: Technology, Politics, and Ethics as Anthropological Problems*, eds. A. Ong and S. Collier. Oxford: Blackwell.

Ross, F.C. 2001. Speech and Silence: Women's Testimony in the First Five Weeks of Public Hearings of the South African Truth and Reconciliation Commission. In *Remaking a World: Violence, Social Suffering and Recovery*, eds. V. Das, A. Kleinman, M. Lock, M. Ramphele, and D. Reynolds. Berkeley: University of California Press.

Ruiz Vilaplana, A. 1938. *Burgos Justice: A Year's Experience of Nationalist Spain*. New York: Alfred A. Knopf.

Ryan, L. 2009. The sins of the father: The destruction of the Republican family in Franco's Spain. *History of the Family* 14: 245–252.

Sanford, V. 2003. *Buried Secrets: Truth and Human Rights in Guatemala*. New York: Palgrave MacMillan.

Sant Cassia, P. 2007. *Bodies of Evidence: Burial, Memory and the Recovery of Missing Persons in Cyprus*. New York: Berghahn Books.

Saunders, N.J. 2000. Bodies of metal, shells of memory: "Trench art" and the Great War recycled. *Journal of Material Culture* 5 (1): 43–67.

Saunders, N.J. 2002. Excavating memories: Archaeology and the Great War, 1914–2001. *Antiquity* 76 (1): 101–8.

Saunders, R. 2002. Tell the Truth: The Archaeology of Human Rights Abuses in Guatemala and the Former Yugoslavia. In *Matériel Culture: The Archaeology of Twentieth Century Conflict*, eds. J. Schofield, W.G. Johnson, and C.M. Beck. London: Routledge.

Scarry, E. 1985a. *The Body in Pain*. New York: Oxford University Press.

Scarry, E. 1985b. Injury and the structure of war. *Representations* 10: 1–51.

Schnapp, J., M. Shanks, and M. Tiews. 2004. Archaeology, modernism, modernity. *Modernism/Modernity* 11 (1): 1–16.

Sevillano, F. 2007. *Rojos: La representación del enemigo en la Guerra Civil*. Madrid: Alianza Editorial.

Shanks, M., D. Platt, and W.L. Rathje. 2004. The perfume of garbage: Modernity and the archaeological. *Modernism/Modernity* 11 (1): 61–83.

Sharrock, D. 2004. Spain digs over painful past. *The Times*, January 23.

Sieder, R. 2001. War, Peace, and Memory Politics in Central America. In *The Politics of Memory: Transitional Justice in Democratizing Societies*, eds. A. Barahona de Brito, C. Gonzaléz-Enríquez, and P. Aguilar. Oxford: Oxford University Press.

Silva, E. and S. Macías. 2003. *Las fosas de Franco: Los republicanos que el dictador dejó en las cunetas*. Madrid: Temas de Hoy.

Silva, E., A. Esteban, J. Castán, and P. Salvador, eds. 2004. *La memoria de los olvidados: Un debate sobre el silencio de la repression franquista*. Valladolid: Ámbito Ediciones.

Sofaer, J.R. 2006. *The Body as Material Culture: A Theoretical Osteoarchaelogy*. Cambridge: Cambridge University Press.

Sontag, S. 1979. *On Photography*. London: Penguin.

Sontag, S. 2004. *Regarding the Pain of Others*. London: Penguin.

Stallybrass, P. and A.R. Jones. 2001. Fetishizing the glove in Renaissance Europe. *Critical Inquiry* 28 (1): 114–132.

Steele, C. 2008. Archaeology and the Forensic Investigation of Recent Mass Graves: Ethical Issues for a New Practice of Archaeology. *Archaeologies* 4 (3): 414–428.

Stover, E. and G. Peress. 1998. *The Graves: Forensic Efforts at Srebinica and Vukovar*. New York: Scalo.

Tarlow, S. 1997. An archaeology of remembering: Death, bereavement and the First World War. *Cambridge Archaeological Journal* 7: 105–121.

Tarlow, S. 1999. *Bereavement and Commemoration: An Archaeology of Mortality*. Oxford: Blackwell.

Taylor, T. 2002. *The Buried Soul: How Humans Invented Death*. London: Fourth Estate.

Thomas, H. 1990. *The Spanish Civil War*. London: Penguin.

Tilley, C. 1990a. Michel Foucault: Towards an Archaeology of Archaeology. In *Reading Material Culture: Structuralism, Hermeneutics and Post-Structuralism*, ed. C. Tilley. Oxford: Blackwell.

Tilley, C. 1990b. On Modernity and Archaeological Discourse. In *Archaeology After Structuralism: Post-Structuralism and the Practice of Archaeology*, eds. I. Bapty and T. Yates. London: Routledge.

Torres, F. 2008. The images of memory: A civil narration of history. A photo essay. *Journal of Spanish Cultural Studies* 9 (2): 157–175.

Tremlett, G. 2006. *Ghosts of Spain: Travels through a Country's Hidden Past.* London: Faber and Faber.

Tremlett, G. 2007. After Franco, the forgetting. *The Guardian*, November 3.

Trinch, S. 2003. *Latina's Narratives of Domestic Violence: Discrepant Versions of Violence.* Philadelphia: John Benjamins.

Valis, N. 2007. Civil War Ghosts Entombed: Lessons of the Valley of the Fallen. In *Teaching Representations of the Spanish Civil War*, ed. N. Valis. New York: The Modern Language Association of America.

Vázquez Montalbán, M. 2003. *Cronica sentimental de España.* Barcelona: Debolsillo.

Verdery, K. 1999. *The Political Lives of Dead Bodies: Reburial and Postsocialist Change.* New York: Columbia University Press.

Vinyes, R. 2002. *Irredentas: Las presas políticas y sus hijos en las cárceles de Franco.* Madrid: Temas de hoy.

Vinyes, R. 2010. La reconciliación como ideología. *El País*, August 12.

Wagner, S.E. 2008. *To Know Where He Lies: DNA Technology and the Search for Srebrenica's Missing.* Berkeley: University of California Press.

Webster, J. 2003. El valle de Dios. In "El silencio en boca de todos," special issue, *Granta en Español* 1: 135–159.

White, H. 1992. Historical Emplotment and the Problem of Truth. In *Probing the Limits of Representation: Nazism and the "Final Solution,"* ed. S. Friedlander. Cambridge: Harvard University Press.

Whitehead, G. 1990. The forensic theatre: Memory plays for the post-mortem condition. *Performing Arts Journal* 12 (2–3): 99–109.

Wilde, A. 1999. Irruptions of memory: Expressive politics in Chile's transition to democracy. *Journal of Latin American Studies* 31: 473–500.

Wilson, R.A. 2001. *The Politics of Truth and Reconciliation in South Africa: Legitimizing the Post-Apartheid State.* Cambridge: Cambridge University Press.

Winter, J. 1995. *Sites of Memory, Sites of Mourning: The Great War in European Cultural History.* Cambridge: Cambridge University Press.

Yates, F. 2001. *The Art of Memory.* Berkeley: University of California Press.

Young, J.E. 1997. Toward a received history of the Holocaust. *History and Theory* 36 (4): 21–43.

Young, J.E. 1998. The Holocaust as vicarious past: Art Spiegelman's *Maus* and the afterimages of history. *Critical Inquiry* 24: 666–699.

Index

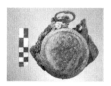

About the Author

Layla Renshaw is a senior lecturer in the School of Life Sciences at Kingston University, UK, where she teaches forensic archaeology and anthropology. She received her PhD in anthropology from University College London. Her research interests include postconflict investigations and representations of the traumatic past, the political and theoretical significance of forensic archaeology, and its representation in the media.

Printed in Great Britain
by Amazon

22273932R00145